An Interactive Guide to College

Diane S. Fitton
Monroe Community College

PEARSON

Prentice
Hall

Upper Saddle River, New Jersey
Columbus, Ohio

Library of Congress Cataloging-in-Publication Data

Fitton, Diane.
  On campus : an interactive guide to college / Diane Fitton.
      p. cm.
  Includes index.
  ISBN 978-0-13-514573-9
1. College student orientation. I. Title.
  LB2343.3.F56 2009
  378.19'8—dc22

                                              2007052313

Vice President and Executive Publisher: Jeffery W. Johnston
Executive Editor: Sande Johnson
Development Editor: Jennifer Gessner
Editorial Assistant: Lynda Cramer
Design Coordinator: Diane C. Lorenzo
Cover Designer: Diane C. Lorenzo
Managing Editor: Pamela D. Bennett
Project Manager: Kerry J. Rubadue
Production Coordination: Aptara
Operations Specialist: Susan Hannahs
Director of Marketing: Quinn Perkson
Marketing Manager: Amy Judd
Marketing Coordinator: Brian Mounts

This book was set in Life Roman by Aptara Inc. It was printed and bound by Courier/Stoughton. The cover was printed by Phoenix Color Corp./Hagerstown.

Pearson Education Ltd.   Pearson Education Australia Pty. Limited
Pearson Education Singapore Pte. Ltd.   Pearson Education North Asia Ltd.
Pearson Education Canada, Ltd.   Pearson Educación de Mexico, S.A. de C.V.
Pearson Education—Japan   Pearson Education Malaysia Pte. Ltd.

10 9 8 7 6 5 4 3 2 1
ISBN-13:   978-0-13-514573-9
ISBN-10:   0-13-514573-2

Preface

Attending college to acquire an education is an opportunity of a lifetime. Education, once realized, not only changes the way a person perceives and reacts to the world, but it also provides a foundation for future opportunities.

Often, the difference between the student who successfully takes advantage of a college education and the student who flounders or fails is a matter of applied strategies and acquired skills. This book focuses on outcomes designed to maximize student success in college.

From my years teaching college orientation, I believe students learn best by example and personal involvement. For that reason, *On Campus* contains concrete examples from professors across the nation. Whether the example is from a small four-year liberal arts college, a comprehensive two-year community college, or a large university, all illustrate how expectations equate with student responsibility. Throughout the text, students are engaged in activities that require reflection. Authentic case scenarios motivate students to share values and explore issues related to their success.

On Campus is actually several books in one. The textbook is designed as a work text, and the *On Campus* Student Website contains an online reader and exercises that encourage interactive learning with the text. With a comprehensive approach to content and pedagogy, *On Campus* addresses topics covered in many separate textbooks, where each one typically focuses on a single topic, such as college survival, student success, study skills, critical thinking, learning strategies, or freshman orientation.

Whether a college freshman is straight out of high school or a returning adult, college orientation is a pivotal experience. Many years ago Mark Twain commented, "I was seldom able to see an opportunity until it had ceased to be one." *On Campus* can help students see the value of higher education while it is still an opportunity.

I would like to acknowledge the numerous students from my classes at Monroe Community College who reinforced my efforts to write a comprehensive student success book. Special thanks go to Leah Santirroco Dyer, Assistant Director of Public Safety, who provided thoughtful suggestions regarding campus safety issues.

My sincere gratitude is extended to the Prentice Hall team, Sande Johnson, Lynda Cramer, Kerry Rubadue, and Kelly Ricci, who worked hard to publish an outstanding textbook. I am indebted to Linda Thompson, who on the shortest of timelines, provided expert editing. Although we live across the country from one another, I felt we were kindred spirits. I also would like to extend my appreciation to Kevin Keating, Broward Community College; Cathy Lysy, Boston University; and Jacqueline Robinson, Milwaukee Area Technical College, for their insightful reviews.

To my husband, John, the cute guy I met 40 years ago at the University of Connecticut Student Union on his first day of college, I am indebted for a lifetime of unwavering encouragement and assistance.

Brief Contents

Contents

CHAPTER 8   Academic Writing   179

COURSE SYLLABUS

Many things are lost for want of asking.
~ *English proverb*

On the first day of college in classrooms across the United States, you share similar experiences with all students. Entering the classroom, you find a seat and wait for class to start. There is usually a feeling of tension and excitement as you anticipate the beginning of a new semester. When the professor enters and walks to the front of the classroom, all eyes follow. In many of your minds, there is an unanswered question: How hard will this professor and course be? The answer becomes evident as the professor either hands out the course syllabus or explains how students can access a copy online.

As you attend your classes the first week, you will notice differences in the way your professors introduce their courses. Some professors explain the course syllabus in great detail by reading and explaining each point. Other professors, preferring that students read the course syllabus on their own, may talk about the course in general, involve students in an ice breaker, or lecture on a course topic. Regardless of a professor's style, all professors have the same expectation: You are, without exception, responsible for following the course syllabus.

The course syllabus you receive in each course should comply with guidelines set by the college. Its purpose is to communicate the learning content and the instructor's requirements. Think of the course syllabus as a learning plan that you can use to set personal goals and to manage your time. Imagine what students must have thought in 1919 when they read the syllabus for *Contemporary Civilization,* a course still offered at Columbia University. Here is a brief description of its content:

> It is difficult to overemphasize the uniqueness of these early CC syllabi. A modern syllabus usually fills only a few pages and lists class requirements and readings, sometimes grouped under general headings. For its first 20 years, however, the CC syllabus was something much more vast and impressive, a detailed outline of the content of the entire course, published as a bound volume by Columbia University Press.[1]

COURSE SYLLABUS DOCUMENT

A **course syllabus** is an official college document that explains the course content, requirements, and expectations for a specific course. Don't bury the syllabus among your papers or toss it away. Read each syllabus carefully and thoughtfully. Because you may need to refer to your syllabi periodically throughout the semester, keep them in a location that you can readily access.

Even after you have completed a semester, keep the course syllabi with your college records. In the event that you transfer to another college, a course syllabus will provide more detailed information than the course title or catalog description. If the course titles are different at each college, a syllabus may be used to determine whether or not you can transfer credit.

In some colleges the terms *course syllabus* and *course information sheet* are used interchangeably. Be sure you know what the terms mean at your college.

COURSE SYLLABUS CONTRACT

Many colleges treat the course syllabus as a written legal covenant that outlines responsibilities involving the student, instructor, and college. You may be required to sign a **course syllabus agreement** to indicate that you have read the syllabus, understand its content, and are aware of your obligations and responsibilities for that course.

EXAMPLE

I, the undersigned, hereby indicate that I have read and fully understand the terms and conditions of the Course Syllabus and I unconditionally agree to abide by the terms of the Course Syllabus.

Course Number _____

Date _____

Signature _____

COURSE SYLLABUS TOPICS

A course syllabus is typically organized under major headings that address fundamental questions:

What are the course title, course number, and credit hours?

How can students contact the instructor?

What are students expected to learn in the course?

How is the course information presented?

How does the instructor measure what students have learned?

What are students' responsibilities and rights?

GENERAL COURSE INFORMATION

General course information includes the course number, title, and description and identifies any prerequisite or corequisite. A **prerequisite** may be specific courses, test scores, and/or grade level that must be completed before taking a particular course. A **corequisite** is a course or lab that must be taken either simultaneously with or prior to taking another course. When you sign up for a class, be sure to double-check that you have the required academic background and that you have registered for the correct course.

Course numbers indicate if a course is lower division or upper division. Lower division courses are usually completed in the first two years of college. Upper division courses designate advanced level of study in the sophomore, junior, and senior years. Typically 100-level courses are lower division; 200-level are upper division.

Each course is assigned a number of **credits** or points that you can earn after you complete the semester. The number of credits corresponds to the number of hours of instruction in traditional courses during a semester term. Typically there are 15 hours of instruction for each credit hour. Courses with labs may meet more hours than the number of credits they carry. In Chapter 10, you will learn how different types of course delivery change the number of faculty to student instruction time. A trimester system designates credits with **quarter hours**. The term **credit** is also called **semester hour, unit hour,** or **unit**.

If you would like to take a course without earning credit or a grade, you can arrange to **audit** the course. Your college may require that you first obtain permission to audit a course from the professor who teaches that section. Usually, permission is granted if seats are available. You still have to pay tuition for the course. An "AU" or similar designation next to the course appears on your transcript to indicate you audited the course.

Besides credit-bearing courses, colleges may offer **noncredit** courses, which appear on your transcript. These courses, taught by college faculty, may be developmental-level courses designed to remediate academic skills or workforce-related courses to upgrade skills. Depending on the college, these credits may or may not count toward your grade average; however, the course titles and credits will still appear on your official transcript.

INSTRUCTOR INFORMATION

This section provides specific details describing who is teaching the course, how the instructor can be contacted, and when the instructor is available outside of class. The information should include the following about the instructor:

- Full name
- Title
- Office location and telephone number
- Office hours
- E-mail address
- Web site address (if applicable)
- Teaching assistant's name and contact information (if applicable)

COURSE DESCRIPTION

In contrast to the brief catalog course description, the course syllabus describes the course more fully. Your syllabus may explain the professor's teaching methods as well as how you will be involved in the learning process.

COURSE GOALS, OBJECTIVES, AND OUTCOMES

Goals, objectives, and outcomes express the skills and knowledge that students are expected to gain from taking the course. Sometimes the terms *goals* and *objectives* are used synonymously. In general, **course goals** state the broad purposes of the course, **course objectives** describe specific purposes of the course, and **learning outcomes** explain how students are to demonstrate their knowledge or skills.

TEXTBOOKS AND SUPPLIES

This section includes a detailed list of items students need to purchase or reserve:

- Required and optional textbooks, with the specific title, author, and edition
- Required and optional supplies such as a calculator, notebook, or binder
- Books and materials on reserve at the library and on electronic reserve

COURSE POLICIES

Course policies explain the dos and don'ts of the course—what actions are tolerated and expected and what actions are restricted and penalized. Typical topics include

- Attendance
- Promptness
- Participation
- E-mail assignments
- Classroom etiquette
- Rules of behavior
- Missed tests

- Missed or late assignments
- Cell phones/pagers
- Audio/video recordings of the instructor or the class

COURSE GRADING

This section provides a clear understanding about how the final grade is calculated, based on assessments and grading criteria. The syllabus should indicate what topics are evaluated and whether extra credit is offered. Typical methods of assessment include

- Homework or assignments
- Quizzes, tests, and exams
- Papers
- Class presentations or projects

In Chapter 2, you will learn more about how the weight and value of each assessment affect the final grade.

COLLEGE POLICIES

College policies, sometimes stated as course policies, govern rules and regulations for all college students. These policies include

- Accommodations for students with disabilities
- Withdrawing from courses
- Student code of conduct
- Academic integrity
- Emergency closings

STUDENT SUPPORT SERVICES

Colleges provide a wide array of services to assist students. Your instructor may list those services that are particularly relevant for the course. These may include

- Library services
- Learning centers
- Tutoring
- Online resources and services

In Chapter 12, you will learn more about college services.

COURSE CALENDAR OR SCHEDULE

A course calendar or schedule may be part of the syllabus or may be a separate attachment. This schedule provides an outline of the sequence of course topics, assignment deadlines, quiz and test dates, and which topics or materials are included in each test. The syllabus may also indicate whether or not all quizzes are scheduled or announced ahead of time.

 FOR DISCUSSION

Read the example of a freshman American history course syllabus from Baruch College (NY)[2] to determine what information is provided. In the left column, enter the *number* of the question (listed below) next to the section in the syllabus that answers the question.

1. What are the course title and section number?
2. How can students contact the instructor?
3. What are students expected to learn in the course?
4. How is the course information presented?
5. How does the instructor measure what students have learned?
6. What are students' responsibilities?
7. What are students' rights?

	History 1000 **Themes in American History** Prof. _____ Building 11, Room ____ (Box D-) Office Hours: By appointment; I am on campus 5 days a week. **Description and Objectives** Spanning approximately 200 years, from the formation of the United States until the 1970s, this introductory course in American history focuses upon the

formation and sources of American nationalism. Our primary concern is political history, but we will spend a great deal of time examining issues of race and the rise of the United States as a world power. We will also explore the United States' dedication to democracy and democratic values. The questions we ask will demand attention to social, economic, and cultural concerns.

History is not the memorization and recitation of dates and facts. Instead, history calls for the gathering and assessment of information and the creation and testing of arguments. The assignments and activities in this course are designed accordingly. The course's objective is to expose students to a range of historical material in both primary and secondary sources and to help them to make cogent arguments about that material—doing history.

Requirements
Active participation is required in the classroom and attendance is essential. Classroom discussions will be enhanced with occasional in-class assignments, and some assignments will be on Blackboard. I encourage you to meet with me once in a one-on-one setting during the semester, and it would be best if that meeting happens earlier in the term.

Four absences will result in a grade of WU. Assignments are due at the beginning of each class meeting. Assignments may be emailed to me. A full grade will be deducted for each day an assignment is late; after four days, no credit will be given for late assignments.

In addition to providing material in a typed or electronic format, you must familiarize yourself with Blackboard and the Web. URLs (Web addresses) for pertinent sites will be provided, and the vast majority of the class information will be available electronically. Furthermore, some assignments may be completed online. An extraordinarily rich variety of historical information can be accessed through the Internet. If you need an e-mail account, obtain one by following the instructions on the Baruch College home page. Almost all the course material will be available through Blackboard, Baruch's online course-delivery system. We will review Blackboard, which is available from the college's home page.

Be considerate to your colleagues. Before entering class, turn off all cell phones and beepers. If you are late or have to leave early, choose a seat that will not disrupt discussion.

Learning history does not offer much in the way of shortcuts. Most historical knowledge is obtained through reading and reading takes time. A good rule of thumb is that you will need at least

2-3 hours of study for each hour spent in the classroom. The pace of the course demands that you keep up with the readings and other assignments. If you have difficulty maintaining the schedule, difficulty meeting deadlines, or any other problems relating to the course, contact me immediately. I am on campus 5 days a week and am always available through e-mail.

Grading
Your grade for the course will consist of the following:
- Participation: attendance, active contributions to discussions, and classroom exercises (in person and on the Web), as well as one substantive discussion/exchange with me (10%)
- Midterm Exam: essay/short answer (10%)
- Final Exam: essay/short answer (10%)
- 4 Quizzes: multiple choice (20%)
- 5 Writing Assignments (50%)

Required Texts
Purchase the following textbooks, all of which are available in the Baruch Bookstore:
Eric Foner, *The Story of American Freedom* (NY: Norton, 1998)
Gary Gerstle, *American Crucible* (Princeton, 2002)
Other required readings and handouts will be posted via Blackboard on the Web.

Recommended Texts

Students unfamiliar with U.S. history are strongly encouraged to consider purchasing a survey textbook. Many are good; but I recommend

Berkin, Carol, et al., *Making America* (Houghton Mifflin)

Also, there is a wealth of information and strategies available in the following handbook:

Berkin, Carol, and Anderson, Betty S., *The History Handbook* (Houghton Mifflin)

Schedule of Classes

(Subject to Revision)

1—January 27 Introduction: American values and colonial America

Introductory Quiz

2—January 29 Revolution and the creation of the United States

Read: AF 1-28 ("Birth of American Freedom") Declaration of Independence; Smith on reserve; Study Guide 1(HIS 1000 assessment)

3—February 3 Read: AF 29-46 ("To Call It Freedom")

Read U.S. Constitution and the Federalist papers (#10 in particular)

4—February 5 Constitution and Federalist Papers Draft

Writing Assignment 1

STUDENT RESPONSIBILITIES AND RIGHTS

As you read each course syllabus, analyze it. What impression does the syllabus convey? Does the course appear to be what you expected? Or, are you concerned about your ability to complete the course requirements?

If you have any questions or concerns, make an appointment to speak with your professor as soon as possible. Your professor will ask you questions about your academic background and may make recommendations. That way, you can make an informed decision as to whether you will do well to stay in the course or if you should drop that course and add a different one.

A college professor expects you to read the course syllabus carefully and to ask any questions you may have about its content. Because many college professors treat their courses as preprofessional experiences, they hold you responsible for meeting deadlines for assignments, papers, projects, and tests, without exception. When policies are explained in the syllabus, a professor has little or no patience for such remarks as, I didn't know you took off points for being late or I didn't realize my attendance counted towardsparticipation.

For instance, in the following example, students would be hard pressed to claim they did not know the consequences of handing in late papers and assignments after reading their course syllabus.

A Communications Course at Ohio University

Papers and other assignments are due at the assigned due dates and times. No makeup or alternative exams will be given. Students who turn in papers late gain an unfair advantage over their classmates who meet the assigned deadlines. Therefore, except in very rare circumstances, late papers will be penalized 1 letter grade for each 24-hour period after the due date. (The clock starts running at the assigned due date and time.)[3]

Sometimes, a course syllabus is subject to change as the demands of the course require. These changes are either announced in class and/or e-mailed to students. Failure to attend class or read course-related e-mail does not excuse you from your responsibility to be aware of these changes.

Just as a course syllabus details your responsibilities, the syllabus provides an understanding of your rights. For instance, you should know what topics will be covered in the course. Also, you have a right to know what you can expect in terms of assignments and grading procedures. In other words, if a course syllabus states that all tests are weighted equally for the final grade, the instructor may not arbitrarily change this weighting during the semester.

After you read the course syllabus, make sure you clarify any aspect of the syllabus that is either unclear or perhaps not addressed at all. If the syllabus is missing information that was not presented in class, you have a right to find out those details.

OBLIGATIONS AND RESPONSIBILITIES

In general terms, an **obligation** is something that you are committed to or required to do. **Responsibility** is, in effect, your *response* to your obligations. The more you respond to your obligations, the more maturity you demonstrate. For example, it is your obligation to buy books for your courses, but it is your responsibility to read them. Similarly, it is your obligation to follow the code of conduct at college, but it is your responsibility to behave civilly.

 FOR DISCUSSION

Reread the chapter and examine it from the perspective of what you believe your obligations and responsibilities at college are. Make a list of each and then check off those that you believe are both an obligation and a responsibility.

ACTIVITIES AND EXERCISES

Log onto the On Campus Student Website at www.prenhall.com/fitton to determine how well you have studied and what you still need to learn.

1. **Defining Terms**
   Write the meanings of the following words.

   Course syllabus _____

   _____

   Course syllabus agreement _____

   _____

Course goals, objectives, learning outcomes _____

_____

_____

Credit _____

_____

Noncredit _____

_____

Prerèquisite _____

_____

Corequisite _____
Audit _____

_____

2. **Checking Your Understanding**
   a. In what ways does a course syllabus protect students' rights?

   _____

   _____

   _____

   _____

   b. In what ways does a course syllabus imply faculty responsibilities?

   _____

   _____

   _____

   _____

3. Knowing Your Campus

Consolidate and organize the information provided in the syllabus for each of your courses. Use a separate table for each course.

Course Title & Credit	
Course Prefix & Number	
Instructor	
Office Location	
Office Phone Number	
Email Address	
Office Hours	
Attendance Policy	
Assignment Policy	
Late Policy	
Make-Up Policy	
Classmate Contact Name/E-mail/Phone #	

Final Grade Calculation

Criteria	Percent or Point Value	Important Notes
Class Participation		
Assignments/Homework		
Papers		
Projects		
Quizzes		
Tests		
Final Exam		
Other		

Course Title & Credit	
Course Prefix & Number	
Instructor	
Office Location	
Office Phone Number	
Email Address	
Office Hours	
Attendance Policy	
Assignment Policy	
Late Policy	
Make-Up Policy	
Classmate Contact Name/E-mail/Phone #	

Final Grade Calculation

Criteria	Percent or Point Value	Important Notes
Class Participation		
Assignments/Homework		
Papers		
Projects		
Quizzes		
Tests		
Final Exam		
Other		

Course Title & Credit	
Course Prefix & Number	
Instructor	
Office Location	
Office Phone Number	
Email Address	
Office Hours	
Attendance Policy	
Assignment Policy	
Late Policy	
Make-Up Policy	
Classmate Contact Name/E-mail/Phone #	

Final Grade Calculation

Criteria	Percent or Point Value	Important Notes
Class Participation		
Assignments/Homework		
Papers		
Projects		
Quizzes		
Tests		
Final Exam		
Other		

Course Title & Credit	
Course Prefix & Number	
Instructor	
Office Location	
Office Phone Number	
Email Address	
Office Hours	
Attendance Policy	
Assignment Policy	
Late Policy	
Make-Up Policy	
Classmate Contact Name/E-mail/Phone #	

Final Grade Calculation

Criteria	Percent or Point Value	Important Notes
Class Participation		
Assignments/Homework		
Papers		
Projects		
Quizzes		
Tests		
Final Exam		
Other		

Course Title & Credit	
Course Prefix & Number	
Instructor	
Office Location	
Office Phone Number	
Email Address	
Office Hours	
Attendance Policy	
Assignment Policy	
Late Policy	
Make-Up Policy	
Classmate Contact Name/E-mail/Phone #	

Final Grade Calculation

Criteria	Percent or Point Value	Important Notes
Class Participation		
Assignments/Homework		
Papers		
Projects		
Quizzes		
Tests		
Final Exam		
Other		

Course Title & Credit	
Course Prefix & Number	
Instructor	
Office Location	
Office Phone Number	
Email Address	
Office Hours	
Attendance Policy	
Assignment Policy	
Late Policy	
Make-Up Policy	
Classmate Contact Name/E-mail/Phone #	

Final Grade Calculation

Criteria	Percent or Point Value	Important Notes
Class Participation		
Assignments/Homework		
Papers		
Projects		
Quizzes		
Tests		
Final Exam		
Other		

4. Applying Chapter Concepts

a. Above each number in the table, write the course prefix and number for each of your courses. Then, use the details you collected in Exercise 1.3 to check off the information provided by each syllabus.

		Course Prefix & No.				
1	2	3	4	5	6	**Check if your course syllabus explains**
						Instructor information
						General course information
						Course description
						Course goals, objectives, outcomes
						Textbooks and materials
						Course policies
						Course grading
						College policies
						Student support services
						Course calendar or schedule

b. Based on course information that is missing from the table, what questions do you now have regarding course expectations?

_____

_____

c. Which of your course syllabi do you prefer? Why?

_____

_____

5. Writing for Reflection

Explore your feelings about responsibility in college. Write at least one paragraph in response to the following quotation or a meaningful sentence you select from the chapter.

For the want of a nail, the shoe was lost; for the want of a shoe the horse was lost; and for the want of a horse the rider was lost, being overtaken and slain by the enemy, all for the want of care about a horseshoe nail.

Benjamin Franklin

6. **Concerning College Athletes**

Make a special effort to find the name of a classmate who will let you photocopy missed notes and will tell you about any other important information, such as changes in the syllabus regarding assignments and test dates.

7. **Reading Further**

The reading selections on the On Campus Student Website at www. prenhall.com/fitton explore different aspects of chapter topics. At the end of each reading selection are critical thinking questions. Your instructor will let you know whether you should print out your responses or use the online feature to e-mail your answers.

A Letter to My Students Bill Taylor

Read this selection to understand why the author wrote a letter to his students at the beginning of the semester.

Notes

[1] Columbia College. *Core Curriculum.*, http://www.college.columbia.edu/core/oasis/history0.php (accessed March 17, 2004).

[2] David Potash, *The Baruch College Faculty Handbook Suggestions for Creating a Good Syllabus, History 1000*, Baruch College, The City University of New York, http://www.baruch.cuny.edu/facultyhandbook/syllabus_items.htm (accessed March 1, 2004).

[3] Judith Yaross Lee, *Communications syllabus.* Ohio University, http://www.ohiouedu/~leej/inco234/syllabus.html (accessed April 12, 2003; site now discontinued).

Notes

Notes

COLLEGE GRADES

2

Results are what you expect; consequences are what you get.
~ Anonymous

One of the inescapable occurrences at college is being graded. At the end of the semester, all that remains to document both your effort and understanding of a college course is a single grade. Many systems have been used in the past to notate grades. For example, in 1780, Yale University used a 4-point grading system; later in 1830, Harvard adopted a 20-point grading scale. Some colleges preferred descriptive terms when sending reports home to parents. In 1817, William and Mary College mailed this type of "report card" to parents:

> The Society took into consideration the situation of the different Classes, and the demeanors and improvement of each of the Students during the Course which has just terminated, Whereupon Resolved that a Communication to the following effect be transmitted to the Parent or Guardian of every young man at the Institution.
>
> No. 1. (Names listed) The first in their respective classes, orderly and attentive and have made the most flattering improvement.
>
> No. 2. Orderly, correct and attentive and their Improvement has been respectable.
>
> No. 3. They have made very little improvement and as we apprehend from want of Diligence.
>
> No. 4. They have learnt little or nothing and we believe on account of escapade and Idleness.[1]

Today, most colleges no longer send reports home to parents. Therefore, you alone must be responsible for understanding how college grading works in general and how it works, in particular, at your college.

WHY GRADES MATTER

For many reasons—personally, professionally, and practically—it makes sense to strive for good grades. Although grading is an imperfect system, over the long haul a GPA is a fairly good demonstration of your academic achievement. True, you may receive a grade that you believe does not represent what you have learned, or you may take a test that you believe is unreasonably hard. For the most part, however, it is not typical to receive a C instead of an A or a D instead of a B. Low grades are the result of many factors and typically stem from the choices you make regarding your study habits, time management, and attitude toward learning.

Your course grades can impact opportunities you may have in the future. For example, when you submit a résumé for a job, your GPA makes a statement about your overall commitment and achievement while in college. Many employers believe your GPA is an indication of the kind of employee you will be because it reflects on your work habits. Employers look carefully at both your overall GPA and your GPA in your major. Additionally, if you want to transfer to another college, you will find most colleges usually require a grade of C or better in order to accept a course for credit transfer. For these reasons, make decisions throughout the semester that enable you to earn the best grades you are capable of achieving.

Remember this rule: It is much easier to maintain a good GPA than to turn around a low GPA in subsequent semesters.

For example, as a first-semester student, suppose you earn 15 credits with a 1.9 GPA. The second semester, you want to raise your GPA to at least a 2.5. To accomplish this, you have to earn at least a 3.1. To raise your cumulative GPA to a 3.0 at the end of the third semester, you would have to earn all A's. Given your past academic performance, this might not be a realistic expectation.

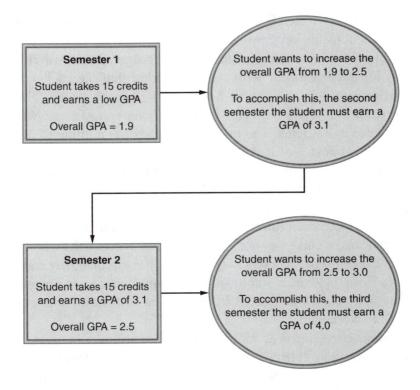

With a starting 1.9 GPA the first semester, in order *to* graduate with a 3.0 GPA, you must earn a minimum 3.2 GPA each subsequent semester for a bachelor's degree (124 credits) and a 3.3 for an associate's degree (64 credits). From this example, you can understand the importance of working hard your freshman year to achieve your best grades.

PERSONAL MOTIVATION

There is an old Zen motto:

> If you want to get someplace, you've got to give up wanting to get to that place.
> In order to achieve something, you've got to stop waiting for it to happen and get into the process of achieving it.

In other words, you must replace *wanting* good grades with *working* for good grades.

People are motivated by extrinsic and intrinsic motivation. **Extrinsic motivation** depends on contingent rewards that are not part of the activity. For instance, many elementary school teachers give children stickers for good behavior with the expectation that the sticker award (which has nothing to do with behavior) will motivate the child to behave well. Employers may give incentive bonuses to factory workers who produce more items. The monetary reward has nothing to do with making the product, but it will motivate workers to work faster. Similarly, you might work extra hard if your parents offered to pay for your spring-break vacation with the condition that you earn at least at 3.5 GPA.

Extrinsic motivation can be effective, but it has limitations. Take away the stickers, and a child may not want to behave. Remove the work incentive at the factory, and workers may slow down more than they had prior to the extrinsic motivator. Return to college after your spring break, and you may find yourself distracted from studying without another enticing incentive to work hard.

In comparison, intrinsic motivation is a far stronger motivator than extrinsic motivation. **Intrinsic motivation** draws on your desire to perform the task for its own sake. If you are intrinsically motivated, you do things just for the personal satisfaction you derive accomplishing those tasks. For example, most people who exercise are intrinsically motivated. Notice the determination displayed by people who go to the gym at 5:30 a.m. each morning to work out and then get to their jobs on time. For your college experience, determine the intrinsic factors that motivate you the most.

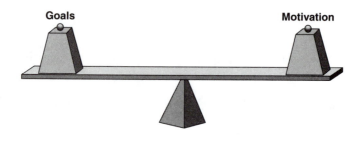

FOR DISCUSSION

Understanding what motivates you will help steady your resolve to stay committed when you are faced with competing distractions. Check off those reasons that apply to you. Then, compare your reasons with those of other participants in your discussion group.

Reasons for Good Grades

1. To feel satisfied with the knowledge you have learned
2. To stay in college
3. To be admitted to certain majors
4. To make the dean's list
5. To enroll in certain courses
6. To qualify for graduation
7. To graduate with honors
8. To participate in certain college activities
9. To maintain athletic eligibility in certain sports
10. To maintain financial aid
11. To qualify for financial scholarship
12. To qualify for the college honors program
13. To study abroad
14. To be considered for certain internships
15. To be admitted to graduate and professional schools
16. To qualify to become a graduate assistant
17. To obtain a job interview with the company where you want to work

COURSE GRADES

As you might expect, grading in college is quite different from that in high school. In high school, you had many opportunities to improve your grades. In college, the grading system reflects higher expectations that come with increased adult responsibility. Look at a comparison chart compiled by Southern Methodist University (TX)[2] that highlights key differences between high school and college grading.

High School	College
Grades are given for most assigned work.	Grades may not be provided for all assigned work.
Consistently good homework grades may raise your overall grade when test grades are low.	Grades on tests and major papers usually provide most of the course grade.
Extra-credit projects are often available to help you raise your grade.	Extra-credit projects cannot, generally speaking, be used to raise a grade.
Initial test grades, especially when they are low, may not have an adverse effect on your final grade.	Watch out for your first tests. These are usually "wake-up calls" to let you know what is expected—but they also may account for a substantial part of your course grade. You may be shocked when you get your grades.
You may graduate as long as you have passed all required courses with a grade of D or higher.	You may graduate only if your average in classes meets the departmental standard—typically a 2.0, or C.
Guiding principle: "Effort counts." Courses are usually structured to reward a "good-faith effort."	**Guiding principle:** "Results count." Although "good-faith effort" is important in regard to the professor's willingness to help you achieve good results, it will not substitute for results in the grading process.

Many colleges have instituted collegewide guidelines for faculty to follow that communicate a course's grading policies.

EXAMPLE

Union County College (NJ)

The faculty has adopted a collegewide grading policy, which requires each instructor to give students a written statement regarding his or her grading policy at the beginning of each academic term. Students who have failed to receive such information prior to the end of the second week of classes should approach the instructor with a special request for a statement outlining the grading policy to be followed.[3]

When you start a new semester, you should know exactly how your final grade is calculated for each of your courses. In particular, you should understand the **rubric,** a detailed description of standards that the professor uses to evaluate work. That way, you can make informed decisions as to how to study for each subject. If your instructor does not provide information about how your final grade is calculated, ask for these details and make sure you understand them. You do not want to spend the semester second-guessing how your grade is determined.

Grading Example

Participation (panels, performance, discussion)	25%
Response papers – 2	25%
Research paper	25%
Final exam	25%

In this first example, four grades are averaged equally for the final grade, with all grades having a significant impact on the final grade. The final exam presents an additional risk because there are no tests during the semester. Students with test anxiety or whose test taking skills need strengthening should attend college workshops on test-taking skills.

Grading Example

1 5-page paper	10%
1 15-page paper	35%
Class participation	15%
Oral presentation and annotated bibliography	15%
Electronic discussion forum	10%
Final exam	15%

In Example 2, the requirements emphasize discussion and written assignments. Students who like to "sit back" and listen to others will need to push themselves to become more actively involved. Additionally, students who find writing challenging may want to visit the college writing center.

Grading Example

Test 1 Chapters 1 & 2	10 points
Test 2 Chapter 3 & 4	25 points
Test 3 Chapters 6, 10 and 11	25 points
First book report	5 points
Second book report	5 points
Final Chapter 5	10 points
Cumulative	20 points

In Example 3, test scores weigh heavily, providing no opportunity for students to raise a grade with class participation. Students who do not perform well on the first test, however, have an opportunity to increase their average by improving their study habits.

Grading Example

Assignment	Points	Course Grade	Total Points Earned
Portfolio	400 points	A	930+
Essay 1	80 points	A−	900–929
Essay 2	100 points	B+	870–899
Essay 3	130 points	B	830–869
Response papers (6)	150 points (25 pts. each)	B−	800–829
Peer reviews (3)	75 points (25 pts. each)	C+	770–799
Conferences (3)	15 points (5 pts. each)	C	730–769
Participation and attendance	50 points	D	600–729
		F	Below 600

The fourth example shows an elaborate grading system that assigns specific point values for each type of task. As illustrated from an English course at the University of New Mexico, the total points earned are assigned a range of letter grades.[4] When your professor uses a point system, make sure you understand how it works at the beginning of the semester.

Grading on a curve means the instructor distributes numeric scores in such a way that their graph, when plotted as a curve, resembles a bell shape. Because most of the grades are centered around the grade C, for every A, someone else receives an F. Consequently, you are graded relative to how well you perform when compared to others who take the test rather than on absolute numerical test scores.

When an instructor grades on a bell curve, you will earn an A only if you are significantly above the class average. These courses are typically more competitive because you must "compete" with each other to earn a higher grade.

Notice how the bell curve resembles a bell shape.[5]

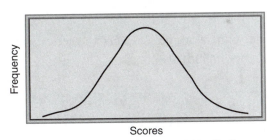

Scores

Theoretical Normal Curve of Distribution

GRADE POINT AVERAGE

Your grade point average is a measure of your academic performance. The average is calculated by dividing the total credit points attempted by the total points earned. Course grades are averaged at the end of each semester to determine your grade point average (abbreviated GPA). The terms **grade point average (GPA)** and **quality point average (QPA)** are often used interchangeably. **Cumulative grade point average** is the weighted mean value of all grade points you have earned for all semesters you were enrolled in college.

LETTER GRADES

Most U.S. colleges use letter grades to indicate a level of academic performance.

A = excellent

B = good

C = fair

D = barely passing

F = failure

P = passed at a minimum level of C−

NP = not passed

S = satisfactory, passed at a minimum level of B−

U = unsatisfactory

I = work incomplete due to circumstances beyond the student's control

W = withdrawal from the course

The grades A, B, C, and D may be modified by plus (+) or minus (−)

POINT VALUE

To calculate a grade point average, convert the letter grades to points. Colleges may or may not include A+ or D−.

Letter Grade	Point Value
A	4.0
A−	3.7
B+	3.3
B	3.0
B−	2.7
C+	2.3
C	2.0
C−	1.7
D+	1.3

(continued)

Letter Grade	Point Value
D	1.0
D−	0.7
E/F	0.0
W	—

CALCULATING GRADE POINT AVERAGE

To figure out your semester GPA, multiply the number of credits given for each class by the point value of the letter grade that you earned in that class. That product determines your grade points for each class. Next, add the grade points in all your classes for that semester and divide it by the total number of registered credit hours.

EXAMPLE

Class	Conversion Grade Point Value	Credits	Points
MTH 165	B+ = 3.3 points	× 3 credits =	= 9.9 grade points
ENG 101	C = 2.0 points	× 3 credits =	= 6.0 grade points
HIS 110	A = 4.0 points	× 3 credits =	= 12.0 grade points
BOT 140	B = 3.0 points	× 3 credits =	= 9.0 grade points
HED 148	A− = 3.7 points	× 2 credits =	= 7.4 grade points
	Totals:	**14 credits**	**44.3 grade points**
GPA Calc =	**44.3 grade points**	**divided by 14 credits**	**= 3.16 GPA**

In the next two examples, notice how a one-credit course can make a significant impact on the GPA.

Even though all the three-credit courses are a C, a one-credit course grade of F results in a 1.85 GPA. In many colleges, a GPA of less than 2.00 results in academic probation.

Class	Conversion Grade Point Value	Credits	Points
MTH 165	C = 2.0 points	× 3 credits =	6.0 grade points
ENG 101	C = 2.0 points	× 3 credits =	6.0 grade points
HIS 110	C = 2.0 points	× 3 credits =	6.0 grade points
BOT 140	C = 2.0 points	× 3 credits =	6.0 grade points
PEC 101	F = 0 points	× 1 credit =	0.0 grade points
	Totals	**13 credits**	**24 grade points**
GPA Calc =	**24 grade points**	**divided by 13 credits**	**= 1.84 GPA**

In contrast, in the next example, all C's plus a one-credit course grade of A results in a 2.15 GPA.

Class	Conversion Grade Point Value	Credits	Points
MTH 165	C = 2.0 points	× 3 credits =	6.0 grade points
ENG 101	C = 2.0 points	× 3 credits =	6.0 grade points
HIS 110	C = 2.0 points	× 3 credits =	6.0 grade points
BOT 140	C = 2.0 points	× 3 credits =	6.0 grade points
PEC 101	A = 4.0 points	× 1 credit =	4.0 grade points
	Totals	**13 credits**	**28 grade points**
GPA Calc =	**28 grade points**	**divided by 13 credits**	**= 2.15 GPA**

GPA Calculators

Many college Web sites provide reliable online GPA calculators to make calculating your grade points a simple task. Try typing the words "GPA Calculator" on your college Web site, or use the GPA calculator provided on the *On Campus Student Website*.

FOR DISCUSSION

What might be the **extrinsic** and **intrinsic values** of earning good grades in college?

ACTIVITIES AND EXERCISES

Log onto the On Campus Student Website at www.prenhall.com/fitton to determine how well you have studied and what you still need to learn.

1. **Defining Terms**
   Write the meanings of the following words.

   GPA, QPA _____

   _____

   _____

   Cumulative grade average _____

   _____

   _____

   Grading on a curve _____

   _____

   _____

   _____

   Rubric _____

2. **Checking Your Understanding**
   a. How does the grading in this course compare to the four text examples? What do the requirements in this course emphasize?

   _____

   _____

   _____

   _____

   b. Explain why it is easier to maintain a good GPA than to turn around a low GPA.

   _____

3. **Knowing Your Campus**

   a. What is the grading policy at your college?

   _____

   _____

   _____

   b. Does your college have midterm grades? If so, how are the grades reported?

   _____

   _____

4. **Applying Chapter Concepts**

   a. Calculate the GPA using the grades indicated.

Course	Conversion Grade Point Value	Credits	Points
ENG 101	C =	× 3 credits =	_____ grade points
HIS 110	B− =	× 3 credits =	_____ grade points
MTH 165	D+=	× 3 credits =	_____ grade points
BIO 126	C+ =	× 4 credits =	_____ grade points
HED 101	A =	× 2 credits =	_____ grade points
	Totals =	_____ credits	_____ grade points
GPA	_____ **grade points**	**divided by** _____ **credits**	= _____ **GPA**

b. Keep a record of the grades you receive this semester. Include all scores that will be used to calculate your final average in each course. Enter these grades in the following chart, or create your own table to track your grades.

Courses						
1						
2						
3						
4						
5						
6						
7						
8						
9						
10						

5. **Writing for Reflection**

Explore your feelings about college grades. Write at least one paragraph in response to one of the following quotations or a meaningful sentence you select from the chapter.

"By nature, men are nearly alike; by practice, they get wide apart."
Confucius

"It's not that I'm so smart, it's just that I stay with problems longer."
Albert Einstein

6. **Concerning College Athletes**

What are the GPA requirements for maintaining your athletic eligibility and/or scholarship?

7. **Reading Further**

The reading selections on the On Campus Student Website at www.prenhall.com/fitton explore different aspects of chapter topics. At the end of each reading selection are critical thinking questions. Your instructor will let you know whether you should print out your responses or use the online feature to e-mail your answers.

a. *College at Work: Outlook and Earning for College Graduates, 2000–10,* Bureau of Labor Statistics

As you read this report prepared by the Bureau of Labor Statistics, draw your own conclusions as to how good college grades can improve the quality of your life.

b. *More Education: Lower Unemployment, Higher Pay,* Bureau of Labor Statistics

Read the Bureau of Labor Statistics report to learn about the correlation between education, salary and employment.

Notes

[1] M. L. Smallwood, *An Historical Study of Examinations and Grading Systems in Early American Universities* (Cambridge: Harvard University Press, 1935), 44.

[2] *How is College Different from High School?* Southern Methodist University, http://www.smu.edu/alec/whyhighschool.html (accessed March 28, 2003).

[3] Union County College Academic Policies and Regulations, Union County College, http://www.ucc.edu/grades.htm (accessed March 21, 2004; site now discontinued).

[4] *Freshman English at the University of New Mexico (2002–2003),* University of New Mexico, http://www.unm.edu/~english/docs/101syllabus.doc (accessed January 18, 2004; site now discontinued).

[5] Jonathan Dolhenty, *A Basic Guide to Statistics,* from the Jonathan Dolhenty Archive Web site, http://radicalacademy.com/statistics4.htm (accessed January 18, 2004).

Notes

Notes

CAMPUS COMMUNITY

3

Although the size, appearance, and culture of colleges have changed dramatically over centuries, the goals of American colleges, to educate and credential people for positions in society, continue. As explained by Cardinal John Henry Newman in 1854, higher education is a place that encompasses a community of learners.

If I were asked to describe as briefly and popularly as I could, what a University was, I should draw my answer from its ancient designation of a Studium Generale, or "School of Universal Learning." This description implies the assemblage of strangers from all parts in one spot; from all parts; else, how will you find professors and students for every department of knowledge and in one spot; else, how can there be any school at all?[1]

INSTITUTIONAL MISSION

From the smallest college with fewer than 100 students to the largest university with almost 50,000 students, institutions of higher education offer a range of advanced courses, certifications, and degrees. Beyond a common mission to provide an excellent education, colleges formulate their institutional mission based on their goals, geography, history, and tradition.

The mission statement of a community college, which includes the unique requirements and characteristics of its surrounding community, is different from that of a land-grant college, which has its historical charge of teaching, research, and service to the people of the state. Likewise, the mission statement of a religious-affiliated college, which promotes religious traditions and beliefs, differs from that of a public institution that has no such affiliation. The institutional mission guides how decisions are made in every office, school, and department within a college.

For example, at Beloit College (WI), a commitment for the values and traditions of a strong liberal education is articulated in their mission statement.

> Our primary aim at Beloit College is to provide a learning and living environment dedicated to the cultivation of liberally educated persons.[2]

The college mission statement at Babson College (MA) describes an innovative undergraduate program designed to meet changing global conditions.

> Babson College educates men and women to be entrepreneurial leaders in a rapidly changing world. We prepare them to identify opportunities and initiate actions that result in genuine accomplishment.[3]

Practical, hands-on learning experiences and internships support Montana Tech's mission at the University of Montana to educate "well rounded, competent, responsible and ethical professionals."

> Montana Tech of The University of Montana is a comprehensive university emphasizing science and engineering with a national and international reputation for excellence.[4]

Because its institutional mission statement furnishes each college with a sense of identity, purpose, and direction, the feel and focus of your college is related to its mission statement.

COLLEGE CULTURE

Until the late 1960s, colleges operated in loco parentis, a view that colleges should act on the behalf of parents to oversee the health, welfare, and morality of students. Spurred on by the civil rights movement and the

Vietnam War, students rebelled against these college restrictions. During the 1970s, colleges began to relinquish their controls regarding dress codes, curfews, and socializing with the opposite sex. This relaxation of control resulted in a more permissive environment that allowed students unrestricted personal and social freedom. By the beginning of the 21st century, many of these relaxed college rules brought increased student problems with alcohol and drugs. Virtually every campus community has been affected by these changes. As a result, many colleges now have reinstituted consequences for students who abuse established campus codes of conduct.

College culture expresses the beliefs, traditions, and behaviors of the college campus. This culture is often enshrined in the college's goals and mission statements and is reflected in periodic strategic plans issued by faculty and administration. Never static, college culture represents and reacts to changing social forces. As U.S. culture evolves, so does college culture. Within a college culture, there are *subcultures*—groups who have their own set of beliefs, traditions, and behaviors. Sometimes, a predominate college culture emerges, influencing the behaviors of individuals and groups within the college. College culture may be barely visible, or it may be prominent, coloring the college scene with established traditions, celebrations, events, ceremonies, and college themes.

TRADITIONS

College traditions, like familial traditions, are activities repeated by a group of people year after year. Many times, the origins of a tradition are long forgotten, but the satisfaction of following the tradition is sustained. For example, students who graduate from Bennington College (VT) are sure to remember the caring community that was part of their college culture:

> Near the end of term, when deadlines for final projects loom, fire engines from the local volunteer fire department drive through campus, sirens blaring and lights flashing, just as the clock strikes midnight. Loudspeakers announce the arrival of a twice-annual event at Bennington: midnight breakfast. Students—most interrupted in the middle of work on end-of-term projects—head for the dining halls, where faculty and staff members, dressed in aprons, serve them eggs, waffles, and coffee. Midnight breakfast celebrates the term that is coming to an end and the work that students have accomplished.[5]

CELEBRATIONS AND EVENTS

Homecoming, when alumni return to celebrate their alma mater, is a time-honored annual event at many colleges. Today, most college homecoming celebrations coincide with sports. At Oregon State University, one homecoming celebration tradition continues to be part of their college culture:

Aside from the game itself, the oldest tradition associated with Homecoming is the bonfire, known early on as the "Rook Bonfire" because it was the responsibility of the freshman class to both gather the wood and guard the stack from pranksters who might want to torch the pile early. No one knows the date of OSU's first Homecoming bonfire, but school records confirm the practice goes back to at least the year 1907.[6]

A college winter carnival held at Middlebury College (VT) is the oldest and largest student-run carnival event in the country. At Hendrix College in Arkansas, a candlelight carol service is an annual event inscribed in their college culture:

Almost 40 years ago, the Hendrix College Choir began presenting a Service of Lessons and carols modeled after the one presented at King's College in Cambridge, England. The Candlelight Service has since become an important Hendrix tradition. Each year more than 1,200 people travel to the College to experience one of the five on-campus presentations.[7]

CEREMONIES

Time-honored ceremonies, such as Silver Taps at Texas A&M University, enrich college culture:

The first Silver Taps was held in 1898 and honored Lawrence Sullivan Ross, the former governor of Texas and president of Texas A&M College. Silver Taps is currently held in the Academic Plaza and honors a deceased student. On the day of Silver Taps, a small card with the deceased student's name, class, major, and date of birth is placed as a notice at the base of the academic flagpole, in addition to the memorial located behind the flagpole. Around 10:15 that night, the lights are extinguished and hymns chime from Albritton Tower. Students silently gather at the statue of Lawrence Sullivan Ross. At 10:30 p.m., the Ross Volunteer Firing Squad marches into the plaza and fires a 21-gun salute. Buglers then play a special rendition of Silver Taps by Colonel Richard Dunn. Taps is played three times from the dome of the Academic Building: once each to the north, south, and west. It is not played to the east because the sun will never rise on that Aggie again. After the buglers play, the students silently return to their homes. Silver Taps is a sacred tradition that Aggies hold dear.[8]

THEMES

College culture may be expressed in college *themes*. For instance, since 1991, the University of Puget Sound (WA) has sponsored an annual Diversity Theme Year to engage the campus in lectures, arts events, programs, and activities that address issues of diversity and promote acceptance and tolerance of differences among people.[9]

2005–2006 Diversity Theme: Liberty and Justice for Some . . .

From the large campus at Notre Dame University in Indiana, where incoming freshman are told that they are now "part of the Notre Dame family" to the small campus at Whitman College (WA), students respond positively to an inviting cultural presence.

There is a spark at Whitman, a powerful sense of community. On a visit, you'll see it in the friendly greetings from people you've never met. As a Whitman student, you'll know it from the pride you develop for this special place of learning. Once you feel this spirit, you'll never forget it.[10]

DIVERSITY AND PLURALISM

Diversity is about differences. At college, you experience diversity when you meet people in classes, residential halls, and campus activities. You see differences in race, culture, gender, religious preference, sexual orientation, age, and life experience. The college campus reflects our multicultural and multireligious U.S. society.

Learning about and appreciating diversity enriches your college education. The liberal arts subjects you study—literature, history, anthropology, sociology, psychology, art, and music—represent individual and combined efforts and achievements of people from around the world. The more you understand diversity, the more you may appreciate these disciplines.

Appreciating differences in others begins with knowing who you are. What cultural, religious, and ethnic attributes define who you are? Once you understand how your identity affects your perceptions of the world, you can appreciate how people may see things differently. You may find that the more you learn about different cultures, religions, beliefs and values, the more you can learn about who you are. You learn to see the exotic in the familiar and the familiar in the exotic. You discover that people share human traits common to you—being nurturing, loving, and inquisitive.

Beyond the classroom, valuing diversity prepares you well to dialogue intelligently in a global community. Regardless of your career path, at some point you may work with colleagues whose backgrounds are not at all like yours. Effective communication depends on replacing bias, stereotypes, and prejudices toward differences with understanding, interest, tolerance, and kindness. When you look past differences, you may realize that differing perspectives can contribute positively to any decision.

Pluralism suggests you look at differences with understanding, respect, and even *engagement*. Pluralism is not about renouncing your individual and cultural identity, but rather it is about accepting diversity in others. The Rochester Pluralism Project at Monroe Community College explains this distinction by answering this question: How is pluralism different from diversity?

Good question! Most of us are aware of the existence of people whose faiths differ from our own. We notice the turbans worn by certain men, the head coverings or colorful saris worn by women. We're aware also that some folks discard their shoes on entering their house of worship, perhaps facing a certain way during prayer; still others sit silently in chairs or on cushions. For some, the holy day is Friday; for others, Sunday is set aside as "sacred" time. We notice tall minarets or graceful domes soaring above our cornfields or rising in our cities, yet we're not sure exactly what all this represents. In short, we've become increasingly conscious of changes in our cultural—especially religious—landscape, our remarkable diversity. Pluralism, on the other hand, asks us to engage in that diversity and actively begin to consider how these new faiths are changing America, how to make these differences into strengths that enrich our national and civic cultures, rather than tearing us apart.[11]

CIVILITY ON CAMPUS

Before you start reading this section, take a few minutes to think about the last time you noticed simple acts of civility: when a person held a door open for someone walking right behind or when a driver motioned for a waiting car to move into a lane. These simple acts of civility are part of what it means to be civil.

On campus, you share community space with hundreds—even thousands—of individuals. You come in contact with people, ideas, and experiences you might otherwise never have encountered. You meet individuals with beliefs, attitudes, and personal values that may or may not be similar to yours. Some students you may like; others you won't. With some students, you agree with what they have to say; with others you completely disagree. You may be assigned to live or work closely with students not of your choosing. Either way, each student deserves to be treated with politeness and respect. Within the campus environment, each individual has a right to study in peace and to socialize in a calm environment devoid of strident noise and profanity.

Every semester, you prepare academic work for a new slate of professors, each with his or her own set of requirements and preferences. Some professors you may like; others you may not. Some professors are approachable; others seem distant. On a college campus, civility is a reciprocal relationship, in which professors, administrators, and students treat each other with respect.

Campus civility is a behavior that all people deserve. When individuals feel they are entitled to behave as they please, unmindful of others around them, they are being rude. Rude behavior is both offensive and hurtful. When individuals participate in hate and bias-related incidents, they are being abusive. Abusive behavior is against all codes of decent, moral behavior. None of these behaviors have a place in civilized society and cannot be tolerated.

Civility is a social responsibility that contributes to the public good and the quality of life. Civility implies a concern for other people's welfare and a willingness to act decently and thoughtfully toward others. It is also an ethical and moral choice people make because they believe it is the right thing to do. Your college has codified their expectations in a formal code of behavior. You will learn more about these regulations in Chapter 11, "College Policy."

 FOR DISCUSSION

Part 1

The following list gives student behaviors that occur periodically in college classes. Read the list and circle five behaviors that you believe clearly demonstrate lack of civility towards other students and faculty.

Part 2

Meet with your group to discuss the behaviors each person has chosen. Next, make a combined list of the behaviors chosen by group members and agree on a ranking from most offensive (1) to least offensive. Discuss how the situations can be handled civilly. Be prepared to present your group's conclusions to the entire class.

1. Student leaves class repeatedly to take cell phone calls.
2. Student text-messages during lecture.
3. Student misses many classes for important personal issues and then is angry because the absences lower his or her final grade.
4. Student eats food in class.
5. Student argues with the professor about a grade.
6. Student talks loudly on cell phone in hallway.
7. Student cleans out book bag on classroom desk.
8. Male student makes crude remarks to passing female student.
9. Student leaves trash on desk.
10. Cell phone goes off repeatedly after student has been asked to silence it.
11. Student demands an extension for a late paper.
12. Students are talking to one another in class during instruction.
13. Student puts feet on table before class starts.
14. Student makes loud snide remark after faculty repeats request to stop talking.
15. Student utters a profanity when he or she receives a zero for handing in homework at end of class.

16. Student gets publicly angry after receiving a low test score.
17. Student pays no attention in class while working on a homework assignment.
18. Student challenges the professor's knowledge during class.
19. Student makes sarcastic remarks or gestures, such as yawning out loud.
20. Student dominates the class discussion.
21. Student wears headphones in class.
22. Student applies makeup in class.
23. Student sleeps during class.
24. Student noisily enters classroom and interrupts instruction.
25. Other example

ETIQUETTE

Don't confuse civility with etiquette. **Etiquette** is a socially accepted way of doing things at a particular time in a particular society. Initially, you learn etiquette from your family. As society changes, rules of etiquette evolve as well. For example, at one time it was considered proper etiquette for a female to wait for a male to open a door for her. Today, both females and males open doors for each other.

Civility and etiquette are not reciprocal. You can be civil while being ignorant of etiquette, and you can show fine manners and etiquette, yet behave uncivilly. Civility is behavior that emanates from within a person. Etiquette is behavior that responds to social customs.

NETIQUETTE

In the 18th century, Benjamin Franklin wrote,

"A slip of the foot you may soon recover, but a slip of the tongue you may never get over."

Had he lived in the 21st century, Franklin would most likely have revised his quotation to read:

"A slip of the foot you may soon recover; a slip of the tongue you may never get over; a slip of "send" you may regret forever."

With Internet communication, as soon as you press *enter* on your computer, whatever words you typed can be replicated, forwarded, and distributed a thousandfold without your knowledge or consent. For that reason, you should be particularly aware of what you write when using your college e-mail or participating in online courses.

Netiquette, a word that blends two words, Internet and etiquette, refers to the civil and respectful way to communicate electronically with other people. Learn the following protocols:

- Using all capitals is considered shouting.
- To emphasize a point, use *asterisks* around the word.
- Humor may be misunderstood on the Internet.
- Sarcasm usually leaves the wrong impression.
- Use Standard English for academic or business communications.
- Never write anything on the Internet that you recognize would be disrespectful if spoken to a person.

Although shortcuts and abbreviations are common text-messaging protocol, remember to capitalize I and to use an apostrophe with contractions, such as don't. Set your computer options to automatically spell-check before you send off a message or participate in an online discussion.

Notice the difference between the tone and language in the following email examples.

1.

Dear Professor,

I am in your section 002 class. I will not be attending class on Thursday because of a medical problem. I will complete the assignments that are due this week, but I wanted to make sure I keep up with class activities as well. Could you please let me know when it is a good time to talk to you about what I will miss so I can have the classwork done by the next class? Thank you.

Your student,

Natalie F.

2.

I dont know if you received my phone call but im writing you just in case you didnt. its regarding my final grade i received from you. i understand that i didnt work up to my complete ability but the grade i received i can't accept.

Tania N.

PERSONAL SAFETY AND SECURITY

Students at U.S. colleges and universities are participants in a campus culture that to a large extent mirrors our society as a whole. Unfortunately, like our society, the college community is not immune to the dangers and threats of the 21st century. College campuses are equally vulnerable to theft, violence, and terrorism.

Safety on a college campus is everybody's responsibility. Students, faculty, and staff must work together to prevent crime and make their campus a safe and secure environment for all. Campus public safety departments, with the combined efforts of the college community, can help protect and safeguard campuses. In addition to reading the recommendations presented in this section, visit your campus public safety department and your college's Web site. Obtain updated safety information and learn about security measures specific to your campus.

The following charts give essential recommendations and strategies to help you become responsible for your safety and security. Take time to think about what you are reading. In the left column, make a check next to each suggestion that you find particularly valuable because of the following:

- ☑ You did not know this information.
- ☑ You intend to incorporate the suggestion in your routine.
- ☑ You want to share this information with friends.

HOW TO PROTECT YOURSELF

The Auburn University Campus Safety Web site (AL) provides students with a thorough compendium of safety tips.

Your Property[12]

Follow these recommendations to protect your property.

1. Use a combination padlock on all storage units. Check the unit periodically to make sure nothing has been disturbed.
2. Don't mark your key chain with your name, address, and license number. Lost keys can lead to theft. Take care of keys; don't give anyone the chance to duplicate them.
3. Engrave all valuable personal property with your name. Keep a detailed list of all valuables and their serial numbers.
4. Move valuables out of view from windows and doors.
5. Lock your vehicle at all times.
6. Copy all important papers and cards that you carry in your purse or wallet, including your driver's license. Keep the copies in a safe place. The information will be invaluable if anything is stolen or lost.
7. Copy your vehicle ID (VIN) and tag number. If your vehicle is stolen, it cannot be entered into the nationwide law-enforcement network without this information.

At Your Residence[13]

Whether you live in a residence hall or in an off-campus apartment, incorporate these proactive measures. If you come from a neighborhood where you never locked the door to your house, you must be particularly careful to change those habits while living in a college campus.

1. Keep doors and windows locked at all times, even if you are only away for a few minutes. Do not prop open doors in residence halls.
2. Be assertive and demand that any unwanted person in your residence leave, or leave yourself. Anyone who refuses to leave is a trespasser. If you live in a women's residence hall, report any unescorted males to security.
3. Make sure hallways, entrances, garages, and grounds are well lit. Leave porch lights on all night.
4. Keep blinds and curtains shut after dark and never dress in front of a window. When you expect to return after dark, leave an interior light on, with the shades drawn. If you live on campus, report any malfunctioning light to the physical plant.

	5. Know who is at your door before you open it. Campus staff carry identification and solicitors (generally) are not allowed on campus. Require proper identification from any repair or utility people.
	6. If you live off campus, install a peephole in your front door.
	7. Make calls for strangers who want to use your phone. Don't open your door or let them in.
	8. List initials and last names only on your mailbox or door and in the telephone book. Don't leave your name on your door or answering machine if you live alone. Don't have the recording state you are away or when you will return.
	9. Get to know your neighbors. If you live off campus, join a neighborhood watch system and share information on suspicious circumstances.
	10. When you go home on breaks, have someone pick up your mail, newspaper, etc. Install timers and leave on all outside lights. Make your residence appear lived in.
	11. If you come home and see a broken window or a jimmied door, don't go inside. Confronting a burglar can be dangerous. Phone police immediately.

Fire Safety at Your Residence

Get Out and Stay Alive is a U.S. FEMA (Federal Emergency Management Agency) program designed to help save your life in case you find yourself in a fire situation. This program focuses on three main topics: Getting Out, Prevention, and Protection.[14]

Getting Out

If you get caught in a fire situation, survival is your top priority. You should do the following.

	1. FEEL THE DOOR HANDLE If the door handle is hot, don't open it. Go to a window and call for help. If the handle is not hot, open the door cautiously. Check for smoke or fire before going out.

(continued)

	2. GET OUT OF THE BUILDING BEFORE PHONING FOR HELP Don't take time to phone before leaving. Get out and find a phone.
	3. PULL THE FIRE ALARM ON YOUR WAY OUT
	4. DON'T LOOK FOR OTHER PEOPLE OR GATHER UP YOUR STUFF Knock on doors as you leave. Yell "**FIRE!**" as you leave. Don't hesitate or stray from your path as you leave.
	5. CRAWL LOW TO THE FLOOR Thick smoke can make it impossible to see. Toxic chemicals from smoke can be deadly in minutes.
	6. CLOSE THE DOOR BEHIND YOU You may help keep the fire from spreading. You may protect your possessions from fire and smoke damage.
	7. IF YOU CAN'T GET OUT, GET SOMEONE'S ATTENTION Yell and scream. Hang a sheet from the window. Stay low, there is less smoke and fewer poisonous gases close to the floor.

Prevention

Fires can be prevented from starting if you take responsibility for some simple precautions.

	1. Assign a nonimpaired "event monitor".
	2. Clean up immediately after parties and take all trash outside.
	3. Do not overload electrical outlets.
	4. Keep space heaters and halogen lamps away from flammables.
	5. Put out candles and incense when unattended.
	6. Extinguish all smoking materials thoroughly. Use deep ashtrays and soak ashes in water before disposal.
	7. Don't smoke while tired or impaired.
	8. Keep a fire extinguisher in your residence, and know how to use it.

Protection

You can also protect yourself from becoming trapped in a fire situation by following some important suggestions.

1. CHECK SMOKE ALARMS Be sure they are in proper working condition. Install new batteries at the beginning of each semester.
2. PLAN ESCAPE ROUTES Know where all exits are located in the building. Practice your escape plan.
3. TAKE FIRE ALARMS SERIOUSLY Do not ignore fire alarms. Do not wait to see fire or smoke. Do not worry about grabbing your stuff.

Make a Plan

You can make a plan for your own fire safety and protection as soon as you get home. Use the following checklist.

1. Check to make sure your smoke alarms are working. Change the batteries.
2. Find all possible exits from your room or residence.
3. Make a fire escape route plan that includes two escape routes.
4. Practice your fire escape route plan.
5. Perform a "home inspection" for fire and safety hazards.
6. Tell your roommates about your plan.
7. Call your local fire department for more information about student housing fire safety.

Away From Your Residence[15]

Being smart about how you conduct yourself can increase your personal safety.

1. Walk or jog with a friend. Avoid jogging after dark. If you must jog at night, stay in well-lit, well-traveled areas.
2. Carry a whistle and don't hesitate to use it to alert others you need help. Vary your pattern frequently.

(continued)

	3. Don't wear headphones when jogging or biking. They significantly reduce your ability to hear and, thus, your awareness.
	4. Tell someone where you are going and when you will return.
	5. Don't fight back if your purse or wallet is snatched. Throw it in one direction and run in the other rather than risk personal injury. Call the police immediately.
	6. Be careful when and where you patronize ATM machines. Accessing ATM cash machines in remote locations, particularly at night, could increase your risk of robbery and personal injury. While you are standing at the machine, keep turning around so you are aware if people approach you or linger around.
	7. Avoid working or studying alone in a building other than your residence at night.
	8. Stand and walk tall with a brisk, purposeful stride. Make brief eye contact with someone who makes you feel uneasy to let them know that you see them and are not afraid, but don't stare too long or prolong your glance.
	9. Trust your instincts.

In Your Car[16]

Along with the tremendous mobility and independence a car provides, driving a car involves potential risks. Be vigilant before, during, and after you drive.

	1. Check the back seat before entering your car.
	2. Keep your vehicle's doors locked at all times, even when driving in daylight, so no one can jump in at a red light.
	3. Be suspicious of people approaching your car asking for directions or change or handing out flyers.
	4. When stopping in traffic, leave enough distance between your car and the one in front of you so you can quickly pull away if necessary.
	5. If another driver bumps your car or your tire goes flat, keep the doors and windows closed and wait for police to arrive, or slowly drive to the nearest police station.
	6. Keep enough gas in your tank for emergencies.
	7. Don't offer rides to anyone you don't know, even if he or she claims to be a student.

	8. Honk your horn if someone suspicious approaches your vehicle.
	9. If your car breaks down, lift the hood, turn on the flashers, and wait inside the car for help with the doors locked. Ask people who stop to call the police or AAA. Don't go with anyone that you don't know well.
	10. Don't stop for stranded motorists. You are of greater help to them by calling the police.
	11. Keep valuables in the trunk of your vehicle, not on the seats.
	12. Park your car in well-lit areas.
	13. Remove all keys from your vehicle. Thieves look for keys under fenders and in magnetic key cases. Walk with your keys in your hand.
	14. Remember to buckle up.

At Work[17]

These behaviors will help you stay alert to theft and to the threat of danger at the workplace.

	1. Avoid working or studying alone in a building at night.
	2. When working late, make sure doors are locked.
	3. Keep your purse in a locked cabinet or drawer. Never leave it on or underneath a desk.
	4. Avoid using stairs in remote sections of the building.
	5. Do not hold the door open for strangers after normal business hours.
	6. Ask people you don't recognize if you can help them. Report suspicious activity to campus police.
	7. Be careful what you leave on your desk and on your computer screen when you step away from your desk.
	8. Keep passwords in secure places.
	9. It is very important for you to have a plan if an attacker tries to steal your bag or attack you from behind or your car breaks down at night, etc. Knowing how you would handle situations if you should ever have to face an attacker could save your life. Always be on your guard.

Date or Acquaintance Rape[18]

The following recommendations emphasize the importance of communication, personal responsibility, and intervention regarding date or acquaintance rape. Your college campus may offer specific counseling resources and provisions for victims.

Awareness + Common Sense + Early Planning = Best Prevention

	1. Be aware of your surroundings and instincts.
	2. Expect to be respected. Assert your rights.
	3. Clearly communicate your thoughts and beliefs through actions and words.
	4. Meet social or business acquaintances in public places; arrange to have your own transportation or travel with good friends.
	5. Carry money to meetings and on dates in case you need to use the phone or pay for transportation.
	6. Control your environment. Don't let yourself get put in a dangerous location such as an alley or back room.
	7. Know your date's first and last names, address, and business.
	8. Especially with new people, watch how much alcohol or drugs both you and your date consume. Alcohol and drug use may increase your vulnerability by lowering your awareness and ability to react.

If you find yourself in a potentially bad situation, consider:

	1. The object is survival. Do whatever you can to survive. Try to remember as much as you can about the attacker: height and weight compared to yours, scars, tattoos, accent, etc.
	2. As in prevention, clearly assert your rights through your words and actions.
	3. Criticize your date's actions, not him personally, so that he will understand what behavior to stop. For example, say, "I'm not ready for sex" or "I have enjoyed our date until now, I don't want to do this."
	4. If he does not listen to you, leave.
	5. Do not let embarrassment for him keep you from doing what is right for you.

	6. Choose effective means to get yourself out of the situation.
	7. Act with a purpose. Try to keep your composure; avoid falling apart.
	8. At the first opportunity, escape from the situation and go to a safe place and call for help.

Active intervention methods:

	1. Bite, scratch, kick, pull, twist, and punch in vulnerable areas—stomach, sides, face, eyes, shins, hands, and the groin area.
	2. Run away.
	3. Attract attention by continually screaming and yelling "FIRE," "HELP," or "I DON'T KNOW THIS PERSON."

Passive intervention methods:

	1. Talk yourself out of a situation. Give a "convincing story." Tell your attacker you have a contagious venereal disease, you're pregnant, or a friend is expected to appear at any moment.
	2. Pretend to cooperate until an opportunity for escape presents itself. Put your attacker off guard.
	3. Act in a bizarre and/or repulsive manner (feign insanity or convulsions, urinate, or vomit.)
	4. Do what is best for you and your situation.

After the attack:

	1. Try to be as calm as possible in order to think more clearly.
	2. Call 911 immediately and ask to speak to a rape counselor, or call a crisis center.
	3. Do not disturb any evidence, including that on your body. Do not bathe, brush your teeth, douche, clean your fingernails, or change clothes. Take a change of clothes with you to the hospital.
	4. You, as a student, have the option to report a rape, and the campus security authority has the responsibility to help you report it to the proper people.

If you know someone who has been attacked:

	1. Be there. Your presence means you care and helps counter feelings of helplessness, guilt, and isolation that victims often experience.
	2. Listen to the victim. Don't be judgmental of his or her actions.
	3. Offer to accompany the victim to the hospital or police station.
	4. Encourage the victim to seek help from a victim's assistance program.

Date-Rape Drugs

Often referred to as *club drugs,* the most widespread illicit drugs used for sexual assault are GHB, Ketamine, Rohypnol, Ecstasy, LSD, and Methamphetamine. A club drug facilitates rape because it can be easily slipped into someone's drink. When the drug dissolves, it is often colorless and odorless and may be tasteless. The person drinking the drugged drink becomes much more vulnerable and defenseless and may black out.

Although date-rape drugs are most frequently used to victimize females, their use on male students is a potential threat. The motive for this might be robbery or some other illicit reason, including malicious pranks.

In addition to protecting yourself from drugs, do not consume alcohol if you are under age. If it is legal for you to drink, drink responsibly. Irresponsible drinking accounts for much crime particularly sexual assault and abuse, that occurs on college campuses.

	1. Don't go out by yourself.
	  a. Go to parties, clubs, or raves with a trusted friend and watch out for each other.
	  b. If you arrive with a friend or a group, leave with your friend or group.
	  c. Never leave with someone you just met.

	2. If you forget and leave your drink unattended, even for a few seconds, don't finish it. Get a new one.

	3. Always pour your own drink.
	  a. Don't take drinks from large open containers, such as a punch bowl.
	  b. Do not accept an opened drink—even water—from anyone.
	  c. If you order a drink in a bar, make sure you watch the bartender open the bottle or mix your drink.
	  d. Don't share or exchange drinks.

	4. Date-rape drugs produce a variety of symptoms. If you feel any of these symptoms or see someone with these symptoms, get help. Doing so may mean the difference between safety and assault, life and death. ■ Agitation; aggressive or violent behavior ■ Convulsions ■ Dizziness ■ Disorientation ■ Drowsiness ■ Hallucinations ■ Loss of consciousness ■ Loss of coordination ■ Loss of inhibition ■ Nausea ■ Problems talking ■ Seizures ■ Visual disturbances
	5. Never go outside alone with someone (or a group) you have just met to get some fresh air or smoke a cigarette. Make sure you have friends who go with you.

HOSTILE SITUATIONS

Most people are not prepared to deal with acts of violence. By thinking about the potential problems beforehand and knowing how to respond, you can greatly reduce your chances of serious injury or even death.

The public safety department at Monroe Community College[19] (NY) provides comprehensive guidelines in the event of an active shooter incident on campus. Be sure to check with your college campus public safety office to see what additional recommendations are provided for protecting yourself and alerting campus officials about suspicious behaviors. Remember in any hostile situation the importance of remaining calm.

Secure the immediate area:

	Lock the door, if possible, whether it is a classroom, bathroom, or office.
	Block the door using whatever is available—desks, file cabinets, books, other furniture, belt, etc.

(continued)

	After securing the room, people should be positioned out of sight and behind items that might offer additional protection—walls, desks, file cabinets, etc.
	If the shooter enters your room and leaves, lock/barricade the door behind him.
	Close blinds and block windows.
	Turn off radios and computer monitors if necessary.
	Silence cell phones.
	Signs can be placed in interior doors, windows, but remember the shooter can see these.
	Place signs in exterior windows to identify the location of injured persons.
	Keep occupants calm and quiet.
	If safe, allow others to seek refuge with you.

Opening doors:

	The shooter will not stop until his objectives have been met, unless engaged by law enforcement.
	Consider the risk exposure created by opening the door.
	Attempts to rescue people should only be made if that can be done without further endangering the persons inside a secured area.
	The shooter may bang on the door and yell for help to entice you to open the door.
	Remember the safety of the masses versus the safety of a few.
	If there is any doubt to the safety of the individuals inside the room, the area needs to remain secured.

Unsecured areas:

	If you find yourself in an open area, immediately seek protection.
	Put something between you and the shooter.
	Is escape your best option? Do you know where the shooter is? Is escape immediately available? If in doubt find a safe area and secure it the best way you can.

As soon as you can, contact emergency personnel by dialing Emergency 911 or x2911

WHAT TO REPORT

Your specific location:
 Building name
 Office/classroom number
 Number of people at your specific location
Injuries:
 Number of people injured
 Types of injuries
The dispatcher may provide instructions on how to care for injured until medical assistance can be provided.
Details about assailant(s):
 Specific location
 Number of assailant(s)
 Race and gender
 Clothing color and style
 Physical features – height, weight, facial hair, glasses
 Type of weapons (rifle/shotgun, handgun)
 Backpack
 Do you recognize the shooter? What's his name?
 Have you heard explosions separate from gunshots?

LAW ENFORCEMENT RESPONSE

 Law enforcement will immediately respond to the area.
 It is important for you to convey to others that help is on the way.
 Remain inside the secure area.
 Law enforcement's goal is to locate, contain, and stop the shooter.
 The safest place for you to be is inside a secure room.
 The shooter will not flee when law enforcement enters the building, instead he will have new targets to shoot.
 Remember the shooter's mindset is not escape. His goal is to kill and injure.

INJURED PERSONS

Initial responding officers will not treat the injured or begin evacuation until the threat is neutralized.

You may need to explain this to others in an attempt to calm them.

Once the shooter is contained, officers will begin treatment and evacuation.

EVACUATION

Safety corridors will be established. This may be time consuming.

Remain in secure areas until instructed otherwise.

You may be instructed to keep your hands on your head.

You may be searched.

You will be escorted out of the building by law enforcement personnel.

THE INVESTIGATION

Information will be released to the college community and media as quickly as possible.

The entire area will be treated as a crime scene.

Once you have been evacuated you will not be permitted to retrieve items or access the crime scene.

After evacuation you will be taken to a holding area for medical care, interviewing, counseling, etc.

The Security Home Page at Saint Mary's College, Notre Dame (IN) lists additional warning signs you should be aware of while on campus.

What is a heightened security state of alert?[20] A mindset that leads you to notice unusual or suspicious behavior or circumstances and reporting your observations to authorities in a logical, rational and timely manner.

Heightened security is not intended to induce fear and panic. People should go about their normal business while paying particular attention to their surroundings.

Be aware of and report the following to security.

Suspicious Behavior/Circumstances:

	1. People in buildings or areas who do not appear to be conducting legitimate business
	2. People monitoring areas, buildings, or entrances

	3. Unauthorized people in restricted, sensitive, or private areas
	4. People requesting information with no apparent need for that information
	5. People wearing clothing not consistent with the weather conditions at mass population events (bulky coat in warm weather, etc.)
	6. Abandoned parcels or other items in unusual locations or high-traffic areas
	7. Individual attempting to access utility locations (water, electrical, petroleum, telecommunications, information systems)
	8. Multiple persons who appear to be working in unison, committing any of the above

Be Alert to:

	1. Abandoned vehicles
	2. Vehicles parked near buildings or public and common areas
	3. Unexpected/unfamiliar delivery trucks
	4. Unfamiliar vehicles parked for long periods
	5. Vehicles containing unusual/suspicious parcels or material
	6. Vehicles arriving and being left behind at off hours
	7. Substances leaking or spilling from vehicles

The availability of information about criminal activity on and around campus is a matter of federal law. Being informed about criminal activities and security issues heightens your sense of awareness about your surroundings and helps to minimize your exposure to these risks.

THE CAMPUS SECURITY ACT[21]

The Crime Awareness and Campus Security Act requires all postsecondary institutions participating in Title IV student financial aid programs to disclose campus crime statistics and security information. In 1998 this act was renamed as the Jeanne Clery Disclosure of Campus Security Policy and Campus Crime Statistics Act in memory of a student who was slain in her dorm room in 1986.

The Clery Act requires higher education institutions to give timely warnings of crimes that represent a threat to the safety of students or employees and to make public their campus security policies. It also requires that crime data be collected, reported, and disseminated to the campus community and also be submitted to the U.S. Department of Education. The act is intended to provide students and their families, as higher education consumers, with accurate, complete, and timely information about safety on campus so that they can make informed decisions.

FOR DISCUSSION

1. How do your checked items compare with those of other students?
2. What other suggestions can you offer that are not listed in this section?
3. How will learning this information alter your behavior?
4. How can you become more involved with campus safety?

ACTIVITIES AND EXERCISES

Log onto the On Campus Student Website at www.prenhall.com/fitton to determine how well you have studied and what you still need to learn.

1. Defining Terms
   Write the meanings of the following terms.

   Institutional mission _____

   _____

   _____

   Civility _____

   _____

   _____

   Etiquette _____

   _____

   _____

Netiquette _____

_____

_____

2. **Checking Your Understanding**
   How are diversity and pluralism similar? How are they different?

   _____

   _____

   _____

   _____

3. **Knowing Your Campus**
   a. What is the mission statement for your college?

   _____

   _____

   _____

   _____

   b. Describe one tradition, celebration, ceremony, theme, or symbol that is a part of your college culture.

   _____

   _____

   _____

   _____

   _____

   c. Is there a predominant culture on your campus? Explain.

   _____

   _____

   _____

   _____

   _____

d. What is the college civility statement on your campus?

_____

_____

_____

_____

e. Become informed about safety and security on your campus.
What is the name of the campus public safety department?

_____

Where is it located? _____

What is the phone number? _____

What type of campus safety department does your college have?

_____ A full police department

_____ Nonsworn, unarmed officers employed by the college

_____ Contract employees from a private security department

How do you report a crime? _____

_____

_____

What is your college's crisis plan? _____

_____

_____

_____

What security services does the public safety department provide?

_____

_____

_____

How are students informed of dangerous situations?

_____

_____

_____

Where are the lighted areas when walking at night?

_____

_____

_____

Where are emergency telephones located?

_____

_____

_____

In the event of an emergency, how does the college communicate with the campus community?

_____

_____

_____

What resources does the college or university have in place to assist persons in crisis or need of other help?

_____

_____

_____

How does your college comply with the Clery Act?

_____

_____

_____

4. **Applying Chapter Concepts**
    On your campus, does the civility you experience satisfy, exceed, or fail to meet your expectations? Give examples.

    _____

    _____

    _____

    _____

    _____

5. **Writing for Reflection**

Explore your feelings about civility. Write at least one paragraph in response to one of the following quotations or a meaningful sentence you select from the chapter.

"Caring about others, running the risk of feeling, and leaving an impact on people, brings happiness." Harold Kushner

"Being civil means being constantly aware of others and weaving restraint, respect, and consideration into the very fabric of this awareness." P. M. Forni

6. **Concerning College Athletes**

a. Does your college sport project an image of civility? Explain.

_____

_____

_____

_____

b. Do you believe your college supports the view that participation in intercollegiate athletics is viewed as a privilege that must be earned, not a guaranteed "right" of students?[22] Explain your reasons.

_____

_____

_____

_____

7. **Reading Further**

The reading selections on the On Campus Student Website at www.prenhall.com/fitton explore different aspects of chapter topics. At the end of each reading selection are critical thinking questions. Your instructor will let you know whether you should print out your responses or use the online feature to email your answers.

a. *George Washington and Rules of Civility* George Washington
Read this selection to see how rules of civility never go out of date.

b. *Respect in Action* P.M. Forni
Read this selection to learn how living according to the principle of respect can add harmony to people's lives.

Notes

[1] John Henry Newman, 1854, History and Archival Resources in Higher Education Web site: http://www.higher-ed.org/resources/newman-university.htm (accessed February 24, 2004).

[2] *The Beloit College Mission Statement,* Beloit College, http://www.beloit.edu/%7Eacadaffa/policy/chap2.html#mission (accessed February 17, 2004).

[3] *About Babson,* Babson College, http://www3.babson.edu/About/ (accessed February 17, 2004).

[4] *Building the Future While Honoring Our Heritage. Mission Statement,* Montana Tech Web site at University of Montana, http://www.mtech.edu/WHY_ CHOOSE_ TECH/mission.htm (accessed February 17, 2004; site now discontinued).

[5] *Life on Campus,* Bennington College, http://www.bennington.edu/main.htm (accessed February 18, 2004; site now discontinued).

[6] G. P. Edmonston, Jr., *Up Close and Personal: OSU's Homecoming Tradition,* Oregon State University, http://alumni.oregonstate.edu/eclips/carry/nov1_2002.html (accessed March 28, 2004).

[7] Candlelight Service, Hendrix College, http://www.hendrix.edu/choir/candlelight.html (accessed March 28, 2004).

[8] *Aggie Traditions,* Texas A&M University, http://aggietraditions.tamu.edu/silvertaps.shtml (accessed February 18, 2004).

[9] *Diversity Theme Year,* University of Puget Sound, http://www.ups.edu/x638.xml (accessed February 15, 2007).

[10] *Whitman Admission,* Whitman College, http://www.whitman.edu/admission/about.cfm (assessed March 25, 2004; site now discontinued).

[11] D. Day, *The Rochester Pluralism Project,* Monroe Community College, http://www.monroecc.edu (accessed March 24, 2004).

[12] Auburn University, Campus Safety Web site, http://www.auburn.edu/administration/public_safety/campus-safety.html (accessed July 1, 2007; site now discontinued).

[13] Ibid.

[14] "Getting Out and Staying Alive," U.S. Department of Homeland Security, FEMA, U.S. Fire Administration, http://www.usfa.dhs.gov/downloads/pdf/publications/fa-280.pdf (accessed November 10, 2007).

[15] See note 12 above.

[16] Ibid.

[17] Ibid.

[18] Ibid.

[19] *The Active Shooter Prevention and Response.* Powerpoint presentation by Lee Struble, Director of Public Safety Department. Monroe Community College, Rochester, New York, April 16, 2007.

[20] Saint Mary's College, Notre Dame, Security Home Page, http://www.saintmarys.edu/~security/emergency.html (accessed June 30, 2007).

[21] U.S. Department of Education, Office of Postsecondary Education, *The Handbook for Campus Crime Reporting,* Washington, DC (2005), 17.

[22] Allan Hancock College Department of Intercollegiate Athletics, Student-Athlete Handbook (2003–04), Allan Hancock College, http://athletics.hancockcollege.edu/Default.asp?page=717 (accessed January 16, 2004).

3
CAMPUS
COMMUNITY

Notes

MISSION TO GOALS

4

Even a small star shines in the darkness.
~ Finnish proverb

Realizing a dream, instead of just imagining what your life could be like, can happen if you work hard and focus on accomplishing your goals. Nancy Mace realized her lifelong dream when she graduated magna cum laude in 1999 as the first female from The Citadel, The Military College of South Carolina. Nationally recognized and highly regarded, The Citadel is known for its rigorous academic standards and strict military discipline.

When Mace started at The Citadel, her goal was to beat out as many men as possible so she would be seen as an equal. She did not want any special treatment because of her gender. During her first physical training test, Mace was the only female in her platoon. Only four cadets passed the test that day, and Mace was one of them. She not only surpassed the maximum expectations for female cadets, but she also surpassed the expectations for males. Mace wanted to fit in with the other cadets, but the fact that she was a woman made her stick out. The single most important lesson Mace said she learned was that when faced with adversity, you must stick to your morals and not compromise yourself.[1]

LOOKING *IN*, LOOKING *OUT*

You are entering a period in your life when, for a few wonderful years, you focus on your college experience. You are presented with new ideas, meet friends, and acquire knowledge, all of which are colored by your life experiences up to that point.

Achieving your dream starts with *looking in*—thinking about who you are, understanding how important your goals are, and planning how you can accomplish those goals. Regardless of who you are, whether you are a freshman straight out of high school or a returning adult, whether you are living in a dorm, an apartment, or at home with your family, your decision to attend college results in personal change. Sometimes, the process is subtle. At some point, you may think the people who you have known all your life are changing, when, actually, you are the one who has changed. Your education changes the way you consider issues, approach challenges, and understand complex ideas.

Today's college students have many roles and responsibilities. In addition to being a college student, you may be working either part-time or full time; you may be an athlete competing in collegiate sports; you may be a parent of one or more children; you may be a returning adult learner, looking to upgrade your skills or find a new career, or you may be a student from another country. These added responsibilities may, at times, slow you down. Sometimes, you may encounter obstacles that will challenge your resolve and commitment. For this reason, you must start your academic journey both with a focus on short-term achievements and with the long-term goal of graduation in mind. As you read this chapter, be steadfast in learning how your personal mission can make you unstoppable and believe in yourself!

KNOW YOUR PURPOSE

In a 1980 Winter Olympics hockey game, when the relatively unknown American team played against the indomitable Soviet Union team, fans screamed with delight as they watched Mike Eruzione score the winning goal. From one goal to the next, the U.S. team went on to beat the Finnish team and advance to fulfill their mission—winning the first U.S. Olympic Gold in hockey. What started as a dream became a reality.

You, too, can make your dreams become reality. Start by analyzing your purpose for attending college. If the pleasure of having good times and socializing outweighs your desire to become a more educated person, you may be hard-pressed to find the time required for the demanding and time-consuming academic tasks associated with college courses. Your reasons for attending college impact your level of motivation and commitment in college. If you fail to do your work, you may ultimately fail to be able to work in a career that gives you personal satisfaction.

 FOR DISCUSSION

Check off the reasons that explain why you are attending college. Then, compare your choices with students in your class. How do the reasons you selected impact your personal motivation?

Reasons for Attending College

☐ Prepare for a career
☐ Discover new strengths
☐ Learn a new trade
☐ Secure a better job
☐ Increase earning potential
☐ Fulfill requirements for a profession
☐ Learn new ideas
☐ Be intellectually challenged
☐ Gain knowledge
☐ Socialize and have a good time
☐ Get away from home
☐ Meet family's expectations
☐ Be the first college graduate in family
☐ Find a husband, wife, or life partner
☐ Help humankind
☐ Learn more about myself and others
☐ Participate in sports
☐ Meet new people

DECIDE WHAT YOU WANT TO ACCOMPLISH

Your reasons for attending college frame your **personal mission statement.** Written in a single sentence or a few paragraphs, a personal mission statement is an affirmation of what you value, what you believe, and what you want to accomplish.

As you read the following examples, see how the reasons become the basis of a personal mission statement that reflects each person's value system.

EXAMPLE

Michael, married with three children, was a well-paid supervisor in a factory that specialized in building boilers. After the plant moved overseas, Michael no longer had a job. He decided to open his own home-remodeling business because he already had many carpentry skills. To round out his capabilities, he wanted to learn heating and air-conditioning. Michael was the first person in his family to attend college, and the decision was both nerve-wracking and exhilarating. His reasons for attending college were (1) to deal with losing a job, (2) to open up his own business, and (3) to learn specialized trade skills for his business.

Michael's mission statement reflects his personal experience and needs: *I intend to earn a college degree in AC/HV with at least at 3.0 GPA so I can open my own business and provide for my family. I want to be a role model for my children. That way they can witness the value of an education and the results of my hard work.*

EXAMPLE

Growing up in a home where college was part of her family's experience, Janice knew in high school that she wanted to attend college. Janice's reasons for attending college were (1) to prepare for a career teaching physical education, (2) to meet people, (3) to enjoy social activities, and (4) to discover and develop her own talents.

Janice's personal mission statement included several of her reasons as well as an additional intention: *I want to graduate from college with a BS in physical education and a high GPA so I can be competitive finding a teaching position. I want to make sure I stay physically fit in college because I think fitness is personally and professionally important.*

EXAMPLE

Living in a house with an alcoholic father and submissive mother, Marquise's goals were to avoid confrontations with her father and to avoid attention in school. After living with an abusive husband for seven years, Marquise's mother finally left. She struggled financially to start again with her two daughters. Marquise gave birth to her son in her senior year of high school and then worked at various low-paying jobs. When

Marquise decided to attend college, her reasons were (1) to get out of poverty, (2) to provide for her son, (3) to find a fulfilling career, and (4) to help other females take immediate action when abused.

Marquise's personal mission statement reflects her priorities in life: *I want to graduate from college with a degree in counseling so I have a fulfilling, rewarding career. I want to provide for my son and to help other women take the imitative to leave a dysfunctional relationship sooner rather than later.*

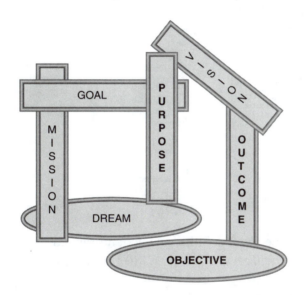

YOUR PERSONAL MISSION IN COLLEGE

Your personal mission statement, much like the North Star, is a constant point of reference. By referring to your personal mission statement for guidance, you can evaluate how decisions you make either support or work against your ultimate achievement. Take time to articulate your mission statement. You want your mission statement to be a source of inspiration and direction in college. Carry it with you and post copies in visible places at home or work. Revise and evaluate your mission statement as you continue in college to make sure it always reflects what you want to achieve.

SET GOALS TO ACCOMPLISH YOUR MISSION

After you *know* your mission, you have to work to *make it happen*. You do this by aligning goals with your personal mission statement. Without goals, your mission statement is an empty wish.

A **goal** is a quantifiable, or measurable, outcome that you hope to achieve. You will find some goals easy, others difficult, some goals time consuming, others quick. Some goals are more compelling than others. In other words, when you believe there is high value associated with accomplishing a goal, your commitment to its success increases.

If you are unable to accomplish a goal, consider *why*. To succeed you may need to revise your goal and then try again. Setting goals is a dynamic, ongoing process that changes as you do.

Effective goals are specific, achievable, and measurable.

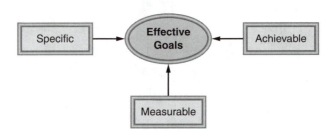

SPECIFIC

Your goal must be clear, definite, and action oriented. For example, *I will study* is vague; *I will rewrite my notes after each history class* is specific.

ACHIEVABLE

Make goals that can be achieved. For example, *I will write a 10-page research paper in one evening* is unreasonable and self-defeating. In contrast, *I will start my 10-page research paper two weeks in advance and work on it one hour each evening* is achievable.

Plan for success by ensuring you have all the information you need to make your goals work. The goal *I will make the dean's list* necessitates that you know the criteria to make the dean's list. Or, *I will go the learning center twice a week* requires that you know the hours the center is open. To avoid frustration, obtain the necessary details to make your goals achievable.

MEASURABLE

Phrase your goals in a way that you can measure what you achieve. Replace a generic goal such as, *I will read each night* with a measurable one, *I will read 15 pages from my psychology text each night this week.*

This way, you can gauge your results. This will also allow you to assess objectively whether or not your goals are realistic and whether they are helping you to achieve your mission.

Goals can be short term, midterm, intermediate, and long term. In general, **short-term goals** can be accomplished in an hour, a day, a week, or a month. For instance, *I will read and take notes from my 20-page sociology assignment Thursday evening* is a clearly articulated short-term goal. Some short-term goals are steps that lead to midterm or long-term goals. **Long-term goals** are goals you plan to accomplish by the end of semester or in one or more years. For example, *I will make the dean's list this semester* is a long-term goal.

Spend time thinking about your goals. A written goal is a record of what you intend to accomplish. Along with your personal mission statement, keep your goals visible. Your goals become the basis for many of your daily and weekly activities.

The example that follows shows the relationship of a personal mission statement to setting long- and short-term goals. Accomplishing one's personal mission requires many goals, which are adjusted according to life events.

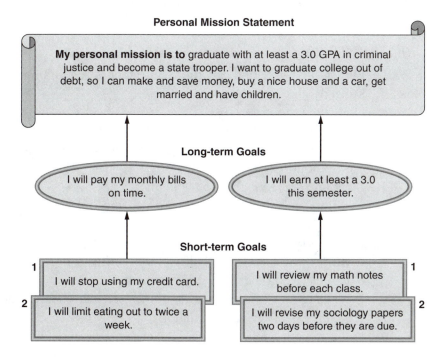

Personal Mission Statement

My personal mission is to graduate with at least a 3.0 GPA in criminal justice and become a state trooper. I want to graduate college out of debt, so I can make and save money, buy a nice house and a car, get married and have children.

Long-term Goals

I will pay my monthly bills on time.

I will earn at least a 3.0 this semester.

Short-term Goals

1 I will stop using my credit card.

2 I will limit eating out to twice a week.

1 I will review my math notes before each class.

2 I will revise my sociology papers two days before they are due.

FOR DISCUSSION

Read the following sentences. Check each sentence that is an effective goal statement. Rewrite each goal that is vague or ineffective to make the goal specific, achievable, and measurable.

LONG-TERM GOALS

☐ 1. I will find a major that interests me.
☐ 2. I will be an officer in a college social club by my fourth semester.
☐ 3. I will work next semester to earn money.
☐ 4. I will graduate from college with a degree in communications.
☐ 5. I will study abroad in France during my third semester.
☐ 6. I will transfer to another college.
☐ 7. I will audit one computer-related course each semester next year to improve my computer skills.
☐ 8. I will take two humanities courses during summer session.
☐ 9. I will volunteer to work on an urban service learning project during my second semester.
☐ 10. I will put $20.00 from each paycheck into the bank to save so that I have enough money to pay for my books next semester.

SHORT-TERM GOALS

☐ 1. By Friday, I will find out the requirements for joining tae kwon do club sports.
☐ 2. I will start a study group.
☐ 3. I will do all my reading assignments.
☐ 4. I will meet with a counselor on Tuesday to discuss my interests and options.
☐ 5. I will find someone to help me in math.
☐ 6. I will make flash cards for my biology vocabulary words to study from this weekend.
☐ 7. I will work on my chemistry lab three hours this week.
☐ 8. I will set my alarm clock half an hour earlier and get to my 8 a.m. class on time every day this week.
☐ 9. I will go to the library right after dinner, so I can research and write my history paper due tomorrow.
☐ 10. I will find out about getting a scholarship.

ACHIEVE COLLEGE SUCCESS

By creating a personal mission statement for college and setting goals that help you to achieve your mission, you are being **proactive**. People who are successful follow proactive behaviors, that is, they think through each situation, anticipate any problems or difficulties, consider their options, and do whatever needs to be done. In contrast, both **reactive** and **passive behaviors** limit choices and opportunities for success.

Your definition of success reflects your beliefs and values. For instance, some people measure success by how much money they earn; others measure success by knowing they have a group of friends they can count on. As you grow older, you may reaffirm what you believe success means, or you may reevaluate and change what signifies success. In college, success can be viewed many ways:

Success is making lifelong friends at college.

Success is meeting and communicating with people different from you.

Success is figuring out what you want to major in.

Success is learning how to write a research paper.

Success is minimizing college debt.

Success is getting involved in a college club.

Success is learning the skills to figure out things on your own.

Success is passing a difficult course with a C.

Success is getting your child to daycare, going to college, and studying for a test.

Whether you define college success as passing all your courses or earning a GPA that will enable you to get the job and salary you want, there are fundamental skills to help you achieve the level of success you want in college. By reading and implementing the guidelines and principles in this textbook, you will

- understand your responsibility in achieving your goals;
- manage your time to ensure you achieve your goals;
- understand how to earn a college degree;
- know how to learn information and demonstrate your knowledge;
- make the most of college resources and opportunities.

 ## FOR DISCUSSION

How do you define college success? Compare your definition with others in your group. What similarities and differences do you see?

ACTIVITIES AND EXERCISES

Log onto the On Campus Student Website at www.prenhall.com/fitton to determine how well you have studied and what you still need to learn.

Log onto the On Campus Student Website at www.prenhall.com/fitton

1. **Defining Terms**
   Write the meanings of the following terms.

   Personal mission statement _____
   _____
   _____

   Short-term goal _____
   _____
   _____

   Long-term goal _____
   _____

   Proactive behavior _____
   _____
   _____

2. **Checking Your Understanding**
   What are qualities of an effective goal?
   _____
   _____
   _____
   _____

3. **Knowing Your Campus**
   What are the mission and goals for the college orientation course you are taking? How do they relate to your personal mission and goals?
   _____
   _____
   _____
   _____

4. Applying Chapter Concepts

a. Write a personal mission statement that reflects your reasons for attending college. Then, write long- and short-term goals that align with your mission. Make sure each goal is *specific, achievable,* and *measurable.* Use the following graphic or create your own.

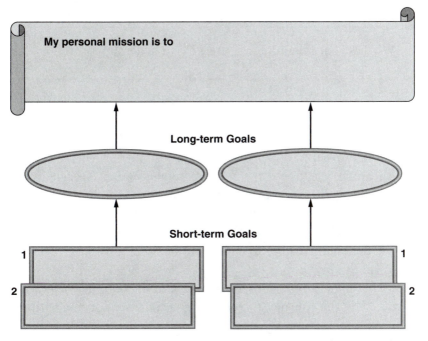

b. Create a personal vision board collage that represents your personal mission and makes a statement about who you are. Use poster board or PowerPoint to present this information to your class.

5. Writing for Reflection

Explore your feelings about your personal mission in college. Write at least one paragraph in response to one of the following quotations:

We are what we believe we are.

Benjamin Cardozo

First say to yourself what you would be, and then do what you have to do.

Epictetus

Great minds have purposes; others have wishes.

Washington Irving

6. **Concerning College Athletes**

a. How does your role as a college athlete impact your college mission statement?

_____

_____

_____

b. What is your mission for sports? What goals support this mission?

_____

_____

_____

7. **Reading Further**

The reading selections on the On Campus Student Website at www. prenhall.com/fitton explore different aspects of chapter topics. At the end of each reading selection are critical thinking questions. Your instructor will let you know whether you should print out your responses or use the online feature to email your answers.

a. *Revel In The Journey Or Skip The Trip* Marvin Karlins

Read this selection from the textbook *Romancing The Clock* to find out why the journey to reach a goal is as important as the goal itself.

b. *Achieving Happiness* Andrew DuBrin

Read this selection from the textbook *Human Relations* to discover "keys" to happiness.

c. *Developing Self-Discipline To Achieve Goals And Stay Motivated* Andrew DuBrin

Read this selection from the textbook *Human Relations* to see why self-discipline is important in achieving your goals.

Notes

[1] Dawn Miller, (2003). Citadel's First Female Graduate (2003), Grady College Alumni Web site, http://www.grady.uga.edu/alumni/GradyNews/Winter2003/FemaleGraduate. pdf (accessed February 19, 2004; site now discontinued).

Notes

Notes

TIME MANAGEMENT

5

One hour today is worth two tomorrow.

~ Latin proverb

After students have studied their course syllabi and understand the expectations for each course, the amount of time required for college study often comes as a surprise to many freshmen. Compared to high school, the hours spent reading text material and writing papers may double or even quadruple. In sharp contrast to the 21st century, college students in the 13th century had little to say about how they spent their time during the day.

A student's daily routine began about 4:00 a.m. each weekday with Mass. The first "ordinary" lecture attended would commence at 5:00 or 6:00 a.m. and last about two hours. Customarily, lecturing broke off by 9:00 in the morning and was followed by two "extraordinary" or "review" lectures in the afternoon, extending perhaps until around 4:00 or 5:00 p.m. A student would join in disputations until suppertime; later he would attend an organized recitation or a review session or perhaps go off to read on his own. He retired by 9:00 in the evening.[1]

Within the last few decades, students have enjoyed opportunities that allow them to decide how they spend their time at college. With this freedom, however, often come increased responsibilities, such as needing to earn money for college and family obligations. Although you cannot really "manage" time, you can learn to manage your behaviors so that you have sufficient time to study in college.

Time management is similar to managing a budget, but there are significant differences. With a budget, you determine how much money you have and subtract the money you need for fixed expenses. The remainder represents the amount of money you have for other items. If you spend more money than you have, you may borrow money on credit. If you do not pay your loans, you may go bankrupt. It is not quite so simple with time management. Unlike the amount of money that is available to you, the hours each day are immutable. You cannot borrow time in advance. From the 24 hours in each day, you subtract the number of hours you need for sleeping and fixed commitments, such as classes, work, and personal obligations. The difference represents your **discretionary time,** blocks of time you have for studying and for scheduling other activities.

COMPLETE A MASTER SCHEDULE

A **master schedule** includes all repeatable fixed activities and obligations, such as classes, practice, work, and childcare. Although eating and personal hygiene are repetitive routines, the time periods for accomplishing those tasks can vary. If, for instance, you need at least eight hours of sleep a day to function well or consider certain activities, such as working out, as fixed, then include those items in your master schedule. Draft a new master schedule each semester or when regularly scheduled time commitments change.

As you see in the following master schedule example, time for fixed activities is indicated; however, time allotted for sleep is not. If you require more or less sleep, your schedule should reflect your needs.

SCHEDULE STUDY TIME

Study time in college includes time for reading assignments in textbooks, journals, and reserved books as well as online. It involves writing papers, answering questions, working on projects, and presentations. As you will learn in Chapter 7, study time requires rehearsing and memorizing information. By identifying fixed activities on a master schedule, you can clearly see what time slots are discretionary. These are the "free" blocks of time that you can schedule for study and personal activities.

Master Schedule

Time	Monday	Tuesday	Wednesday	Thursday	Friday	Saturday	Sunday
7:00 a.m.	Commute		Commute		Commute		
8:00 a.m.	BIO 126	SOC 101	BIO 126	SOC 101	BIO 126	Gym	
9:00 a.m.	MTH 165		MTH 165			Gym	
10:00 a.m.		LAB				Gym	
11:00 a.m.							
Noon	ENG 105		ENG 105		ENG 105		
1:00 p.m.	ART 104	PED 148	ART 104		ART 104		
2:00 p.m.							
3:00 p.m.					Commute		
4:00 p.m.	Commute	Commute	Commute	Commute	Work		
5:00 p.m.	Work	Work	Work	Work	Work		
6:00 p.m.	Work	Work	Work	Work	Work		
7:00 p.m.	Work	Work	Work	Work	Work		
8:00 p.m.					Work		
9:00 p.m.					Work		
10:00 p.m.					Work		
11:00 p.m.					Work		

If you plan your time correctly, you may have more time than you realize. Maximizing your time depends on the *way* you fill in your unscheduled blocks of time. Imagine, for a minute, a tall jar, a pile of sand, several golf balls, and some small marbles. If you try to pour the sand in first, followed by the marbles, and then the golf balls, not everything will fit. However, if you first place the golf balls in the jar, followed by the small marbles, you can pour the sand in as well. You might even have room for water. Remember this image when you arrange the things you do in your life. How you sequence activities can have a significant impact on your efficiency.

Preparing a master schedule and allocating time for study doesn't mean you are locking yourself into a regimented schedule, but rather it means you are prioritizing what is important in your life while finding time for relaxation and personal activities.

By shading or coloring the fixed items in the master schedule example, the free slots of time are more readily apparent.

one week = 168 hours

fixed activities = 55 hours

sleep = 8 hours/day = 56 hours

unscheduled time = 57 hours

Although your instructors may have provided a schedule of assignments, be sure you use a **monthly calendar** to keep track of major projects, papers, and tests. By consolidating all due dates in one calendar, you will know at a glance when you will have many major assignments due at the same time and whether you need to work on resolving time conflicts. In addition to the monthly calendar, use a **weekly planner** to insert assignment due dates. This visual reminder will keep you organized and on task. Give consideration to what type of weekly planner you want to use. Should it be a large conspicuous binder that you cannot easily misplace or a small, pocket calendar you can carry everywhere? Would you prefer an electronic day keeper with a reminder buzzer? Choose a style that you know will help you remember what you must do.

PRIORTIZE THINGS TO DO

As you have experienced in life, two things can compete for your time. You sit down to start reading your textbook, and a friend calls to chat. You are on the way out the door to meet your friend, and your mother calls needing

Master Schedule

Time	Monday	Tuesday	Wednesday	Thursday	Friday	Saturday	Sunday
7:00 a.m.							
8:00 a.m.							
9:00 a.m.						Gym	
10:00 a.m.	MTH 165	LAB	MTH 165			Gym	
11:00 a.m.	MTH 165	LAB	MTH 165				
Noon							
1:00 p.m.							
2:00 p.m.							
3:00 p.m.							
4:00 p.m.							
5:00 p.m.							
6:00 p.m.							
7:00 p.m.							
8:00 p.m.							
9:00 p.m.							
10:00 p.m.							
11:00 p.m.							

a ride to the doctor's. Sometimes two "good" things compete for your attention: You made plans to go out for dinner with a friend, but another friend suddenly has a free ticket for the college football game. Deciding which choice to make or which one to do first depends on your priorities.

Your **priorities** are measured against the goals and missions you have established for yourself. Each time you prioritize, you are making a decision. **Decision making** involves evaluating *what* you are doing compared to *how* you are doing. For instance, if you go out for the evening instead of working on your studies, ask yourself, Does this place me closer to or further from my goals? Staying home to study may involve sacrificing socializing with your friends in order to get closer to your goals and your mission. Additionally, your decision to study may be a service to your friends by setting a good example of commitment and determination.

If you *intend* to study but find that you become easily sidetracked, ask yourself three questions:

1. What do you spend most of your time thinking about?
2. How do you spend your money?
3. What do you do with your free time?

Your answers to these questions tell you whether or not you are committed to your personal mission statement.

Keeping a **to-do list** is the simplest way to remind yourself of what needs to be done right now and what you can work on later. As you look at your list of things you need to do on a daily or weekly basis, you decide which activities are most and least important. Regardless of how tempted you may be to work first on tasks that may be easier or more pleasant, be resolved to complete those things that are most important. Let your personal mission statement and goals direct your decision making.

One way to create a to-do list is to list things you have to do and then number the items sequentially in the order of importance. As you complete each task, you can check it off or cross it out.

EXAMPLE

1. ~~Call Health Services about immunization.~~
2. ~~Schedule appointment with Prof. Gleason.~~
3. Read short stories, pp. 110–163. Write 100-word summaries for each.
4. Complete biology lab report.
5. Buy basketball tickets.
6. Read sociology pp. 35–75. Answer questions.
7. Change cell phone service.

Another way to keep a to-do list is to list things to do and then assign each one a letter value: A = ASAP; B = soon; C = no rush. Complete all "A" items; then do all "B" and then all "C" items.

EXAMPLE

c Read sociology pp. 35–75. Answer questions.
b Read short stories, pp. 110–163. Write 100-word summaries for each.
b Buy basketball tickets.
a Schedule appointment with Prof. Gleason.
c Change cell phone service.
a Call Health Services about immunization.
b Complete biology lab report.

As you go through the semester, you may experience what Robert Burns eloquently expressed about life: "The best laid schemes o' mice an' men/Gang aft a-gley." In other words, no matter how carefully you may plan out your day or week, something may happen to change everything. For example, the person who was going to give you a ride to school can no longer help you. Your two-year-old child is hospitalized with bronchitis. Your boss decides to change your work schedule without discussing it first. Your computer crashes with all your research notes. When things go "a-gley," consider all your options. Problem solving involves examining obvious solutions as well as considering whether there are solutions that are less obvious. Weigh the pros and cons of each potential solution, keeping your personal mission in sight. Work through any obstacle or roadblock as best as you can. Talk to a college counselor or professor who may be able to help you with difficult challenges.

 ## FOR DISCUSSION

For each of the following situations, discuss these four questions:

1. What is the decision the student faces? What makes it difficult?
2. What are the choices available to the student in this situation? Are there more than two possible choices?
3. What are the consequences of each choice the student can make? Are there both positive and negative consequences?
4. How could the student have been proactive rather than reactive? What steps could the student have taken before this situation arose that might have prevented or lessened the time conflict the student faces?

Situation 1

After serving three years in the Army, John is determined to graduate with honors with a degree in business. In high school, John wasn't motivated, but now that he attends college, he sees this time as his opportunity to make a life change. John has an important test tomorrow at 10:00 a.m. in his statistics course. Although the course is challenging, John wants to earn an A. He is up to date on his assignments and intends to work the entire evening on the review handouts the professor provided in class. He has just started the first problem when his friend Sonia calls, sounding very upset. Her mother, who lives in a different state, is in the hospital. Sonia needs a ride to the airport, a 45- to 60-minute trip.

Situation 2

Stacey has a five-page research paper due tomorrow for her 8:00 a.m. freshman English course. The paper counts toward 30% of the final grade. The week before, Stacey spent several days at the library gathering and copying research articles. During the weekend, she worked on her thesis and rough outline. With a 17-credit load, Stacey has been working long hours trying to keep up with her studies. Stacey intends to write from 7:00 p.m. until 11:00 p.m. She is in the middle of drafting her third page when she gets a phone call. There is a last-minute party going on at a friend's house. From the music and laughter in the background, the party sounds great.

Situation 3

Rueben's recent engagement motivated his decision to return to college. He is recognized at work for his intelligence and commitment, but he has been unable to apply for promotion because of the lack of a college degree. He is also a dedicated, loving single father of two children. One of his courses this term is online, and each week's assignments are due Sunday at midnight. It is Sunday, and Rueben has blocked the day to finish his assignments. His children have the stomach flu that has been going around, so he has been focused on their needs most of the day. Rueben puts them to bed at 9 p.m. and has three hours left before the deadline. He goes to work at 5 a.m. the next day as a result of the flexible schedule his employer has allowed so that he can attend his afternoon on-campus courses. At 9:05 p.m., his fiancée comes by to spend some quality time with him. They haven't seen each other all week.

Situation 4

Charlie has been absent twice in his computer science course, which meets Monday and Wednesday from 1:00 to 2:30 p.m. The attendance policy states that after three absences, the final grade is lowered 10% for each subsequent absence. On Tuesday evening, Charlie receives a frantic phone call from his girlfriend, Liliya. Liliya has a 1:00 p.m. appointment on

Wednesday at the regional U.S. Immigration Office, approximately 150 miles from where they live. The interpreter who was going to accompany Liliya at the interview had to cancel because of a family emergency. Now, Liliya is very worried that she might not understand all the interviewer's questions correctly and, therefore, might jeopardize her application to extend her work visa. She asks Charlie if he can come with her. The Immigration Office does not reschedule an appointment so late.

Situation 5

Jane, a single mother, works as a cashier from 9 a.m. until 5:30 p.m. and is taking classes in the evenings. On the first day of classes, she stopped before class to pick up her math textbook at the bookstore, but she was told her financial aid had not come through. Consequently, she was late for her first class, a 6 p.m. math class, and did not have her book. The professor warned the class that they must have their books and their completed textbook assignment by the next class. She also warned them that she does not tolerate lateness. On the day of her second math class, Jane calls and speaks to the financial aid office during her lunch break. She finds out there is a glitch in her paperwork, so her financial aid still isn't available. Jane will have to stop at the ATM after work to get money for her book and buy it before going to class. This will make her late for class again, without any of her homework completed.

Situation 6

After finishing classes on Tuesday, Mark heads to the library, where he knows he can spend the afternoon studying before he goes to work that evening. On Monday, Wednesday, and Friday, he takes three courses in a row, beginning at 8:00 a.m. His third psychology exam is tomorrow at 10:00 a.m. This test is important to Mark because he scored 75% on the first test and 61% on the second one. He needs a much better grade on this one because there are only four tests for the semester. Twenty minutes into studying at the library, Mark receives a cell phone call from his boss. They are short-staffed and need Mark to start work at 3:00 p.m. instead of 6:00 p.m.

Situation 7

Melanie has an appointment at 3:30 p.m. to speak with her history professor, Dr. Zwick, to discuss her American history tests. Melanie studies hours for each exam, but she still has difficulty answering the multiple-choice questions. When Melanie missed her first appointment with the professor, she sent an e-mail the next day explaining that she was sorry she had forgotten about it. Now, on her way to Dr. Zwick's office, Melanie sees she has a phone message from her ride home. She learns that her ride, Lee, can't wait at school for Melanie's appointment. Melanie has no other means of transportation to get home.

Situation 8

Josh is taking a communications course that requires one individual project and one group presentation. He has never been absent from class. For his individual project, Josh earned a B. For each group presentation, the professor assigns a specific meeting time when she assesses the group's written and oral presentations. Each person in the group earns the same grade. Josh has met with his three group members several times after class to divide the work, research the topic, and outline the presentation. They all agree to practice their individual parts of the presentation on their own time. An hour before the group's presentation, Josh gets a migraine. If he takes his medicine, he will feel better, but he will be too drowsy to attend class.

Situation 9

Yasemin has always dreamed that someday she will be a lawyer. Funds are limited, so Yasemin's goal is to qualify for a full scholarship to law school. During her first semester, Yasemin earned a 3.7 GPA while working part-time and commuting from home. At noon tomorrow, Yasemin will be one of the finalists in a state debate competition. When Yasemin returns from work the evening before the competition, she learns that her younger brother, a junior in high school, has been suspended from high school for fighting. The high school principal has called a meeting for tomorrow at 1:00 p.m. with the counselors, security, and parents. Yasemin realizes that her parents will expect her to translate for them. She also knows that the faculty advisor for the debate team has high expectations for their team.

Situation 10

Janice, a physical education major living in a college dorm, is in her second semester, taking 17 credits. Her human anatomy professor gives voluminous notes for the entire lecture hour. The four exams are based 60%

on lecture notes and 40% on textbook reading. Karli, one of the girls who lives on another floor in the dorm, takes the same course at a different time. A week ago, Karli missed two classes after being sick with the flu. She asked Janice if she could borrow her class notes. After waiting several days to get her notes back, Janice gave her a call. When Karli didn't return the call after a day, Janice went to her dorm room and knocked on the door. When no one answered, she left a message. It's Monday, and Janice has a human anatomy exam on Thursday. She still does not have her notebook.

USE TIME-MANAGEMENT STRATEGIES

Too often at the end of the semester, students faced with the prospect of a D or F urgently meet with the professor and ask, What are my options? The most common reply is, None.

At the start of each semester, you have plenty of options. You can complete your assignments on time, study by yourself or with a group, or get a tutor. As the semester progresses, your options diminish. You can do your best on a final project or paper and study hard for your final. There are no other options at the end of the semester. For this reason, it is important to spell out your options at the beginning of the semester.

The following time-management strategies can save you time as you learn to accomplish things intelligently and efficiently.

☐ STOP PROCRASTINATION

You are, as the saying goes, a creature of habit. Sometimes, you may not even realize that the behaviors you regularly repeat have become habits—watching television while eating, checking e-mail several times a day, or tossing change in a jar. Each habit is a force that pushes you in a direction.

Procrastination is a habit of delaying tasks you want to avoid. The key to replacing procrastination with action is to remember your mission. When you procrastinate, you compromise excellence and risk not accomplishing your goals. If you are someone who procrastinates, write out your reasons to change from a procrastinator to a proactive person. Think through the steps you need to take to achieve this change. With repetition, these behaviors will become a new habit—a positive force that points you in the right direction. Remember, procrastination is a choice you make about how you spend your time. You have control over choices you make, and if you choose to stop procrastinating, it is within your power to do so.

☐ MAXIMIZE SMART SLEEP

A successful time-management schedule includes sufficient time for sleeping. Each of us is born with a preset internal clock that determines how many hours of sleep we need. If you shortchange these hours, you run into time debt. Recent research suggests that most people need at least 8 hours of sleep. You, on the other hand, may require 9 or 9½ hours of sleep. Prolonged sleep deprivation (4 hours of sleep for six consecutive nights) can negatively affect your blood sugar and memory capability.[2] The benefit of sleep was demonstrated in a Harvard Medical School study, which showed that people who sleep after learning new information retained more the next day than people who stayed up all night studying.[3] If you follow your natural sleeping habits and rhythms, you will be more productive during the day, study more effectively, and remain healthier.

☐ SELECT A STUDY SYSTEM

Which subject should you study first, the most difficult subject or the easiest subject? If you tackle your most difficult subject first, you get it out of the way while your energy level is high. On the other hand, you may prefer to work first on your favorite or easiest subject so you have a sense of accomplishment. If working on a difficult subject frustrates you, you may have little patience to tackle other subjects later on. Try both methods, and then decide which system works best for you.

How long should you study? Once again, the length of time you study depends on the individual. Studying in 1-hour blocks of time is convenient to schedule. As a general rule, study for at least 30 minutes at a time. Look at the length of your assignment and break it into manageable parts. Avoid studying for more than 4 hours on one subject at a time because doing so may actually be counterproductive. In other words, mental fatigue may slow you down. When you must study for long blocks of time, such as when you are preparing for finals, be sure to include short break periods.

☐ TEAM UP FOR RESULTS

Consider working with a study partner or in a study group. Not only can studying with someone enhance your understanding of the material and make studying more enjoyable, you may feel motivated to be ready for the other person. Accountability may eliminate or minimize your tendency to procrastinate as well as motivate you to do your best.

☐ REWARD ACTION, NOT INTENTION

Make a list of several 10- to 15-minute activities you can use as rewards for working on a task that you would just as soon avoid doing. For instance, reward yourself for working on your paper or reading your textbook for 50 minutes with 10 or 15 minutes of talking on the telephone, catching up on e-mail, or taking a walk. Just make sure your reward time does not extend into your study time.

☐ MAKE A PACT WITH YOURSELF

Making a written agreement with yourself may seem a little formal, but the process of writing *what* you intend to do and *when* you intend to accomplish a task signifies you mean business. Write it out: *On Thursday, I promise to read my psychology text for two hours.* Keep your agreements up to date and visible.

☐ AVOID TIME TRAPS

You sit down to watch 10 minutes of the news, and before you know it, you flip channels during a commercial and start watching a movie. You want to check your e-mail, and the next time you look at the clock, you realize that you have spent an hour sending and responding to e-mails. A **time trap** is something that captures your attention and sidetracks you to the point that you don't work on something of greater importance. In college, both media and friends are students' biggest time traps. As with any "trap," you must first recognize what makes you vulnerable and then change those behaviors. For example, avoid temptation by not turning on the television or checking e-mail until after you have completed those tasks that bring you closer to your personal mission.

    Multitasking, doing more than one activity at the same time, is a formula for disaster. You cannot effectively read a textbook while watching television or write a good paper while socializing with friends. As scientists have determined, the brain does not function as well with competing stimuli. If you still are convinced you can multitask effectively, try reading your history book while working on math problems.

ORGANIZE FOR EFFICIENCY

Organization can increase your effectiveness and efficiency in college. For instance, if you can easily and quickly find your papers, locate a textbook or journal in your living space, or pick out an outfit right away, you save time. On the other hand, if you have to sort through "stuff" to find what you need, you waste time. Business executives know the value of an organized work environment, and for this reason, many executives hire a professional organizer to help create order in their environments. As a college student, being organized is simply a matter of following three routines.

Routine 1: Downsize

Routine 2: File

Routine 3: Consolidate

ROUTINE 1: DOWNSIZE
✄ ↓ ✄ ↓ ✄ ↓ ✄ ↓ ✄ ↓ ✄ ↓

The 21st century is a highly consumable, materialistic society. You notice this every time you open your mail or e-mail. Both are crammed with unsolicited advertisements for goods, products, and credit-card applications, tempting you to buy more things and spend more money. With the excesses of materialism, it is easy to be overwhelmed by the sheer volume of things around you. The following suggestions will help you reduce clutter.

Stacks of Stuff
- Tear out useful articles from outdated newspapers, magazines, and books. Sell, discard, recycle, or donate what remains.
- Sell or donate CDs and DVDs you no longer listen to or watch.
- Sell or donate clothing and shoes that you no longer wear; discard damaged items.
- Discard medicine that has expired or you no longer use. Make sure to check with the pharmacy about the proper way to discard such medication.

Computer Memory

Stockpiling e-mails and Word documents happens at an incredibly fast pace. One day you have 20 e-mails in your inbox, and a week later, you have hundreds. Similarly, if you save multiple drafts of assigned papers, several semesters later you may end up with a long list of documents that take up disk space and cause you to waste time searching for newer material. If this is your situation, find time each week to delete worthless, outdated e-mails and documents. Make sure you delete the files in your computer's "wastebasket" as well.

ROUTINE 2: FILE

Clutter begins as an innocent accumulation of items—the clothes you wore the day before, the stack of mail you picked up, or course papers you have been working on. To deal with stacks of accumulation can take hours; however, on a daily basis, it takes only minutes sorting through small piles. A filing cabinet or several portable file boxes are a good purchase your first semester.

Use basic filing and labeling categories to organize your materials.

ACADEMIC FILING CATEGORIES

Academic courses, labeled with course name, semester, and year

School correspondence

Letters of recommendations

Résumé

Research papers

School records, such as transcripts and syllabi

PERSONAL FILING CATEGORIES

Income statements (retain seven years)

Credit-card statements (proof of important purchases)

Telephone bills

Utility bills

Insurance documents (current year only)

Bank statements (retain seven years)

Guarantees (staple receipt, if proof of purchase is required)

Instruction booklets

Paid invoices

For your computer, make folders to increase your efficiency.

E-MAIL FOLDERS

Friends

Family

College

Job

Online purchases

WORD DOCUMENT FOLDERS

By course

By semester

ROUTINE 3: CONSOLIDATE

Consolidating things involves combining items into manageable units. Try incorporating the following suggestions:

- Staple together important related papers—paper clips have a way of falling off.
- Get everything together you need for school the night before classes.
- Keep an ongoing list of phone calls you need to make each day.
- Put all bills in one folder or a box and review weekly.
- Keep an ongoing list of groceries you need to buy to minimize extra trips.
- Designate one day a week to run errands.

Follow up on this activity at the end of each semester by going through course materials and discarding unimportant papers. Be sure to save course syllabi, important tests, written work, or notes that you can use for later reference.

 **FOR DISCUSSION**

Your success in college depends on your understanding and assuming your student responsibilities. Reread the chapter and examine it from the perspective of what actions you need to take. Make a list of the responsibilities you must assume for your education.

ACTIVITIES AND EXERCISES

Log onto the On Campus Student Website at www.prenhall.com/fitton to determine how well you have studied and what you still need to learn.

1. **Defining Terms**
   Write the meanings of the following words.

   Master schedule _____
   _____
   _____

   Priorities _____
   _____
   _____

   Procrastination _____
   _____
   _____

2. **Checking Your Understanding**
   Explain how creating a time-management plan for studying is being proactive.

   _____
   _____
   _____
   _____

3. **Knowing Your Campus**
   Use your college's Web site or current catalog to find important dates and enter them on your calendar.

a. When is the last day you can drop and/or withdraw from a class?_____

b. When is the last day of classes? _____

c. When do finals begin? _____

d. When can you register for classes for next semester? _____

4. **Applying Chapter Concepts**

   a. Complete a master schedule for this semester. Use the following blank schedule or create your own. You may, for instance, want to indicate half-hour increments of time in the left column or allow for more time in your chart because you need fewer hours for sleep. Fill in all repeatable fixed activities and obligations, such as classes, practice, work, and childcare.

Semester Master Schedule

Time	Monday	Tuesday	Wednesday	Thursday	Friday	Saturday	Sunday
7:00 a.m.							
8:00 a.m.							
9:00 a.m.							
10:00 a.m.							
11:00 a.m.							
Noon							
1:00 p.m.							
2:00 p.m.							
3:00 p.m.							
4:00 p.m.							
5:00 p.m.							
6:00 p.m.							
7:00 p.m.							
8:00 p.m.							
9:00 p.m.							
10:00 p.m.							
11:00 p.m.							

b. Analyze your weekly time.

Fixed items = _____

Sleep hours = _____

Discretionary hours = _____

c. Using your master schedule as a guide, determine those slots of time each day that you will commit to study. Write these time periods in the following chart.

Day	College Study
Monday	
Tuesday	
Wednesday	
Thursday	
Friday	
Saturday	
Sunday	

d. Describe what type of monthly planner you will use to keep track of your major assignments and commitments this semester and what type of weekly planner you use to keep track of ongoing due dates and appointments.

Monthly planner _____

_____

Weekly planner _____

_____

e. Demonstrate your understanding of scheduling your study time for a two-week period. Include the assignment due dates as well as your hours of study to accomplish those tasks. Use a table similar to the following one.

Time	Monday	Tuesday	Wednesday	Thursday	Friday	Saturday	Sunday

f. Create a weeklong *to-do list* of school and personal related tasks. Decide which tasks can be accomplished each day and rank these according to priority. As you complete each task, cross it off your list.

_____

_____

_____

_____

_____

Reflect on this process before your next class. Were you able to accomplish most of your tasks? Did the process of keeping a *to-do list* help you stay on task? What adjustments, if any, do you need to make in the way you use your to-do list?

5. **Writing for Reflection**
   Explore your feelings about how you manage your time. Write at least one paragraph in response to the following quotation or a meaningful sentence you select from the chapter.

   The heights by great men reached and kept
   Were not attained by sudden flight,
   But they, while their companions slept,
   Were toiling upward in the night.

   Henry Wadsworth
   Longfellow

6. **Concerning College Athletes**
   a. When are your athletic competitions, both home and away?

   _____

   _____

   _____

   b. What sport conflicts do you have this semester with academic responsibilities, such as exams, papers, and projects?

   _____

   _____

   _____

6. **Reading Further**

The reading selections on the On Campus Student Website at www. prenhall.com/fitton explore different aspects of chapter topics. At the end of each reading selection are critical thinking questions. Your instructor will let you know whether you should print out your responses or use the online feature to e-mail your answers.

a. *Do You Manage Your Time or Does Time Manage You?* Christopher Lynch, Ph.D.
Read this selection to understand how to balance your time.

b. *Procrastinators Get Poorer Grades in College* Bruce Tuckman
Read this selection to see how procrastinators risk achieving their academic best.

c. *American Time Use* U.S. Department of Labor
Compare the way you spend time with the average American.

Notes

[1] Christopher J. Lucas, *American Higher Education: A History* (New York: St. Martins Press, 1994), 56.

[2] *Risks of Short Sleeping* (March 2003), ABC News Web site, http://more.abcnews. go.com/sections/2020/2020/2020_010330_sleep.html (accessed April 5, 2004; site now discontinued).

[3] Lisa Lipman, *Sleeping Makes you Smarter? Study: A Good Night's Slumber Helps Memory,* Associated Press (November 21, 2003), ABC News, http://abcnews.go.com/sections/living/DailyNews/sleep_memory001121.html (accessed December 4, 2003; site now discontinued).

Notes

Notes

INFORMATION LITERACY

6

> *Better to write down something one time*
> *than to read something ten times.*
> ~ *Japanese proverb*

With a scarcity of books before the invention of the printing press, taking notes from lectures was the only practical way to obtain information. Bookstores and libraries, as you know and use them today, did not exist hundreds of years ago. Because the few books that could be obtained were very expensive, most students could not afford to purchase books for their classes. Try to imagine sitting in a cold, drafty, medieval university classroom during the 14th century, when teachers were instructed to lecture as quickly as possible:

> Opinion differed on the best way of delivering a lecture. Some masters preferred to speak at a brisk conversational pace, a rate that made students' note taking virtually impossible. Others were willing to dictate from their notes so that students could take down a complete transcription of everything said. For obvious reasons, students tended to prefer the latter approach, despite the fact that authorities strongly disapproved. Thus, in Paris in 1355, legislation was enacted requiring teaching masters to swear formally that they would adhere to the first method; anyone failing to comply was to be deprived for a year "from lecturing and from honors, offices and other advantages of our faculty." For second-time offenders, the penalty was doubled.[1]

The information age, spearheaded by late 20th-century computer technology, has facilitated an explosion of information. No longer restricted to the printed page, vast amounts of text are produced and replicated very quickly. Much of the information is valid and accurate; however, a great deal of the information given out is erroneous and dishonest. **Information literacy** refers to the ability to locate, evaluate, and communicate information in all formats. For that reason, it is a core component of higher education curricula. The American Library Association explains the value of information literacy.

Information literacy forms the basis for lifelong learning. It is common to all disciplines, to all learning environments, and to all levels of education. It enables learners to master content and extend their investigations, become more self-directed, and assume greater control over their own learning. An information literate individual is able to

- determine the extent of information needed;
- access the needed information effectively and efficiently;
- evaluate information and its sources critically;
- incorporate selected information into one's knowledge base;
- use information effectively to accomplish a specific purpose; and
- understand the economic, legal, and social issues surrounding the use of information, and access and use information ethically and legally[2]

THE NATURE OF FACTS

In a television series popular decades ago, a steely faced detective was fond of saying, "Just the facts, ma'am. Just the facts." Not interested in others' opinions or beliefs, this investigator wanted only information that could be checked for accuracy, that is, only information that reasonable people would agree to accept as true. Given the facts, he would put them to use.

What is a fact? A fact is a bit of information, *demonstrably* correct, accurate, or true. Just because a statement *appears* to be accurate does not make it factual. An essential part of information literacy is assuring yourself that the information you read is, indeed, true. In other words, check that what you read is information that would be accepted by other reasonable people. Checking the validity of information is critical if you want to base your thinking on reality. For instance, each of these sentences makes an assertion of truth:

New York City consists of five boroughs.

Rap music originated in Sweden.

There is no such thing as a purple pig.

However, asserting, or stating, that something is true does not make it so. Which of the preceding sentences do you believe are facts? How can you be sure?

RELIABLE SOURCES

As you find information that seems to be factual, consider its source.

What is the writer's credibility?

A star athlete who writes about the best types of financial investments may have a great deal of money, but he or she probably has little more information than the average investor. Always consider how the author of a reference obtained his or her knowledge. Take as fact only data supplied by someone who has learned from professional study or experience. The person who cuts your hair, though certainly knowledgeable in many areas, might cite facts about mortgages, but this person may not be a dependable source of information. However, a certified financial planner can give you reliable information about saving and investing for your future needs.

Does the author have a particular bias?

For example, a person writing that couples must have prenuptial agreements before marrying may include supporting facts. If, however, you learn that this person has been involved in a bitter divorce, there is an obvious bias to the point of view. A disinterested attorney would be a more reliable source of information.

Is the information timely?

The facts written in a text about basic computers published 10 years ago are less reliable than the facts written in an article in last month's *PC Magazine*. Likewise, last week's newspaper is not an especially good source for the times that a movie will be shown in a theater tomorrow.

 FOR DISCUSSION

Explain why you believe each is or is not a reliable source of information.

1. A sports broadcaster, about what football teams will be in the Super Bowl in January
2. A popular actor, about the healthfulness of a weight-loss diet
3. A newly graduated probation officer, about the causes of juvenile delinquency in his or her community

4. A Harvard economist, about the value of life insurance
5. A friend of yours, about whether or not you should register for a particular course next semester
6. Your boss, describing a good place to vacation
7. A food writer, about hydroponics (growing plants in water, not soil)
8. An Olympic athlete, about treatment for a sprained ankle
9. A car dealer, about the merits of a particular model car
10. A librarian, about popular reading materials

FACTS AND OPINIONS

Certain descriptive words are difficult to deal with factually. What is a delicious meal? A boring book? An interesting class? A good friend? An ugly piece of furniture? That a house is beautiful is not factual because it cannot be supported with positive knowledge or truth. The expression "beauty is in the eye of the beholder" means that individuals have their own perception of beauty. Reasonable people will have differing views on what qualities make a house beautiful. Statements such as this movie is great, that professor is hard, and the course is boring are not facts. They are opinions.

A statement about which some knowledgeable people will agree and some will disagree is an opinion. An **opinion** is a statement that gives a reaction to or makes a judgment about something. Words that indicate an opinion include **evaluative words.** You have probably heard that everyone has a right to his or her opinion. Of course, that is true. Some opinions, however, are more valuable than others. The most valuable opinions are those that can be supported by facts. For example, you could provide convincing support for the following:

Cats provide welcome companionship.

Public speaking is a valuable skill.

But you might have difficulty showing these statements:

Everyone should own a cat.

Skill in public speaking is a requirement for success in business.

Opinions are conclusions that need the support of facts. When you are alert and aware of the need to check facts, you are well equipped to use them as a basis for your thinking and learning.

FOR DISCUSSION

Read each statement and decide whether it is a *fact* or *opinion*.

1. Students need a high school degree to earn a college degree.
2. The college catalog describes college courses.
3. English is a required course for all college students.
4. Attending college is too expensive.
5. Students who own their own computers will complete more assignments on time.
6. A junior college grants associate degrees.
7. College is similar to high school.
8. The job of faculty includes instruction.
9. A campus consists of its community and buildings.
10. Information literacy is more important than information technology.

CRITICAL THINKING

Philosophers have argued that it is difficult to think about thinking because in the process, the human brain is required to think or reflect upon its own activity. Although the concept of thinking about thinking may be complex, both philosophers and scientists agree that thinking is the process people use to make sense out of their surroundings. Reading, writing, and thinking provide the basis for college learning. As you have probably realized, reading and writing are closely linked parts of the same whole. What one person writes, another reads, and vice versa. Thinking is the purposeful process that makes sense of reading and writing, completing the communication. A critical thinker demonstrates a genuine curiosity and seeks exposure to new ideas, asking questions and establishing connections among thoughts.

Whatever the purpose, the process of critical thinking is an active one that involves discovering facts as well as making use of them. For instance, the process of writing and submitting a paper involves a variety of specific thinking skills. As you brainstorm ideas about a topic, you are recalling your **knowledge**. Deciding your thesis and organizing ideas to support the thesis demonstrate **comprehension**. Writing and revising are processes that require **application** of your knowledge. More sophisticated kinds of thinking are analysis, synthesis, and evaluation. When you print your document and look at the parts—the font style and size, the spacing, and the margins—you are **analyzing** the appearance of the paper. Next, you decide that your paper would be improved with illustrations. In a separate document, you use shapes to create two graphics. When you insert these graphics into your word document to form a new whole, you are **synthesizing** parts. Finally, you reprint your revised paper, read what you have written, and judge its overall effect. Your **evaluation** of the paper is based on criteria that you established.

METACOGNITION

Thinking about the process of thinking is called **metacognition**. You practice metacognition when you think about what you are learning and how you are learning it. Metacognition helps you manage your thoughts, select thinking strategies, and plan, monitor, and assess your thinking. An awareness of your thinking allows you to be conscious of your progress as a critical thinker, benefiting from self-discovery and self-evaluation. You can try a bit of metacognition by rereading this paragraph and asking yourself, What is metacognition? How will I remember the meaning of this word? What is my reaction to the concept? How can metacognition be useful to me?

College work provides opportunities for you to develop the strategies of an educated thinker. Each discipline or subject area asks you to understand some dimension of human experience. The facts you gather through reading can be related to your previous knowledge and experience. As you read information, be an active thinker by continually asking yourself what you are learning.

INDUCTIVE THINKING

Sometimes in collecting information, you find that you first get the facts and then decide how to use them. Consider the following example.

Facts → General Observation or Conclusion

Inductive thinking is the process of using specific facts to arrive at general observations and conclusions.

Facts.

A student usually met her roommate for lunch. Although the student waited from 12:00 to 1:00, the roommate did not appear. The student went back to the sorority house and noticed that her roommate had not picked up her mail from the hall table. When the student entered their room, she saw that the dresser drawers were open and clothing stuck out of each at rakish angles. The closet door was ajar and through the opening, the student was able to notice items were missing. Under the bunk beds, the student saw an empty space where a suitcase had been stored. Finally, the student walked into the bathroom to see a hastily scribbled note taped to the mirror: "Sorry for the mess. Sister had a boy! See you Sunday."

Conclusion.

Using the facts she has gathered, the student understands why her roommate had not been at lunch. After looking at the disarray in the room and reading the note, the student realizes that her roommate rushed out to be with her family. Using facts, examples, or events to reach a conclusion is called inductive thinking.

 FOR DISCUSSION

To each group of facts add at least one additional fact and a conclusion.

1. A husband comes home early from work.
   He cancels vacation plans for the following month.
   Add a fact _____

   _____

   Conclusion _____

   _____

2. A teenager spends hours each day on the phone.
   The teenager's grades are down from last semester.
   Add a fact _____

   _____

   Conclusion _____

   _____

3. A coworker was laid off last week.
   Your boss wants to speak to you.
   Add a fact _____

   _____

Conclusion _____

_____

4. Your roommate has been partying all week.
   Your roommate did not go to any classes.
   Add a fact _____

   _____

   Conclusion _____

   _____

5. Your best friend did not meet you at the gym.
   Your friend has not returned your phone call.
   Add a fact _____

   _____

   Conclusion _____

   _____

DEDUCTIVE THINKING

Deductive thinking moves in the opposite direction from inductive thinking. Instead of finding facts and then deciding what to do with them, a deductive thinker starts with a conclusion and then attempts to find facts which support it.

General Observation or Possible Conclusion ➔ Facts or Support

Deductive thinking is the process of stating a general observation and finding specific facts for support. Consider the following example.

General Observation or Possible Conclusion

You have an idea that you would like to become a teacher. To confirm your interest, you need facts about teaching.

Fact 1. Teachers must have a master's degree.

Fact 2. Schooling includes specialization in a particular field and student teaching.

Fact 3. An abundance of teaching jobs is predicted over the next decade.

Fact 4. The beginning salary for teachers is $25,000 to $30,000 a year.

Based on these facts and others you discover, you can confirm or reject your observation or theory.

FOR DISCUSSION

What facts would be needed to deduce the following observations?

1. Speaking on a cell phone while driving causes accidents.
2. The bathtub can be a dangerous place.
3. The town needs a new high school.
4. A college degree results in a higher income than a high school degree.
5. Food should not be stored in an open can.
6. Suburban shopping malls have reduced business in downtown stores.

COLLEGE READING

As you start reading this section, you may wonder why you can't simply attend classes and skip the reading assignments altogether. The reality is that, even if class time were doubled or tripled, your professor could not possibly present the volume of information you need to acquire during a semester. Your professor uses class time to expand on or explain information you are assigned to read. To check that you have completed your reading assignments, professors include questions about lecture and reading material on their tests.

UNDERSTAND THE AUTHOR'S PURPOSE

Good reading comprehension begins by making sure you understand the author's purpose. Authors write to provide information (**exposition**), to explain how something works (**explanation**), to tell a story (**narration**), to prove a point (**persuasion**), to entertain a reader, or to achieve a combination of these purposes. As you read, look for the author's purpose. Knowing this information can help you to detect the author's bias towards the subject as well as to see the relationship between the author's purpose and the text that supports it.

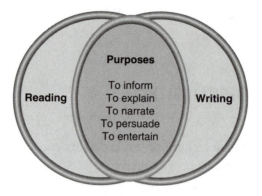

In college, you will spend more time reading information than listening to lectures. Reading material includes textbooks, journal articles, reports, library books, and Web-based information. Notice how the following course syllabi provide guidance and practical suggestions for reading assignments.

EXAMPLE

An English Course at the University of Pennsylvania

Read everything I've assigned on the schedule at the end of this syllabus. Our epics are notoriously large texts, but there are only four of them, and the reading comes in bunches (you get a week off between each text). I strongly encourage you to read the assignments in stages: Cover the entire assignment first at the pace you use for novels, briefly marking points of interest and/or confusion. Then return to the places you've marked and reread them with an eye for detail, making more extensive notes. Such a careful approach to reading will quickly move you away from summary and toward analysis. To help you get through the reading assignments, I'll be giving you regular handouts listing important characters and brief synopses of the key actions in the various books and cantos.[3]

A Philosophy Course at Florida State University

The purpose of this course is for you to understand the major philosophical ideas of the 17th and 18th centuries and to interact philosophically with the major thinkers of that period. This means that you will need to learn to read, write, and critically discuss issues.

Reading: Most of the assignments are short but dense and difficult. For each assignment, you should answer the following before coming to class: (1) What is the central question the author addresses? (2) How would I answer this question? (3) How does the author's answer compare to my own? Raise questions in class if you have them. After the lecture, reread the material. We can meet the goals of this course only if you come to class on a regular basis and complete the reading assignments on time.[4]

Whether you read information from text material or from the Internet, you will improve your reading comprehension by following a four-step process. Use the same reading process when you read material in a text and from the Internet.

6
INFORMATION
LITERACY

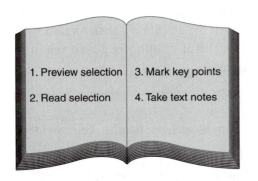

1. Preview selection   3. Mark key points

2. Read selection   4. Take text notes

1. Preview selection
2. Read selection
3. Make hard copy
4. Mark key points
5. Take text notes

STEP 1: PREVIEW THE SELECTION

By **previewing** a reading selection, you are getting an initial quick understanding of what you are going to read more fully later on. Previewing is similar to watching a movie preview. A movie preview is designed to give you just enough background to entice you to see the entire movie. You anticipate what are going to see, and when you watch the movie, if the movie is good, it satisfies your expectations. Similarly, by previewing a reading assignment for a few minutes, you will get a "big picture" of what you are going to read.

To preview a selection, you scan the titles, headings, graphics, and chapter summaries. In text material and on the Web, titles and main headings are often highlighted with bold font. As you turn pages or page down on the computer, glance at any subtitles. *Your goal is to understand the author's outline. When you figure out the outline, you can follow the organization of thought.*

Next, read any introductory paragraph before the main section and/or concluding paragraph at the end. These paragraphs may be set off in boxes or may have a different-style font. *The introductory paragraph tells you what you are going to read, and the concluding paragraph reminds you what you have read.*

After you preview, you are ready to read. Do not try to substitute previewing for reading. In the next step, when you read the selection, you fill in the details of a familiar structure.

STEP 2: READ THE SELECTION

Choose a time and place to read so that you will not be disturbed or sidetracked. Get comfortable. Having spent a few minutes previewing your reading assignment, you are familiar with the selection's structure and are now ready to read thoughtfully. Thoughtful reading is active reading, which involves asking yourself questions.

What is the main idea?

As you read, work on distinguishing main ideas from details. You can identify the main idea in one of three ways.

The main idea is highlighted. The sentence is either in bold, italics, larger-size font, different-color font, or underlined.

The main idea is the first or second sentence of the paragraph. Some paragraphs restate the main idea in the last sentence.

The main idea is woven among sentences in the paragraph. Carefully read the paragraph, sometimes several times, to figure out the main point.

What does this mean?

Think about what you read. If you simply look at words without thinking about the information, you have not learned. To learn from reading, you think about the textual information by considering both its meaning and importance. Reading for ideas requires **reflection**, a deliberate kind of thinking. You can do this by reacting to the text three ways: text to text, text to person, and text to lecture.

Text to Text. Compare what you are reading with other text material you have read on the topic. How is the information similar? What is new? What is different? Is anything contradictory?

Text to Person. Personalize the text information. What experience or knowledge does this remind you of? How can you use this information?

Text to Lecture. Compare what you have read to your lecture notes. What information overlaps? What is new, similar, different, or contradictory?

STEP 3: MARK KEY POINTS

Reread selectively to highlight and underline key ideas. If you are concerned about the resale value of a marked textbook, ask yourself how much your time is worth. *When you are reading material from the WEB or reference material, make hard copies.*

Because you have already created an overview by previewing the selection and have spent time sorting out main ideas from details, you do not need to reread everything. Your goal is to identify important information to study.

To mark your material, follow these guidelines.

1. Be extremely selective in choosing information to mark.
2. Mark or write out only meaningful words, phrases, or sentences.
3. Mark to make information stand out, so it is easier to study later. Typically, no more than 20% of a page should be marked.
4. Personalize your marking by using your own words in the margins of the material.
5. Personalize a system of marks. Decide how you want to use highlighting, double underlines, single lines, brackets, asterisks, circles, and question marks.

In the following text material, *Identity Theft*, there are two purposes: to inform and to explain. Notice how text marking in the first sections highlights these purposes.

IDENTITY THEFT

defn.

→

stealing

Identity theft has been referred to by some as the crime of the new millennium. It can be accomplished anonymously, easily, with a variety of means, and the impact upon the victim can be devastating. Identity theft is simply the theft of identity information such as a name, date of birth, Social Security number (SSN), or a credit-card number.

①

②

③

④

defn.

Identity theft occurs in many ways, ranging from careless sharing of personal information, to intentional theft of purses, wallets, mail, or digital information. In public places, for example, thieves engage in "shoulder surfing," watching you from a nearby location as you punch in your telephone calling-card number or credit-card number or listen in on your conversation if you give your credit-card number over the telephone. Inside your home, thieves may obtain information from your personal computer while you are online and they are anonymously sitting in the comfort of their own homes. Outside your home, thieves steal your mail, garbage, or recycling. Outside medical facilities or businesses, thieves engage in "dumpster diving," going through garbage cans, large dumpsters, or recycling bins to obtain identity information, which includes credit- or debit-card receipts, bank statements, medical records such as prescription labels, or other records that bear your name, address, or telephone number.[5]

defn.

→

Pretexting is the practice of getting your personal information under false pretenses. Pretexters sell your information to people who may use it to get credit in your name, steal your assets, or to investigate or sue you. Pretexting is against the law.

Pretexters use a variety of tactics to get your personal information. For example, a pretexter may call, claim he's from a survey firm, and ask you a few questions. <u>When the pretexter has the information he wants, he uses it to call your financial institution.</u> He pretends to be you or someone with authorized access to your account. He might claim that he's forgotten his checkbook and needs information about his account. In this way, the pretexter may be able to obtain personal information about you such as your Social Security number, bank and credit-card account numbers, information in your credit report, and the existence and size of your savings and investment portfolios.

Keep in mind that <u>some information about you may be a matter of public record,</u> such as whether you <u>own a home, pay your real estate taxes, or have ever filed for bankruptcy.</u> It is not pretexting for another person to collect this kind of information.[6]

Phishing is a form of identity theft that uses e-mail and malicious web sites to obtain personal information. Phishing has become the leading type of Internet-based fraud. The typical phishing attack involves the scammer sending the victim an e-mail message, which appears to be from a legitimate business. The e-mail message requests the victim to update or verify personal information by clicking on a link in the e-mail message. This link will take the victim to what appears to be a legitimate company Web page. However, the Web page is actually a well-designed phony Web page, which only looks authentic. When the victim enters personal information into the Web page, the victim is actually supplying information directly to the scammer.

The most frequently targeted industry by phishing schemes continues to be financial institutions, accounting for approximately 90% of all phishing attacks. The scammer's e-mail message offers what may sound like a plausible explanation for why the victim needs to update

(continued)

or verify account information. One ploy used in the past by phishing scams includes a warning of fraudulent activity on the customer's account, which necessitates account verification or a scheduled software upgrade. A recent phishing scam offered a $50.00 account credit to the victim for simply participating in a short online survey. The scammers are copying and using official bank logos to make the e-mail messages and fake Web pages appear authentic. Customers of Internet-service providers, eBay, and PayPal have also been targeted by phishing scams.

Scammers are always trying to find new ways to steal personal information, including a new form of phishing called vishing. The vishing scheme relies on the fact that it is not unusual for consumers to conduct business transactions over the telephone. Many consumers who are suspicious of e-mail fraud have been banking by phone for years.

Scammers blanket an area using Voice-over Internet Protocol (VoIP))–originated phone calls and leave a message indicating there has been fraudulent activity on the consumer's credit-card account. The victim is directed to call a telephone number immediately to update or confirm account information and to provide personal information, such as a credit card number. Because the phone number has the same three-digit prefix as the consumer's phone number, many consumers believe the phony number is legitimate and become easy targets for this latest scam.[7]

STEP 4: TAKE TEXT NOTES

After you have finished marking your selection, take notes. Your notes should contain main ideas, preferably written in your own words. Your goal is to reduce many pages of print into manageable units of information. When a unit exam approaches, you will discover that studying from several pages of your personal text notes is faster than flipping through hundreds of highlighted text pages.

As you take text notes, make a conscious effort to be neat. Clearly written notes do not require extra time and result in a sharper, cleaner mental image. Label your text notes "TN" and add page numbers for easy reference.

TN pp 124–125

IDENTITY THEFT

- Identity theft is crime of the 21st century!!
- Definition—<u>theft of identity information</u>—name, date of birth, SS#, credit card number

<u>Ways thieves steal identity</u>
1. Careless sharing of personal information
2. Shoulder surfing
3. Steal mail, garbage, recycling
4. Dumpster diving
5. Pretexting

Pretexters pretend to be from a survey firm, ask questions, get info & use info to get more personal information from your bank

<u>Examples of info. on public record</u>
- names of property owners
- real estate tax records
- bankruptcy records

DIFFICULT-TO-READ TEXT MATERIAL

In college you may encounter text material that is hard to understand. One reason may be the difficulty of the subject. Highly abstract, technical, or complex subjects require a great deal of intellectual understanding. Sometimes you may have an insufficient background in the subject content. If this is the case, speak to the instructor and listen to his or her recommendations. Discuss whether you should drop the course and take a prerequisite. Regardless of the reason, work on understanding the author's purpose and use the following suggestions.

1. Read the material, and then explain out loud what it means.
2. Find a study partner to work out the material together.
3. Preread the subject matter using easy-to-read material. For instance, find similar material written on a high school grade level. Read the easier material first, and then read your college textbook.
4. Take excellent class notes and then read the assignment.

5. Use note cards or margin notations indicating your questions. Make an office appointment to see your professor. Your difficulty with the textbook may be resolved by understanding a few key concepts.
6. Divide each reading assignment into several sections. Give yourself a study break after you complete a segment of work to reduce frustration and increase your sense of accomplishment.

READING-RATE FACTORS

At some point you may have read or heard claims about people reading 1000 wpm (words per minute). You may have thought to yourself, *Wouldn't it be great if I could read that fast*! These unbelievable claims are just that—unbelievable. Research has failed to show that a person can *read and comprehend* at 1,000 wpm.

The average rate for reading with good comprehension in college is between 200 wpm and 400 wpm. At rates slower than 200 wpm, reading comprehension decreases because more time is being spent trying to figure out individual words rather than understanding larger units of meaning.

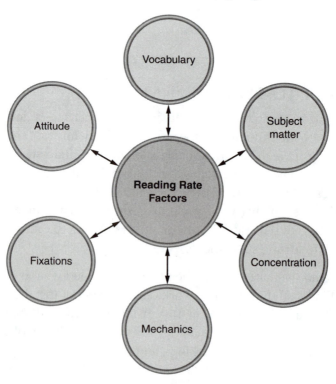

FACTOR 1: VOCABULARY

Your reading comprehension corresponds to your vocabulary. The wider and more extensive your vocabulary, the faster you can read because you are not slowed down trying to figure out what a sentence means. If your general vocabulary is small or your technical vocabulary in a subject area is inadequate, your reading rate will decrease as you struggle to understand each sentence. Skipping over words you do not know on the assumption that it doesn't matter or there's no time to look up the meaning typically results in poor comprehension. Instead, as you read, check or underline unfamiliar words, and look them up. After you have finished reading, study these words by writing each one on a card. Practice using the words until you are sure of their meanings.

FACTOR 2: SUBJECT MATTER

Think about the last time you drove in an unfamiliar place for the first time. You needed time to familiarize yourself with the surroundings. The next time you visited the place, you were able to spot familiar land-marks and go about your way. Similarly, if you lack background in a subject, you spend time learning new concepts as you read. As you become more familiar with the subject—through lectures and reading—you read more fluently. That is why taking required core courses in college provides you with familiar landmarks, called *schema*, that can help you read faster.

FACTOR 3: CONCENTRATION

Your ability to concentrate affects your reading rate—the more interruptions and distractions, the slower the rate. Certain conditions are easily improved. For instance, a messy desk or room may provide distracting visual stimuli. Spend a few minutes tidying up. Vocal music that entertains you during the day may distract you as you read. Research has shown that wordless, steady, or rhythmic music may actually help you shut out casual or irregular sounds. Intermittent sounds, such as the telephone, will certainly distract you. Therefore, turn off the ringer and return phone calls later.

Psychological factors, such as random thoughts—a sudden memory of something you need to do, an upsetting emotional situation—will make it difficult to concentrate while you read. Keep a notepad handy and jot down these distracting thoughts as they arise. Tell yourself that you can visit these issues later when you have time, enabling you to dismiss them from your mind while you read. Most importantly, always *read for information*, looking for ideas and relationships and anticipating content to improve your concentration.

Fatigue impairs your ability to concentrate and will slow your reading rate. Schedule reading during the time of day when your energy level is high. If you start to read and feel fatigued, take a 10-minute catnap. If you are not getting enough sleep, increase the amount of time you sleep by an hour. Additionally, consider the room temperature. It is easier to concentrate in a cooler room than one that is too hot.

Finally, determining ahead of time to read a given selection of material in a specific amount of time results in concentration as you try to complete the reading in the allotted time.

FACTOR 4: EYE FIXATIONS

As you read a line of print, your eyes make stops called **fixations** to register the image. You do not need to stop for every letter or even for every word because your eyes can take in several spaces at a single fixation.

A skilled reader moves his or her eyes in a definite rhythm across the line, stopping to read phrases of words at each fixation. The more fixations you take, the longer it will take to read a sentence. Similarly, the more times you have to go back and reread, the slower your reading rate.

Read the following example, with single-word fixations:

When
you
read
word
by
word
it
slows
you
down.

Notice the difference when you read phrases:

By looking at clusters, or groups of words you can quickly increase your reading rate.

If you take six fixations instead of three fixations for every line, you double the time needed to read the same amount of material. By fragmenting what you read into small pieces, you hinder comprehension. Finally, make sure you swing your eyes quickly from the end of one line to the beginning of the next. This *return sweep* should be accurate and quick. If you skip a line or place your eyes too close to the left or right margin, you are wasting time.

Reading rhythm comes with practice. The more you practice reading, the more skilled you become. To change old reading habits, practice these techniques on easy-to-read material. Try using a note card or your hand to move your eyes faster. Contrary to what you may have been told, this will not slow you down. By moving your note card or hand faster, you can train your eyes to move as fast. You may be spending more time reading than you need, simply for the reason that you never really tried to read faster.

FACTOR 5: MECHANICS

Your eyes can move two to three times faster than your lips can move. If you *vocalize* as you read by moving your lips, you slow down your reading rate. You can read by mentally registering the appearance of the words without pronouncing them. You may think you *have* to say words to yourself, but this may simply be a habit carried over from elementary school. To check for vocalization, place your fingertips on your lips and see if any slight movements occur during reading. With conscious effort, you can eliminate these movements. Be patient with yourself. If you have been vocalizing for many years, it may take several months to change this habit.

Because most of your time studying in college involves reading, do not make assumptions about your vision. Poor eye movements can be symptoms rather than causes of poor reading. Anatomical and functional ocular problems, such as astigmatism, myopia, and eye muscle imbalance, interfere with your ability to read easily for sustained periods of time. Make an appointment with an ophthalmologist or optometrist if you have not had your eyes checked in a few years.

FACTOR 6: ATTITUDE

Your attitude can influence your reading rate. If you approach a reading assignment with the attitude this is so boring or I hate reading this stuff, you are, in effect, sabotaging yourself. It is very hard to concentrate when you bring a negative attitude to the task. Instead, approach your reading assignment determined to learn from it. Remind yourself of your goals. Tell yourself, I don't have to like it; I just have to do it.

COLLEGE LECTURES

You may wonder why you can't simply read about a topic and skip lectures altogether. The reason is simple: Listening to a lecture provides you with information that exemplifies and amplifies what you read in your textbook. With a good lecturer, you become captivated by the subject matter, thus making your learning experience an enjoyable one.

Listening to lectures in high school is different from listening to lectures in college. In high school classes, if you tuned out your teacher while daydreaming about something else, you probably still knew when to take notes because your subject teacher wrote the important information on the board or overhead. Your teacher may have provided handouts containing all the information you needed to know. In high school, the subject matter was usually carefully sequenced to help you learn manageable units of information. If you were absent from class, your high school teacher might have helped you make up the notes you missed.

In contrast, your college professor may lecture for 50 minutes straight, stopping only occasionally to write a term on an overhead projector or a board. Your college professor covers a large amount of information for you to sort out as you listen. If you are absent from class, you must figure out how to obtain the missed notes.

LECTURE NOTES

Your ability to take good lecture notes is a valuable asset in college. Good lecture notes help you to understand the subject content and the textbook and to do well on tests. They can often make the difference of a letter grade. Because your lecture notes are an integral part of your course, be cautious about lending them out. If a student asks to borrow your notes because he or she missed class, offer instead to meet at the copy machine at a convenient time so you can copy the notes. Do not risk losing your notes to someone who does not return to class or misplaces them.

Taking **I-D-E-A-L N-O-T-E-S** is an efficient and effective study skill.

I = INDIVIDUALIZED

Your style of taking class notes should be individualized. Instead of adapting your style to conform to a specific type of note-taking system, adapt the note-taking system to your needs. You will know if your note taking works when you achieve an improved understanding of the content and an increase in your ability to answer test questions successfully.

D = DETAILED

As you listen to a lecture, write down details, such as definitions, examples, reasons, and illustrations that clarify main points.

E = EXPLAINABLE

Your class notes need to be understandable. If you cannot explain your notes at a later time, your notes are worthless. Make it a habit to read over your notes later in the day when your memory of the lecture is still fresh so that you can clarify and add necessary details.

A = ABBREVIATED

Where possible, shorten your sentences to phrases, your phrases to words, and your words to abbreviations. Many professors speak quickly, covering a large amount of information. Although in some instances you may ask permission to tape-record a lecture, tape-recording is an inefficient method because it doubles the time you spend on the lecture. When you rework your notes, make sure you are using abbreviations you understand later.

L = LEVELS

Instead of writing full sentences or paragraphs, make "levels" of notes, indenting for details—much as you would in an outline. That way, when you go back to study your notes, you can see the main points, major details, and minor details from the physical layout of your notes.

N = NUMBERED

Number, label, and date your notes on the top right-hand corner of the page. Start with 1 and continue throughout the semester. Numbering and dating your notes can help if you are absent, if you lend out your notes, or if you have questions. Label class notes "CN" and text notes "TN."

O = ORGANIZED

Use a binder, a folder, or a loose-leaf notebook for each subject. Subdivide large topics within a course with labeled dividers.

T = THOUGHTFUL

Think about your notes. Search for connections, examples, cause-and-effect relationships, reasons, comparisons, and definitions. Consider how your lecture notes are similar to and different from your textbook.

E = EDITED

Let your notes settle in, so to speak, and when you are not rushed, review your notes. Using a colored pen or pencil, mark your notes to highlight important points.

S = SELECTIVE

Your goal in note taking is not to write down everything your instructor says, but rather to select high-value information that you will study from later. Use these guidelines:

1. You do not have to take notes on information you already know *unless* it is being presented in a way that is significant or adds new insight about a topic.
2. Instead of taking notes each time a point is repeated, *highlight the repeated points* in your notes. If your professor reiterates information, that should be a strong clue that the professor thinks the information is important and may be on a test.
3. Don't take notes on *irrelevant* information. Some lecturers sidetrack more than others. If the information being imparted is clearly off the topic, do not write it down.
4. Do take careful notes on information that follows direct verbal signals, such as, *This is important. . ., This you should know. . .,* or *This is a consequence. . . .* or indirect signals, such as a pause, slower speech, or rhetorical question.

Examine the following example to see how lecture notes are written in a personal, useful format for studying.

Internet Fraud and Cyber Crime

Growing nationwide problem

- Internet Crimes Complaint Center (IC3) receives >18,000 consumer complaints per month
- Social Security Admin. Office Fraud Hotline received approx. 62,000 allegations about SSN misuse in 1999

Methods used to obtain identity information

① basic street theft
② organized crime schemes
  - involve computerized databases
  - bribing of employees to access customer personal information

Phishing = fraudulent email

- pretends to come from legitimate businesses or government agencies
- goal is to trick you into giving personal financial information

Phishing attacks

① 1996 –
  - Thieves used phony e-mails as fishing "hook" to trick unsuspecting AOL users to give out passwords
② Phishing e-mails had many spelling, grammar & punctuation errors
③ August 2003 – more-sophisticated-looking fraudulent e-mails
  - Thieves targeted users of online banking, payment services (PayPal) & online e-commerce sites
④ Today –
  - Fraudulent emails pretend to be from popular online merchants
    Phony order number on subject line

(continued)

6 INFORMATION LITERACY

- Fraudulent e-mails warn you credit-card security has been breached

  Scare tactic: Must provide password & log on or account will be suspended

Pharming attacks

- Fraudulent Web sites impersonate legitimate commercial Web site
- User tricked into entering password or credit card

Identity fraud = huge losses

Secret Service tracked actual losses individuals and financial institutions

$442 million in fiscal year 1995

$450 million in fiscal year 1996

$745 million in fiscal year 1997 ☹!!

DIFFICULT-TO-FOLLOW LECTURES

If you have difficulty following your professor's lectures, try the following suggestions.

1. Preread the text material before the lecture to have a better understanding of the lecture. If the lecture follows the text, use a highlighter or pen, checking off information as the lecture progresses.
2. If the lecture does not follow a text but adds more content information, rework your notes after each class so they make sense to you.
3. See your professor during office hours and clarify: *Professor Smith, I just want to make sure that I understand what you mean about. . . .*
4. Find a study partner in your class. Together, piece together your notes so they make sense to both of you.
5. As a last resort, tape the lecture. Listening to a poorly organized lecture for a second time is time consuming but may provide help.

Get to know a classmate who seems to connect with the course content and/or professor. Speak to the person: *I'm having difficulty keeping up with Professor Smith's lecture. Would you mind if I made a copy of your notes today, so I can see how someone else does it?* If the classmate is reluctant to lend notes, you then might ask if the classmate would be willing to review and discuss the notes with you. Many college students find that sharing information in this manner helps everyone involved in the learning process.

FOR DISCUSSION

Your success in college depends on your understanding and assuming your student responsibilities. Reread the chapter and examine it from the perspective of the actions you need to take. Make a list of the responsibilities you must assume for your education.

ACTIVITIES AND EXERCISES

Log onto the On Campus Student Website at www.prenhall.com/fitton to determine how well you have studied and what you still need to learn.

1. **Defining Terms**
   Write the meanings of the following words.

   Information literacy _____

   _____

   _____

   Metacognition _____

   _____

   _____

   Inductive thinking _____

   _____

   _____

   Deductive thinking _____

   _____

   _____

   Preview reading _____

   _____

   _____

   Eye Fixations _____

   _____

   _____

2. Checking Your Understanding

a. How is critical thinking an active process?

_____

_____

_____

b. Explain the steps involved in reading for information.

_____

_____

_____

_____

_____

c. If you have a difficult-to-read textbook, what strategies can you use?

_____

_____

_____

_____

d. What factors affect reading rate?

_____

_____

_____

_____

_____

e. What do the letters in the acronym IDEAL NOTES stand for?

_____

_____

_____

_____

_____

3. **Knowing Your Campus**
   What credit and noncredit reading courses are offered at your college?

   _____

   _____

4. **Applying Chapter Concepts**
   a. Continue text marking the selection *Identity Theft*.
   b. Use your text marking from the selection *Identity Theft* to write text notes.
   c. Evaluate each of your classes for ease of taking class notes. Which class presents the most challenges? Describe how you will incorporate strategies presented in this chapter to help you meet the challenges.
   d. Analyze the reading demands in one course that you are taking. Explain how each of the six factors that influence reading rate will affect your ability to handle the reading assignments.

5. **Writing for Reflection**
   Explore your feelings about the value of information literacy. Write at least one paragraph in response to one of the following quotations or a meaningful sentence you select from the chapter.
   If you believe everything you read, you had better not read.
                                                        Japanese proverb

   If we think of it, all that a University, or final highest School can do for us, is still but what the first School began doing—teach us to read.
                                                        Thomas Carlyle

   Discovery consists in seeing what everyone else has seen and thinking what no one else has thought.
                                        Albert Szent-Gyorgoi Von Nagyrapolt

6. **Concerning College Athletes**
   a. How will you deal with missed lectures when you are traveling to and from sporting events?

   _____

   _____

   _____

b. For each course, explain your responsibilities for making up tests that you miss because of sports events.

_____

_____

_____

_____

7. **Reading Further**

The reading selections on the On Campus Student Website at www. prenhall.com/fitton explore different aspects of chapter topics. At the end of each reading selection are critical thinking questions. Your instructor will let you know whether you should print out your responses or use the online feature to e-mail your answers.

a. *Preventing Identity Theft* U.S. Dept. of Justice

Read this selection to find out how you can prevent identity theft, and then take notes.

b. *Victims of Identify* Theft U.S. Dept. of Justice

Read this selection to find out what steps are taken for victims of identity theft, and then take notes.

c. *OnGuard Online Quizzes* The Federal Trade Commission (FTC) maintains OnGuardOnline.gov.

Try these interactive quizzes to see how up to date you are regarding threats to your personal information.

ID Theft FaceOff!

Invest Quest

Buddy Builder

Invasion of the Wireless Hackers!

AuctionAction—The game that puts "U" in the Action!

Beware of Spyware—Learn the clues!

Phishing Scams—Avoid the bait.

Spam Scam Slam—Don't be fooled.

Online Lineup—Shop Online Safely.

P2P Threeplay!

Notes

[1] Christopher J. Lucas, *American Higher Education: A History* (New York: St. Martin's Press, 1994), 57.

[2] "Information Literacy Competency Standards for Higher Education," American Library Association, 2006, http://www.ala.org/acrl/ilcomstan.html (accessed January 4, 2007).

[3] R. Barrett, *English 7 Epic Heroes and Underworld Journeys*, 1998, University of Pennsylvania, http://www.english.upenn.edu/~rbarrett/teaching/epic98.syllabus.html (accessed April 12, 2003; site now discontinued).

[4] P. Matthews, Modern Philosophy Syllabus, Florida State University, http://garnet.acns.fsu.edu/~srum9778/ModernPhilosophySyllabus.htm (accessed April 12, 2003; site now discontinued).

[5] "Identity Theft: The Crime of the New Millennium," U.S. Department of Justice, *United States Attorneys' USA Bulletin*, 49(2, March 2001), http://www.cybercrime.gov/usamarch2001_3.htm (accessed January 3, 2007).

[6] "About Identity Theft," Federal Trade Commission, http://www.consumer.gov/idtheft/con_about.htm#pretext (accessed January 3, 2007; site now discontinued).

[7] U.S. Department of Justice Federal Bureau of Investigation Press Release, October 16, 2007, http://springfield.fbi.gov (accessed January 3, 2007).

6
INFORMATION
LITERACY

Notes

LEARNING AND TESTS

7

You, yourself, must make the effort.
The Buddha are only teachers.
~ *Buddhist proverb*

For centuries, faculty drilled students with daily recitations. To prepare for each class, students memorized assigned pages from their textbook. When called on by the teachers, students stood before the class to demonstrate how well they committed passages to memory. As you might expect, not all students excelled in these daily examinations:

> If any student shall persist in the neglect of his studies either through obstinacy or negligence and so frequently fails of making due preparation for recitation and other appointed exercises and if he refuses to submit and reform after due admonition he shall be rusticated, i.e., suspended for a time, and if he does not bring sufficient evidence of his reformation he shall be expelled.[1]

In contrast to past practices, periodic tests, quizzes, papers, reports, and projects have replaced daily recitations, making good study skills critical for success.

STUDYING IN COLLEGE

Studying in college is primarily a solitary process that involves sustained, individual efforts. Too often, students who are not successful in college mistakenly believe they are studying when, in fact, they are going through rituals that look like studying but do not involve actual learning. This is known as **pseudostudying**. The following are common pseudostudying behaviors:

- Simply highlighting words in your textbook is not studying.
- Glancing at your notes is not studying.
- Watching television while reading your textbook is not studying.
- Having perfect class attendance is not studying.

Studying means you are actively engaged in learning. You are acquiring information to the point that you understand fully what the information means and are able to demonstrate this understanding. If you did not study in high school or if you have never seen how A students study, you may not realize the following:

☑ Studying can take a long time.

☑ Studying can get frustrating.

☑ Studying can get overwhelming.

☑ Studying can involve sacrifice.

☑ Studying requires focus, concentration, and patience.

As you will learn in this chapter, studying entails purposeful mental work that is greatly influenced by your attitude and time commitment.

ATTITUDE TOWARD STUDYING

Your attitudes are shaped by your experiences and your reactions to those experiences. These attitudes affect how you approach each task. A negative attitude impairs learning. For instance, students who think it is a "waste of time" to study will resent the time commitment that is involved. Students who think studying is "stupid" are really demonstrating that they don't know what it means to become educated. Students who believe they are "entitled" to get good grades don't realize that most students who earn high grades work very hard for those accomplishments. Finally, students who believe they "cannot" learn a particular subject bring attitudes that work against them. When you struggle with these feelings, remember that millions of students enroll in college each year. Students across the country encounter similar academic challenges and hurdles as you do. If you are not willing to study, there will be other students determined to study hard, so they can graduate and apply for what might be your dream job.

Your attitude shapes your study skills habits. The term **study skills** refers to a group of skills that you use to study. These skills include learning, remembering, time management, listening, taking notes, reading, test preparation, and taking tests. You can replace ineffective study habits with effective ones. To do so requires that you identify the habit, understand why you continue with the habit, and plan a sequence of steps to acquire an effective habit to replace the ineffective one. Given a positive attitude, you will approach your studying with determination and commitment.

EXAMPLE

1. ***I don't take notes in class.***

   You recognize that your habit of not taking notes in class will impact your grade because you will not have sufficient information to study for a test. You determine who in the class regularly takes notes and change your seat to sit next to that person. When the other student takes notes, you take notes. Eventually, you find taking notes becomes automatic, and you no longer depend on watching another student take notes to remind you to take your own notes.

2. ***When I read, I skip over words I don't know.***

   You decide you want to make looking up unknown words in the dictionary a habit. In thinking it through, you recognize that you find looking up words time consuming and inconvenient. Taking advantage of new technology, you buy yourself a slim, portable electronic dictionary. Not only do you find it easy to look up words, you are able to save these words in a memory file for review. As your personal vocabulary increases, you look up fewer words.

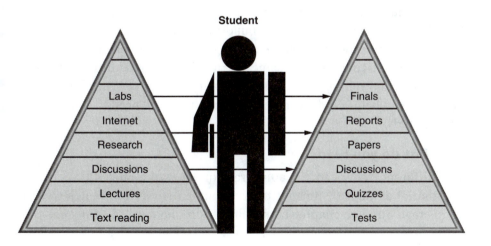

TIME REQUIREMENTS FOR STUDYING

Studying in college includes the time you spend reading, taking notes, writing, working on projects, and learning new information for tests. If you are enrolled in 15 credit hours and spend an average of 30 hours per week on these study tasks, the combined time is equivalent to a 45-hour workweek. Because of the time commitment involved, you can see why working a full-time job *and* attending college full time are challenging for most students and risky for some. If you are working a full-time job, attending college, and parenting one or more children, you *must* cut back on either your job or your credit hours. Use the following guideline until you have been in college for a while and have learned exactly how many credit hours you can handle without sacrificing good grades.

Work Hours	Maximum Credit Hours
40	6
30	9
20	12
10	15

Balancing the time you need to study with other commitments in your life is a challenge shared by most college students. One of the payoffs of studying hard during your freshman year is that you establish a solid knowledge base, upon which you build in ensuing years. You can repeatedly draw on this information, decreasing the time you may need to spend for subsequent courses. The same is true for the foundation courses in your major and minor areas of study. Your answers to the following six questions can help you determine how much time *you* need to schedule for college study.

How fast do you read?

The difference between a reading rate of 100 wpm and 300 wpm is a substantial amount of time. It takes about 2 hours, 40 minutes to read an average 30-page chapter containing approximately 16,000 words. In contrast, it takes about 54 minutes with a reading rate of 300 wpm. With occasional breaks, the total time requirement for each rate is actually longer.

What background information do you bring to the subject?

The academic and experiential background information you bring to a subject affects your reading comprehension. For instance, if you take college preparatory classes in high school, you are prepared to understand more difficult concepts about a similar subject. If you regularly read or watch educational television, you bring a wealth of information to which you can relate new material. In contrast, if this is the first time you have studied a subject, you must spend more time learning new concepts and ideas.

What is the size of the assignment?

Many college assignments are voluminous, requiring you to read a large number of pages and to complete lengthy activities. If your instructor provides an assignment timeline, take advantage of it. Because your instructor knows the typical amount of time students need to read an assignment, the timeline can be a helpful guide.

In the following example, the instructor of an introductory anthropology course at the University of Notre Dame (IN) provided a semester assignment timeline.[2] Approximately 27 pages are assigned for each class meeting.

EXAMPLE

Semester Assignment Timeline					
Date	Day	Lecture Title	Author	Chapter	Page
Mar 4	Mon.	Origins of farming	Kottak	9	210–237
Mar 6	Wed.	Making a living	Kottak	14	344–371
Mar 8	Fri.	Organizing society	Kottak	17	424–456

To know how much time you need to schedule for each reading assignment, clock yourself reading three text pages. Divide that time by 3 to determine approximately how long it takes you to read *one* page. Multiply that number by the total number of pages for the assignment. Using the preceding example, if it takes 20 minutes to read 3 pages, you would need 3 hours to read a 27-page anthropology assignment.

A general guideline is to study two to three hours per week for *every credit hour* you are taking. Some courses may take less than an hour each week for studying, whereas others may require three to four hours a week.

A Philosophy Course at Grant McEwan College, Canada

Weekly reading should take no more than three hours. Work on term paper and preparing for exams will add a few more hours. I expect all students to come to every class prepared to discuss the readings.[3]

How difficult is the assignment?

Some assignments are more complex than others. These types of assignments require more understanding and concentration.

EXAMPLE

An Advanced Accounting Course at the University of Baltimore (MD)

ACCT 301 requires a significant and regular time commitment from the student. You should plan to spend a MINIMUM of 10-12 hours per nonexam week in studying for the course.[4]

What is your aptitude for the subject matter?

Your aptitude in a subject matter impacts the amount of time you may need to spend studying. Can you write with ease and facility? Or, is it a struggle? Is reading scientific material simpler for you than reading historical information? Or, is it the other way around? Can you compute numbers in your head? Or, do you need paper and pencil? Your aptitude in a subject enhances your ability to learn that subject efficiently.

How motivated are you to get a particular grade?

Your motivation ultimately affects the amount of time you spend studying. If nothing less than an A will satisfy you, then you will dedicate the time it takes to learn the material. If, on the other hand, you are satisfied with a C, you will spend less time studying.

 ## FOR DISCUSSION

Listed next are five factors that can influence studying. With the members in your group, discuss a ranking for these factors from most important (1) to least important (5). List your rankings. Be prepared to explain the criteria your group used to rank the factors and the reasons for your ranking.

Attitude

Aptitude

Subject matter

Study environment

Wellness

STUDY SKILL PROCESSES

Once you understand the overall process of studying, as well as its individual steps, you are well on your way to becoming a successful college student. Following these steps does not mean you will whip through your

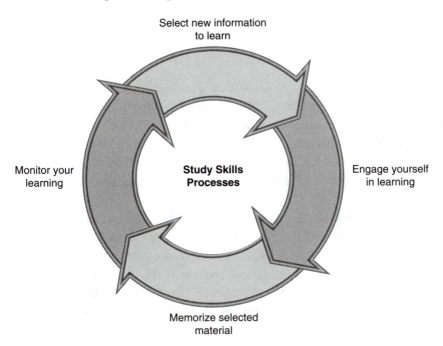

Select new information to learn

Study Skills Processes

Monitor your learning

Engage yourself in learning

Memorize selected material

7 LEARNING AND TESTS

studies in 30 minutes or that you will find the process easy to do. You must tailor each suggestion to your situation and discover what works best. You will know what works best when you achieve the level of success that you want in college.

STEP 1: SELECT INFORMATION TO LEARN

To begin studying, review your **class notes** and **text notes** and reduce them to compact **study notes**. You do this by reading through both your class notes and text notes on the same topic. As you search for connections, **ponder** the material. To ponder means you thoroughly and carefully search for major concepts, definitions, and examples that reinforce and extend your understanding. Now, consolidate your notes by rewriting or retyping them. Label and number these notes *study notes*.

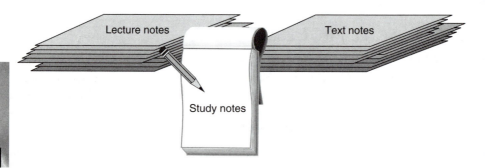

You are studying if you organize your notes, discard unimportant papers, reorder details, think about the information, and write it down. Combining class lecture notes and text notes into study notes reinforces concepts. You can access and see everything you need to learn in one place. When it comes time for finals, you can review the study notes you created during the semester instead of spending time sorting through class notes and text notes.

If you leave a blank column alongside the body of your notes, you have a location for writing questions. This **study question column** can be used like the front and back of flashcards. You cover the body of information on the right column and "test" yourself, rehearsing and monitoring what you learn. Use symbols or a colored pen to circle questions that you have difficulty remembering. You should rehearse highlighted questions extensively.

	SN 5
	10/11
What is identity theft?	Any theft that involves identity information— name, date of birth, SS#, credit card number
How do thieves steal people's identity?	1. careless sharing of personal information **(from CN)**
	2. shoulder surfing
	3. basic street theft (steal mail, garbage, recycling, dumpster diving)
	4. pretexting
	5. organized crime schemes **(from TN)**
	-involve computerized databases
	-bribing of employees to access customer personal information
	6. phishing
	7. pharming
What is the difference between phishing & pharming?	With phishing, thieves send out bogus e-mails that look like the real thing. You have to click on the link or answer the questions. With pharming, you type in the correct URL but it is sent to a bogus Web site that looks like the real thing.

STEP 2: BE ENGAGED IN LEARNING

Staring at words on a page or memorizing lists of words without real understanding is **superficial learning**. To truly learn and store information, you must be involved in the learning process. That is why no one can study *for* you—you have to study for yourself. You become actively engaged when you take the following actions:

Find the Right Study Environment

Before you start studying, scrutinize your **study environment**. Find a place where you can study undisturbed. If necessary, physically remove yourself from distracters, such as loud music and noisy roommates. Be proactive by studying in the library, where quiet is enforced. If you study where you live, turn off the television and shut your door. Block out distracting noises with earplugs or listen to wordless music. Ask your friends not to disturb you. Choosing the right time and place will maximize your mental alertness and ability to stay on task.

Make Personal Connections with New Information

Connecting new information to what you already know results in deep, long-lasting learning.

For example, looking at a persimmon, you might not know whether you would enjoy eating it or not. As you inspect the fruit, you might compare its appearance to a bright orange, medium-sized tomato. Taking a bite, you might say it tasted like a crisp apple. You understand what a persimmon is and what it is not in context of your experiences. The next time you see a persimmon, you will remember what it is. Similarly, when you learn new information, make deliberate attempts to relate it to what you already know.

Learn Something Correctly the First Time

It is much easier to learn something correctly the first time than it is to unlearn or relearn information. For example, a person who learns to type incorrectly using two fingers will find it more difficult to relearn to type using the 10-finger QWERTY method. If you learn something in a fuzzy, incomplete, or incorrect way, it is retained and reproduced in a fuzzy, incomplete, or incorrect way. For that reason, make a point to learn your coursework accurately and completely the first time.

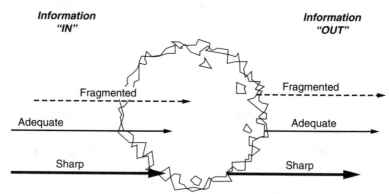

Study by Reading, Writing, and Speaking

To be an effective learner, use as many sensory inputs as possible when you study: visual (reading), auditory (speaking and listening), and kinesthetic (writing). Although you may have a personal preference to learn either by hearing information, seeing words, or doing things, that doesn't mean you cannot learn by using your other senses. If you say to yourself, I can't listen to lecture notes; I have to see the words, or I can't read information; I have to hear it, you set up mental roadblocks and make learning a more difficult chore. If you can see and hear, do not become totally dependent on just one sensory input. Using a less preferred learning modality may take more effort, but the results are well worth it.

The following diagram shows how you learn most effectively.[5] You will see that the more senses you involve, the more you remember.

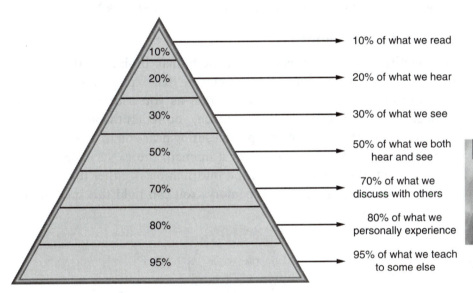

10% — 10% of what we read
20% — 20% of what we hear
30% — 30% of what we see
50% — 50% of what we both hear and see
70% — 70% of what we discuss with others
80% — 80% of what we personally experience
95% — 95% of what we teach to some else

STEP 3: MEMORIZE SELECTED MATERIAL

After you understand a body of information, you decide what parts need to be memorized. For example, in a 20th-century American history course that addresses how greed, power, and hysteria were major issues during McCarthyism, you probably would memorize names of politicians who were involved, names of individuals who were victimized, and legislation that preceded and followed the scandalous witch hunt.

In college you must be able to retrieve previously memorized information so that you can understand new concepts and make correct responses. Your goal is to **recall information**, that is, to retrieve stored information without clues or hints to help you remember. When you recall something, you can easily supply the information. For instance, you probably can easily recall the names of your favorite high school teachers and classmates. Contrast this memory with trying to remember those names from elementary school. Can you recall them? If not, you probably could recognize their names on a list. **Recognition** is the ability to retrieve stored information with clues or hints provided.

Every subject matter has a minimum of facts, terms, and concepts that must be committed to memory. The quantity varies with the subject matter. Some subjects, such as science, contain a large volume of information to memorize. To help you decide what material to memorize, ask yourself, If I gave a test on this subject, what information would I ask?

Principles of Learning

As scientists understand more about the human brain, old theories are revised or discarded and new theories emerge that explain how we memorize information. One explanation is that as you acquire information through sight, sound, taste, smell or touch, you retain the image momentarily. For example, you look at a person sitting near you in a restaurant. If you shut your eyes, you can see for a moment the exact image of that person. From this sensory input, the information is either discarded or goes into working (short-term) memory. You can hold this memory for

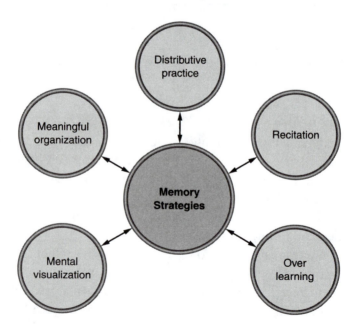

about 20 seconds without rehearsing it. In another example, you see a car drive away from an accident and note the license plate. Unless you keep repeating the license plate number, *KG28XY1904 - KG28XY1904 - KG28XY1904*, the information may slip away in about 20 seconds.

To help transfer short-term memory to long-term memory, so that you can recall information at a later time, use the following strategies:

Meaningful Organization.

Short, recognizable units of information are easier to memorize than long, seemingly unrelated pieces of information. For example, instead of trying to memorize 50 words, break the long list into smaller units, with no more than 7 items in any group.

An **acronym** uses the letters of each word to form a new, memorable word. If the sequence of the words is not important and if one or more of the words contain a word starting with a vowel, an acronym can be relatively simple to construct. As you work on creating an acronym, you are also rehearsing the information.

EXAMPLE
HOMES is an acronym for the names of the Great Lakes: **H**uron, **O**ntario, **M**ichigan, **E**rie, **S**uperior.

An **acrostic** uses either the letters of each word or the words themselves to form a new memorable sentence.

EXAMPLE
Red Or Yellow Gives Big Interesting Value corresponds to **R**ed, **O**range, **Y**ellow, **G**reen, **B**lue, **I**ndigo, and **V**iolet, the colors of the rainbow.

Distributive Practice

If you have ever participated in a team sport, you would think it ridiculous if your coach said, "Hey, guys, since tomorrow's our big day, let's meet early tonight and practice as long as we can." To prepare for the event, athletes spend countless hours practicing and rehearsing routines that become firmly memorized and easily utilized. Similarly, studying in college requires that you spend extended time rehearsing and practicing in order to register information into permanent, long-term memory.

For every hour you study, take a 10-minute break. Then review what you learned before you begin studying again. Make sure not to exceed four consecutive hours of studying a single subject, even with 10-minute breaks. As fatigue and boredom set in, the quality of studying diminishes.

Recitation

Recitation is a method of rehearsing information. One way to recite is to cover your notes and then study the covered material by saying it out loud. After reciting, uncover your notes and check for accuracy. Unless you need to define a term precisely, use your own words to convey information. Alternatively, rather than verbalizing the information, you can cover material and then think or write it. By comparing results, you will know which approach works best. Studying with another person or group to explain and discuss the material may make this process more enjoyable and productive. Guard against social digressions that are counterproductive to learning. Recitation, by yourself or with a group, embeds information and establishes a solid foundation for long-term memory.

Mental Visualization

Visualizing information is a powerful method for retaining information. If you can picture something, you can retrieve the image. For instance, to create a mental visualization for the word *sanguine,* which means having a kindly, joyful, loving disposition, picture a person laughing joyfully and happily with the word *sanguine* written across the person's forehead.

Overlearning

Unlike many of the negative connotations of words that begin with over—overeating, overuse, and overdone—**overlearning** should be your goal. Overlearning means to learn something over again, so that once your initial proficiency is achieved, you reinforce the learned material. Athletes and musicians incorporate overlearning when they repeatedly rehearse their skills. Actors practice their lines over and over, so they can perform in a play with confidence.

When you learn something thoroughly, you should be able to explain or teach the material to someone else. If you cannot do this, then you probably learned the information superficially or insufficiently. Spend more time studying until you are positive you know it completely.

STEP 4: MONITOR YOUR LEARNING

Have you ever taken a test, thought you knew the material, but to your dismay received a test score of D? If this has happened to you, the chances are good that you were *familiar* with the material, but you had only *partially* learned it. With partially learned information, you may be able to recognize bits and pieces, but your learning is incomplete.

To guard against **incomplete learning,** monitor your learning. You should do this every time you study. Stop and ask yourself: What did I just read? What did I just learn?

You check how well you have learned by reciting, using flash cards, taking practice quizzes, and studying with a study partner or group. If you have not learned what you thought you did, repeat Steps 1-3. By constantly monitoring what you learn, you will be well prepared to take college tests with confidence.

 ## FOR DISCUSSION

Discuss an activity either for school, work, or a pastime that you over-learned. How did you monitor your learning?

TEST TAKING

Tests are your opportunity to demonstrate how well you have studied. During a test, you are challenged with questions designed to assess not only *how much you know,* but *how well you know the information.* Timed tests require quick thinking under pressure.

STRATEGIES

1. Before you take a test, find out as much information about the test as you can. You want to know the types and quantity of questions and if there are penalties for guessing. Ask if the instructor gives partial credit. By learning these details beforehand, you can determine how you will prepare for and take the test.

2. The night before your test, make sure you get a good night's sleep. You want to give your brain a chance to *consolidate* what you have studied. You also want to have energy to be mentally

sharp during the test. Taking good care of yourself includes eating breakfast or lunch before the test.

3. Don't overlook basics, such as bringing a supply of pens or pencils (for a Scantron test), allowed aids such as calculators, and, if necessary, writing paper. When you enter the classroom, consider taking a seat on the side of the room furthest from the door to avoid being distracted by students who leave early. As soon as you receive the test, write down your name, the name of the course, date, and whatever is customarily required on the test book. If you have memorized an acronym or acrostic, write these down on the exam sheet or book.

4. If multiple-choice questions constitute only one part of a test, answer that section as quickly as possible. Not only do you need time for other sections, you want time to review your answers and to think through difficult questions.

5. Skip those questions you cannot answer right away. Make sure to mark the question in some way to know where it is when you go back later. As you continue through the test, you may find clues that help you to remember or figure out skipped questions. It is much better to skip questions temporarily than to lose time staring at difficult questions. Sometimes tests have mistakes, and you may be wasting your time trying to figure out an answer that a question that was a proofreading error.

6. Don't leave a test early unless you are satisfied that you have reviewed and answered *all* the questions to the best of your ability.

7. When your test is returned to you, analyze the questions that you answered incorrectly to see if there are patterns in your wrong answers. Did you forget to study a portion of the material on which you were tested? Are there particular forms of questions that you need to practice? Are your incorrect answers the result of incomplete, partial studying? Using your text and lecture notes, can you understand the correct answers? If you cannot determine why you received the given test grade, make an appointment to meet with your professor before the next test.

MULTIPLE-CHOICE TESTS

Many professors prefer multiple-choice questions because the tests are easy to grade and can provide objective assessment of students' knowledge and understanding of course content. For those reasons, the majority of your tests in college will be multiple-choice tests.

Multiple-choice tests supply the *correct answer*. Your task is to *recognize* which answer is correct. The difficulty is that, knowing this, your professor will design a test with **distracters**, incorrect alternatives to make the correct choice less obvious. These distracters include recognizable information from a lecture or text that make them appear plausible, but they are, nevertheless, incorrect. Unless you know the information thoroughly, you may end up selecting a familiar-looking, but incorrect, answer.

Parts of a Multiple-Choice Test

Multiple-choice questions consist of three parts: (1) a stem, which asks a question, poses a problem, or presents an incomplete sentence; (2) the correct answer; and (3) a number of *distracters*, or incorrect alternatives. Use these guidelines for each part.

The Stem

Read each question stem carefully.

1. As you read, underline words such as *not* or *always* to help you remember precisely what it is you are looking for.
2. If the stem contains enough information, cover up the choices and try to anticipate the answer in your own words before you get distracted by incorrect alternatives.
3. Always read each alternative carefully before reaching the conclusion that a particular one is the best.

Distracters

Be on the look out for typical types of distracters.

1. Absolute words such as *always, never, all, none,* or *must*
2. Important sounding words such as *significant* or *accurate*

3. An incorrect choice that is similar in length and complexity to the correct answer
4. Textbook terminology that has the *appearance* of correctness
5. A correct statement but not the best answer to the question stem

Answers

1. Unless there is penalty for guessing, *never* leave a blank on a multiple-choice test.
2. Don't change an answer unless you are positive that a different choice is correct. Stay with your first impulse. Students more frequently change right answers to wrong ones than wrong answers to right ones. In addition, second-guessing wastes time that could be better spent working elsewhere on the test.

Educated Guesses

In answering questions about which you are not sure, use strategy. If there are five answer alternatives and you guess blindly, you have a 20% chance of being correct. If you are able to eliminate one wrong answer, you increase your odds from 20% to 25% correct.

You can make an educated guess by relying on your own good mental abilities, by following your intuition, and by using clues that are inadvertently written in the test.

Clues for Guessing

1. When the last word of a multiple choice is either an or a, it signals whether or not the *correct* choice starts with a vowel.

EXAMPLE

A part-time job during the academic year that provides supervised practical training in a student's field is called an

a. graduate assistant
b. matriculated student
c. work study
d. internship

Answer: Choice (d) is the only word beginning with a vowel.

2. When alternatives are grammatically inconsistent with the multiple-choice stem, select the grammatically correct choice.

A debit card is a type of banking card used

a. to replace checks and cash.
b. it is interest free.
c. and identifying a financial institution.
d. students at state universities.

Answer: Choice (a) is the only one that makes sense when combined with the stem.

3. An alternative with the most words may be the correct answer because it may contain necessary detailed information that makes the answer true.

Why is it important for students to establish state residency when attending a public higher education institution?

a. Public higher education institutions maintain current population enrollment statistics.
b. In-state students receive priority residence hall accommodations.
c. "State residency" determines whether a student will be charged in-state or out-of-state tuition rates at a public higher education institution
d. Out-of-state students may file for an education tax exemption.

Answer: Choice (c) contains detailed information necessary to make the statement true.

4. Select an alternative that repeats key words from the question stem.

In order to receive your full financial aid package,

a. you must purchase a federally guaranteed annuity.
b. you must be at least 18 years old.

c. you must declare a major.

d. you must be enrolled on a full-time basis.

Answer: Choice (d) repeats the word *full*.

5. Select an alternative that sticks out as being different from the other choices.

All the following are examples of financial aid EXCEPT

a. U.S. Federal Government Aid

b. Capital Gains

c. Military Aid

d. National Service

e. Free State Scholarship Lotteries

Answer: Choice (b) is different because all the other choices are government related.

6. Select "None of the above" only if you can eliminate all alternatives as false statements.

According to FAFSA (Free Application for Federal Student Aid) regulations,

a. A student must be admitted before he or she can apply for financial aid at a particular university.

b. To maintain federal aid, a student must maintain an A average.

c. You must apply for federal aid before the first day of classes.

d. Federal aid is awarded on the basis of either race or creed.

e. None of the above.

Answer: Choice (e). Answers (a), (b), (c), and (d) are false.

7. "All the above" is often a good guess.

Which of the following acronyms and terms are correctly linked?

a. FAF   Financial Aid Form

b. FAO   Financial Aid Office

c. FAT   Financial Aid Transcript

d. PLUS   Parent Loan for Undergraduate Students

e. All the above

Answer: Choice (e) can be confirmed if you know *at least two* of the choices are correct.

8. Limiting words, such as all, never, always, and must, are often false. General terms, such as most, some, usually, could, and might, are often true.

EXAMPLE

Which of the following statements about financial aid are correct?

I. A student must be declared an independent to qualify for financial aid.

II. The majority of available student aid comes from the federal government, not private sources.

III. Dropping classes may affect a student's financial aid eligibility.

IV. Changes made to a student's official records are automatically conveyed to the financial aid office.

    a. I, II

    b. II, III

    c. I, IV

    d. II, III, IV

Answer: Choice (b) because I and IV contain absolutes (*must, automatically*) and are false statements.

9. When two out of four choices are opposites, pick one of those two as the best guess.

EXAMPLE

Which statement is true?

a. Financial need is the difference between your school's cost of attendance (including living expenses), as calculated by your school, and your EFC (expected family contribution).

b. Financial need is the sum total of your school's cost of attendance (including living expenses), as calculated by your school, and your EFC (expected family contribution).

c. Private loans offer more flexible repayment plans than Federal loans.

d. Work study is an opportunity to work for credit.

Answer: Choice (a) is the opposite of choice (b), which is incorrect. The correct answer is (a).

10. A double negative occurs when both a question stem and an answer alternative contain a negative. This type of question is tricky. To tackle this, mentally change the negative question stem to a positive statement. If you can, mark negative words in the choices.

EXAMPLE

Which of the following is *not* true?

a. A cosigner on a loan does *not* assume responsibility for a loan if the borrower fails to repay it.

b. FAFSA on the Web *doesn't* require software to be installed.

c. Defaulting on a federal loan means you are *not* eligible for future financial aid.

d. State and Federal loans do *not* automatically renew each year.

Answer: Choice (a). Change the question to *Which of the following is false?* to see that statement (a) contains false information about a cosigner's responsibilities.

SHORT-ANSWER TESTS

A short-answer test is a test of your recall. You supply specific information for a direct question or an incomplete statement. Some short-answer questions are unintentionally vague. For instance, Where is your college located? can be answered by the name of the town, city, state, or country. Each answer is correct. If you encounter this situation on a test, ask your instructor for clarification. Most short-answer tests are constructed to test three types of information.

1. **Terminology**
   An undergraduate with fewer than 30 credits is called a(n) _____.
   What branch of philosophy is concerned with the practice and conduct of individuals and groups?_____

2. **Specific Facts**
   What year was your college founded?_____.
   What is the name of the president of your college? _____.
3. **Method or Procedure**
   To change majors, you need to complete a(n)_____form.
   If you miss your final, what will happen?_____.

TRUE–FALSE TESTS

True–false tests require you to mark *true* or *false, right* or *wrong, yes* or *no,* or *agree* or *disagree* about a statement.

1. Words such as *usually, sometimes, generally,* and often are most likely to appear in true statements.

EXAMPLE

A junior college is often a private institution.

Answer: True

2. Absolute terms such as *always, never, all, none, and only* are more likely to appear in false statements.

EXAMPLE

College admission is always based on scholastic achievement in high school.

Answer: False

3. True statements tend to be longer than false statements because precise information may be needed to make the statement absolutely true.

EXAMPLE

The Big Ten Conference consists of 11 world-class universities that share a common mission of intercollegiate athletics, research, graduate, professional, and undergraduate teaching, and public service.

Answer: True

4. A well-designed true–false test will contain between 40% and 60% true statements.

Knowing this information is helpful. Suppose you have a 10-question true–false test. You are sure that 6 statements are true and 2 are false. Because you believe 60% of the questions are true, you should guess false for the 2 statements you do not know.

MATCHING TESTS

In a matching test, you connect two pieces of correct information. If one of the columns contains an additional item, you know that one of the items is incorrect. Be sure to ask your instructor if you encounter any unclear words on the test. Matching tests are often difficult to construct without misleading clues.

Common types of column relationships include the following.

Column 1	Column 2
Person	Person's accomplishments
Dates	Events related to time
Terms	Definition of words
Principles	Example of each principle or rule
Parts	Functions of how each part works

To save time, always read the column with the longest worded responses once, and then scan up and down the opposite column for a match.

ESSAY TESTS

Essay tests present an excellent opportunity to demonstrate your understanding about a topic. Your professor will have general expectations for essay content and specific ones for in-depth comprehension of the material being questioned. Because there is no *single* perfect answer, you have many ways to approach each question. Technical English (grammar, English usage, and spelling) may count toward the grade. In such instances, outstanding content marred by grammatical errors can result in a low essay grade.

Resist the temptation to rapidly write your essay test. Instead, take a few minutes to make sure you are clear about what you have to do. If you did not find out how many essays you are required to write beforehand, quickly determine the number and the relative value of each. Divide the number of essays you have to write by the total test time to determine the maximum time you should spend on each essay before moving on to the next one. Pay attention to these limitations. You are better off receiving partial credit on three incomplete essays than full credit answering only one out of three essays. For instance, if there are three essay questions and you answered only one perfectly, the best score you could receive is 33%. On the other hand, if you answered three questions incompletely and received 20% for each, you earn 60%.

Begin each essay question by underlining key directions and words that you need to address in your essay. Look for hints that may help you decide ways to answer the question. After you decide your thesis sentence, quickly organize your ideas in a brief outline. The writing skills you need to write an essay test are the same ones you use to write an essay assignment. Chapter 8 in this textbook explains the skills for writing an effective college essay.

 ## FOR DISCUSSION

Discuss the last time you studied for a test, only to get a low grade. According to the chapter, what could be possible reasons?

Which reasons do you believe apply to your situation? Why?

TEST ANXIETY

From pretest jitters and concerns to nervous tension during a test, many students have experienced some degree of test anxiety.

Insufficient test preparation, or incomplete learning, is a major cause of test anxiety. You may think you have studied, when in fact, you have only partially learned the material. Partially learned material results in knowing bits and pieces rather than having a comprehensive, full understanding of all material. Many times, if you prepare insufficiently for a test, you may mistakenly blame your poor test performance on having "test anxiety" rather than on your lack of study. As you learned in the previous section, looking and relooking at notes is not studying. If you overlearn your material, then you will be assured that you can take your test with confidence. With each positive test-taking experience, you will see the benefits of monitoring your learning as part of test preparation.

If you have sufficiently studied for your test but still feel test anxiety, consider whether you feel excessive pressure to succeed or have strong negative associations with test-taking situations. In addition to visiting the counseling center and signing up for test anxiety workshops at your college, try the following suggestions.

REHEARSE TEST TAKING

Practice taking tests will help *assure* you that you know the material. Take as many practice tests as you can. Turn textbook chapter questions and course study guides into tests. Check the library to see if they maintain files of previous tests provided by instructors. These old tests are a way for you to become familiar with the professor's testing style. Find a study partner or form a study group to predict as many test questions as you can. After you have gained confidence in your ability to answer test questions, treat practice tests as if they were real tests. Eliminate distractions and time yourself with testing time limits similar to those in the actual test.

Finally, acclimate yourself to the test environment. Visit the test room, walk around, sit at a desk, and just relax. Your goal is to associate a positive feeling with the testing situation.

CONTROL NEGATIVE THINKING

First, don't spend time listening to negative dialogue. Stay away from uptight classmates who say, "This is going be the hardest test. I heard no one ever passes Prof. Smith's first test. I studied so hard for this, but I know I'm going to fail," or well-meaning friends, "I'm sure you're going to do okay, but even if you don't, it's not that important. You'll do better on the next test. Don't worry about it."

Next, control your inner speech. Don't bother with simplistic phrases such as, I shouldn't worry or I'll try to do my best. Instead, create personally convincing words: I have studied hard, and I will do fine. Use an assertive tone: I *am sure* that I *know* the material. Rehearse your new script. As soon as you begin to worry, think to yourself, *Stop*, and listen to the inner speech you have practiced.

USE POSITIVE VISUALIZATION

Competitive athletes know the value of mental visualization, and they use this technique to form positive thoughts, feelings, and emotions into an unshakable winning mind-set. You, too, can use this technique to boost your confidence and concentration while taking a test. First, find a place and time when you will be uninterrupted. Sit down in a comfortable position, close your eyes, and breathe deeply for a few minutes. Allow yourself to imagine what is going to happen during the exam. Visualize walking into the exam room and taking a seat. When you open the test—although you cannot see the questions—imagine that the answers are perfectly clear. Visualize working through the test, calmly and confidently. After you recheck your answers, you hand in the test paper with a tremendous sense of satisfaction.

Practice this scenario several times before the actual test. Just as athletes improve their athletic performance by regularly using positive visualization, you can dismiss interfering feelings and focus successfully on the task at hand.

BREATHE DEEPLY

Take a deep breath and relax. If you have heard that advice, you will be interested in knowing that deep breathing *does* work. Once you learn how to take a deep, complete breath, you will feel more relaxed *and* energized. The University Learning Center at the University of North Dakota explains two helpful breathing methods to use when test anxiety occurs during an exam.[6]

THE COUNT-OF-THREE METHOD

Through your nose, inhale slowly while silently counting to three.

Hold your breath for the count of three.

Through your nose, exhale slowly while silently counting to three.

With breath out, count to three.

Repeat the cycle (Steps 1 to 4) several times.

Once you have the rhythm, you need not continue counting, but keep up the same timing and the same pauses.

THE DOCTORS' METHOD

Breathe in until your lungs can hold no more.

Take in a quick gasp of air through your mouth.

Breathe out slowly and evenly.

Repeat these three steps seven times.

FOR DISCUSSION

Discuss how to form an effective study group on your campus by answering the following questions:

1. What are the benefits of a study group?
2. How do you find students to be in a study group?
3. Who should be in a study group?
4. What is the maximum number of people in the group?
5. Where should the group meet to study?
6. What issues should you watch out for?
7. What are the tasks in a study group?
8. What are each person's responsibilities?
9. How should you monitor a study group's effectiveness?

ACTIVITIES AND EXERCISES

Log onto the On Campus Student Website at www.prenhall.com/fitton to determine how well you have studied and what you still need to learn.

1. **Defining Terms**
   Write the meanings of the following words.

   Studying _____

   _____

   _____

   Study notes _____

   _____

   _____

   Recall _____

   _____

   _____

   Recognition _____

   _____

   _____

Incomplete learning _____

_____

_____

Meaningful organization _____

_____

_____

Distributive practice _____

_____

_____

Recitation _____

_____

_____

Mental visualization _____

_____

_____

Overlearning _____

_____

_____

2. **Checking Your Understanding**
   Complete this outline of study processes.

   Step 1 Select Information to Learn _____

   _____ A. Review text notes and class notes _____

   _____ B. _____

   Step 2 _____

   _____ A. Find the right study environment _____

   _____ B. _____

   _____ C. _____

   _____ D. _____

Step 3 _____
   A. Meaningful organization _____
   B. _____
   C. _____
   D. _____
   E. _____
Step 4 Monitor your learning _____
   A. Ask, What did I just read? _____
   B _____.

3. **Knowing Your Campus**
   a. What learning centers are available on your campus?

   _____

   _____

   b. How can you receive tutoring at your college?

   _____

   _____

   c. Check your college Web site. When is a study skills workshop offered?

   _____

   _____

   d. Does your college have rooms that can be reserved for study groups? Where are these located? How do you reserve one?

   _____

   _____

4. **Applying Chapter Concepts**
   a. Evaluate your study requirements in each of your courses by answering the following questions about your assignments.
   What is your reading rate for the text material?
   What background information do you bring to the subject?

   _____

_____

_____

_____

_____

_____

_____

b. Check each statement in the following Study Skills Habits Survey that describes you. Based on your responses, what personal insights have you gained? What habits do you want to change? What are your reasons? What is your plan of action?

	Always	Sometimes	Never
I set aside time to review material several times a week.			
I ask questions in class if I do not understand something.			
I take notes from reading assignments.			
I complete homework assignments on time.			
I get help if I don't understand something in class.			
I look up words I don't know in the dictionary.			
I find a quiet place to study.			
I write study notes to prepare for tests.			
If I have time, I check over my answers on a test.			
I begin studying for an exam three to four days before the exam.			
I remove distractions while I do homework.			
I read all the pages assigned in a textbook.			
I look over charts, graphs, and tables when I read a chapter.			
I stick with a difficult assignment.			
I can stay focused when I read difficult material.			

5. **Writing for Reflection**

Explore your feelings about active learning. Write at least one paragraph in response to one of the following quotations or a meaningful sentence you select from the chapter.

Learning is not so much an additive process, with a new learning simply piling up on top of existing knowledge, as it is an active, dynamic process in which the connections are constantly changing and the structure reformatted.

K. Patricia Cross

The most important attitude that can be formed is the desire to go on learning.

John Dewey

6. **Concerning College Athletes**

a. What specific learning resources are available to athletes?

_____

_____

_____

b. Does your college have a directed study hall that mandates attendance and specific hours for athletes? If so, explain its policies and services.

_____

_____

_____

c. How will you keep a positive attitude toward learning while juggling academic and athletic activities?

_____

_____

_____

_____

7. **Reading Further**

The reading selections on the On Campus Student Website at www. prenhall.com/fitton explore different aspects of chapter topics. At the end of each reading selection are critical thinking questions. Your instructor will let you know whether you should print out your responses or use the online feature to email your answers.

a. *Be Aware: Developing Your Thinking* Vincent Ruggiero
   Read this selection from the textbook *The Art of Thinking* to learn what it means to think.

b. *Brain and Mind at Work* Vincent Ruggiero
   Read this selection from the textbook *The Art of Thinking* to consider how the popular notion of learning style may actually limit the way you should be studying.

c. *How We Learn* Daniel T. Willingham
   Read this selection to find out why students sometimes believe they have studied when in reality they have not.

Notes

[1] R. Hofstadter, and W. Smith, Ed., (1961) *American Higher Education A Documentary History* Volume 1, "Laws and Orders of King's College." (Chicago: The University of Chicago Press, 1961), 1755.

[2] University of Notre Dame, Greg Downey, http://www.nd.edu/~gdowney/introsyllabus. html (accessed April 15, 2003; site now discontinued).

[3] Grant MacEwan College, Guillermo Barron, http://www.artsci.gmcc.ab.ca/ courses/phil102gb/syllabus.html (accessed April 12, 2003).

[4] University of Baltimore, Susan A. Lynn, http://www.ubmail.ubalt.edu/~slynn/301/ 301SYL101_1__F03.HTML accessed December 27, 2003; site now discontinued).

[5] W. Glasser, *How We Learn*, Enhance Learning with Technology, http://members. shaw.ca/priscillatheroux/Glasser.htm (accessed April 15, 2004).

[6] University of North Dakota, University Learning Center, http://www.und.edu/dept/ ULC/ASEPKit-WhenTestAnxietyHappens.htm (accessed March 12, 2004; site now discontinued).

Notes

ACADEMIC WRITING

8

By writing you learn to write.
~ *Latin proverb*

*There is an art of reading, as well as an art of thinking,
and an art of writing.*
~ *Isaac Disraeli*

Great works are performed not by strength, but by perseverance.
~ *Samuel Johnson*

A college education intentionally places emphasis on academic writing. First, good academic writing demonstrates skill with language: the ability to formulate and arrange ideas, to word ideas precisely, and to arrange a meaningful string of words with varied structure. Good writing also demonstrates patience: the willingness to write and revise until the final product conveys the intended message. Good writing reflects critical thinking: drawing conclusions, analysis, evaluation, and synthesis of content. Finally, the author's voice and tone—or lack thereof—permeate the written content. It is for these reasons that writing is required in college and is valued by businesses.

Regardless of the workplace—business, technology, science or humanities—your future occupation will involve writing. At the very minimum, you will be writing e-mails to communicate with people within your workplace and to individuals outside. These e-mails, replicated and forwarded, must represent you well. Your writing skills will not only help you retain a job, but they will hold you in good stead for advancement.

When college professors evaluate your writing, they are not looking for a simple listing of facts and figures, but rather they want to read content that conveys knowledge and critical thinking about a specific topic. College writing takes time, but in the process of writing you discover what you understand as you share this knowledge with other people. The information included in this chapter provides valuable strategies and guidelines. Refer to this chapter often as you write in courses across the disciplines.

WRITING ASSIGNMENTS

Writing assignments are as varied as the professors who assign them. Some assignments are spelled out, from topic to font size. Other assignments are more loosely constructed and are designed to assess what you can do on your own. Before you begin a writing assignment, be clear about what the directions mean. If you are uncertain how to proceed, first make a list of questions and then either see your professor during office hours or send an e-mail.

First, be sure to know the day and time the writing assignment is due and mark this on your academic calendar. Of course, your goal is to have your assignment ready on time, but find out the consequences if you miss the deadline and if there is a policy regarding extensions.

EXAMPLE

Agricultural, Environmental and Development Economics Course, The Ohio State University

"On time" means at the beginning of the due-date's class period. Exceptions are possible, but only with the instructor's prior approval and a valid excuse (e.g., a doctor's note or an obituary notice for someone close). Computer difficulties, including faulty diskettes, are not good reasons for tardiness. Without a valid excuse, there is a penalty for late submission—two points per weekday for a section draft and five points per weekday for the final paper.[1]

History Course, Texas A&M University–Kingsville

Late assignments will be accepted for only two class periods following the due date. However the paper grade will be reduced by one letter grade for each late class period. Drafts will be accepted before the due date so that you will have feedback if you feel it is needed. Standards will be rigorous and expectations high, so approach these assignments as learning experiences.[2]

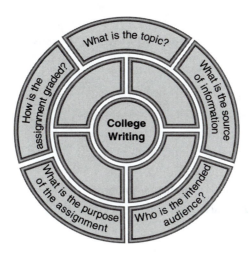

Unlike with tests, which are given at a specific time in a particular place, you choose the time and place for completing a writing assignment. By beginning your assignment early, you may take full advantage of having time to write several drafts and handing in your best writing. Always approach your writing assignments by answering the following five questions.

1. WHAT IS THE TOPIC?

Depending on the subject matter and its complexity, college professors choose either open-ended or specific writing assignments to accomplish their course objectives.

Open-Ended Writing Topic

An open-ended assignment gives you latitude in writing on a topic of your choice. You must narrow the topic yourself; otherwise, you run the risk of taking on too large a topic.

> **EXAMPLE**
> In the following assignment, the professor asks students to submit a thesis before writing the paper.
>
> **Introduction to Classics, Brooklyn College (NY)**
> Following are suggested topics for the paper. If you do not like any of these topics, you can negotiate a topic with me. In any case, I want a brief

paragraph from you containing your working thesis by March 30. Your paper must contain at least 1,000 words, but also please don't equate length with quality.[3]

Topics:

The Olympic Festival: Religion and athletics
Homeric view of athletics
Comparison of modern and ancient sports
The Greek Gymnasium and Palaestra
Importance of chariot racing in ancient Greece
Women and athletics in ancient Greece
Ball games in ancient Greece
Nudity in Greek athletics
Athletes in ancient Greece
Pindar's Olympian 10: An analysis and interpretation

Specific Writing Topic

In contrast, a specific writing topic delineates how to develop the assignment. In the following example, the instructor asks particular questions and gives instructions about the expected response.

EXAMPLE

Introduction to Ethics, Indiana University

How exactly does Hume's theory of obligation relate to that of Locke and Pufendorf? Start by locating the scattered passages in which Hume talks about obligation, and work them into a systematic theory. Then compare this theory with the theory of obligation worked out by Locke and Pufendorf. Where they diverge, what is the reason for the divergence? Which side has the better argument, at the point of divergence?[4]

2. WHAT IS THE SOURCE OF INFORMATION?

Your high school writing experience may have been primarily writing about what you knew personally. In your senior year, you may have had to write a research paper for English or history. In college, most academic writing is based on what you learn from outside sources of information.

Personal Experience

An assignment based on personal experience requires that you draw upon your familial, social, academic, and work experiences to develop your writing.

> **EXAMPLE**
>
> **Introduction to Archaeology, University of Hawaii Manoa**
>
> Most students enrolled in this course have some knowledge about what archaeology is about and what archaeologists do. Tell me what you know about archaeology as a discipline or kind of study and how you learned about it. What other courses in anthropology or related disciplines have you taken? What are your primary interests in archaeology and what do you know about them through archaeology? What issues attract you to archaeology or anthropology?[5]

Single Outside Source

You may acquire information from a single outside source, such as an interview, media, or text material. Whenever you quote or paraphrase from an outside source, cite the source and where you found the source; otherwise, you may run the risk of being accused of **plagiarism**, copying someone else's work without giving proper credit.

> **EXAMPLE**
>
> **American Literature Course, Princeton University (NJ)**
>
> Focusing on a small selection of scenes from one text, write an essay in which you consider the role of gender difference in the book's depiction of moral standards. In what ways does gender matter in questions of morality in this particular work? Why? Are there different moral standards for men and women in the text, or different ways for men and women to meet the same standards? If so, what accounts for these differences? Social position? Moral capacity? Narrative necessity? Something else? Why might the author instead insist that virtue is the same for all, regardless of gender? Be sure to keep your essay focused on your chosen text; be wary of simply making general claims about morality and/or gender.[6]

Multiple Outside Sources

Resource or *research papers* are based on information from multiple outside sources. There are formal academic methods for crediting each source. **MLA (Modern Language Association)** style is typically used to write papers and cite sources for liberal arts and humanities courses. **APA (American Psychological Association)** style is typically used to cite sources within the social sciences. Your professor may indicate on the assignment whether APA, MLA, or a different document style is required. If not, you should inquire if the professor has a preference.

> **EXAMPLE**
>
> **United States History Course, University of Minnesota**
>
> Slavery obviously affected the lives of hundreds of thousands of African Americans, but it also shaped white society in important ways. Drawing specifically from the assigned excerpts from Douglass and Jacobs as well as the other assigned readings (the Boyer textbook and the DOCS), consider how the "peculiar institution" of slavery affected white people in both the South and the North. In particular, what did Douglass and Jacobs have to say about the effect of slavery on white society? How do their perspectives compare to the claims made by George Fitzhugh, Orestes Brownson, and William Lloyd Garrison?[7]

3. WHO IS THE INTENDED AUDIENCE?

When you write your assignment, write for at least two readers. First, you write for your professor to demonstrate that you understand a topic or idea. Secondly, you write for a generally well-educated, intelligent adult who is basically *unfamiliar* with your topic. Your goal is to present your knowledge in a well organized and developed way that avoids assuming the reader already knows the subject. Sometimes your professor designates an intended audience.

> **EXAMPLE**
>
> **Cultural Anthropology Course, Lewis-Clark State College (ID)**
>
> The purpose of this essay is for you to begin to develop an overall view of anthropology so that you will have a framework for understanding new

material as you move forward through the course. Your audience is someone who has not taken an anthropology course.[8]

World History Course, University of Kansas

Imagine yourself an economist being interviewed on a news documentary, and you have only one to two minutes to explain how we should reduce the national debt.[9]

Formal • Traditional • Informal • Colloquial

Legal	Academic	Social	Conversational
Ecclesiastical	Business	Personal	Slang

Styles of writing can be placed on a continuum ranging from formal to colloquial. By understanding these differences, you can choose the one that is appropriate for your audience and situation.

Formal English, at one end of the spectrum, adheres strictly to Standard English and established format. Formal language can be used for legal writing, as in judicial documents and proclamations; for ecclesiastical writings, as in documentations of religious rituals; and for social writing, such as formal invitations and announcements.

Traditional writing, toward the midpoint of the continuum, is widely used by educated people for academic and business writing. This style uses Standard English grammar and sentence structure. Business writing, such as business letters, memorandums, proposals, and professional reports follow established conventions of structure and format.

Informal English follows many of the conventions of Standard English, but the language is more casual. Informal English includes social writing, such as thank you notes and other social correspondence. This style is appropriate in relaxed situations, often when you know the intended readers.

Colloquial English, ranging from conversational to slang, is more often spoken than written. When it is written, it is an attempt to create spoken language. If you keep a journal, your thoughts may be written in colloquial English. Colloquial English may include sentence fragments, run-ons, and other nonstandard grammar and usage. The use of jargon or slang can make colloquial English so specialized for a particular audience that someone outside the group may have difficulty comprehending its meaning.

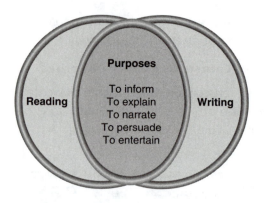

4. WHAT IS THE PURPOSE OF THE WRITING ASSIGNMENT?

Writing can be communicated either privately to oneself, such as in a journal, or publicly to others. You may write to provide information, to explain how something works, to tell a story, to prove a point, to entertain a reader, or to achieve a combination of these purposes. As you will read later in the chapter, there are a many ways to develop and support each of these purposes.

Writing to Inform—Expository Writing

The majority of writing for college classes, as well as for professional and everyday life, relies on *exposition*. Expository writing provides information by illustrating and describing facts. Your source may be your own experiences and observations or outside resources. Whatever form it takes, exposition is informational writing with an emphasis on the topic, not the writer.

In the following expository assignment, students are asked to provide information about an underdeveloped country.

> **EXAMPLE**
>
> **Agricultural, Environmental and Development Economics Course, The Ohio State University**
>
> In the term paper, you will address problems and policies related to population, food, and agriculture, and the environment as they relate to one country that is experiencing either development or transition (from communism). The country you choose to study should have a per-capita

GDP under $5,000 as well as a population above two million. Specific topics to be addressed—with reference to key concepts dealt with in lectures and in readings—follow.[10]

Writing to Explain—Explanatory Writing

When the purpose of your writing is to explain how something occurs or works or why something has happened, you are giving instructions. Explaining relies on analysis. You divide your topic into parts and then explain how each part interrelates or proceeds. Although this may seem like a simple task, explanatory writing requires critical thinking to make sure a part or step is not overlooked. Explanatory writing is used in highly technical subjects as well as in liberal arts courses. You will continue to use explanatory writing for many professional careers.

Writing to Persuade—Persuasive Writing

To *persuade* is to convince someone to look at an issue differently or to act in a particular way. Advertisements, editorials, and political statements are examples of persuasion in everyday life. In academics, persuasive essays promote the value of a particular point of view. By providing compelling reasons, you can persuade readers that you are a credible writer, that they are being told the truth, and that they can benefit by accepting an opinion or acting in a particular way. Effective persuasion anticipates and addresses counterarguments.

A further distinction is often made between **persuasion** and **argumentation.** Persuasion emphasizes emotions and feelings; argumentation emphasizes logic and intellect. Be sure you understand this distinction when an assignment tells you to write a persuasive paper. In the following example, students need to determine whether to use persuasion or argumentation as the primary approach.

EXAMPLE

Classics Course, Skidmore College (NY)

In this essay you will fashion an argument based upon the literary evidence. Your objective is to argue a position by marshalling the evidence and describing it when appropriate, comparing and assessing conflicting sets of data, and then constructing a coherent and persuasive argument.

The Greeks defeated the Persians in the Persian Wars (499–479 B.C.) due to heroic action, divine support, and Greek unity.[11]

Writing to Relate an Experience—Narrative Writing

As a college student, you may be required to report or narrate what happened for a variety of courses, such as lab sciences, social sciences, or humanities. This type of narration is a record of actual events, unlike a fictional narrative, which is a story created from the imagination, often assigned in a creative writing class. Narrative essays and other accounts of actual events are a part not only of academic writing but also of personal and business communication.

Many narratives are written in first person, using I, we, and related pronouns. That is, the writer tells what happened from a personal perspective. Some narratives report what a writer has observed, such as what happened to someone else. In this case, the writer uses the objective third person: he, she, they, and related pronouns.

The following assignment requires students to use narration creatively, based on historical facts.

EXAMPLE

Women in U.S. History, 1620–1865, California State University, San Bernardino

You are a woman who was born in the latter decades of the 18th century. It is 1859 and you are writing your memoirs so that your daughters and granddaughters will have a written record of what it meant to be a woman in this period of history. You should include information on the political, economic, and social conditions during this time. You want to tell them about your work, family life, and culture, but you want to be sure to give them a balanced account (this means writing about the positive as well as the negative aspects) of your experiences.[12]

Writing to Entertain

Unless you are enrolled in a creative writing or journal-writing course where your purpose is to amuse the reader, you will not be asked to write to entertain.

5. HOW IS THE WRITING ASSIGNMENT GRADED?

Academic writing follows recognized standards and conventions. Content, language, writing mechanics, and format are assessed in each writing assignment. Your professor decides the relative value for each of these criteria. If this information is not explained on the course syllabus or assignment, make a point of finding this out.

> **Writing grade =**
> **Content + Language + Writing mechanics + Format requirements**

Content

Both *quality* (how well the content develops the main idea) and *quantity* (to what extent the content develops the main idea) are evaluated in a writing assignment. Well-written content demonstrates three principles of good writing: unity, coherence, and order.

Unity

Unity refers to oneness of thought. All paragraphs within an essay relate to and support the main point. Likewise, sentences within a paragraph develop a topic sentence that is either expressed or implied.

Coherence

Coherence refers to connection of thought. Every sentence in the paragraph relates to the preceding sentence. Similarly, every paragraph relates to the preceding paragraph. Connections are provided with transitional words, phrases or sentences, repetition of key words, and synonyms for key words.

Order

Order refers to organization of thought. The introduction clearly introduces the main point. Within the body of the paper, topic sentences and supporting sentences are logically ordered. The conclusion provides a satisfactory ending.

Transition words help link ideas within and between paragraphs.

To show addition	Also, next, another, and, in addition, moreover, further, furthermore, finally, besides, and then, likewise, nor, too, again, equally important, last, incidentally
To show contrast	But, yet, however, still, nevertheless, on the other hand, to the contrary, even so, in contrast to, otherwise, nonetheless, instead, although, like, one difference, another difference, whereas, notwithstanding
To show similarity	Like, likewise, similarly, both, one similarity, another similarity, in comparison, additionally, furthermore
To show classification	Another, another kind, another group, another type, first kind, first group, first type, second kind, second group, second type
To show spatial order	Beyond, nearby, around, behind, below, opposite, adjacent, across, left, right, next to, between, by, over, under, above, ahead, beside, down, east, north, south, west, in, on, overhead, toward
To show a change in direction	But, however, yet, in contrast, although, otherwise, still, to the contrary, on the other hand
To show cause	Because of, due to, if, when, since, as a result of
To show effect	Therefore, consequently, hence, as a result, thus
To show emphasis	Indeed, in fact, without a doubt
To show example	For example, for instance, that is, in other words, specifically, such as, also, another, as an illustration, to illustrate, for one thing, in addition, in the following way, namely
To show summary or clarification	In summary, in conclusion, in brief, after all
To show sequence or time	After, as, at last, before, during, eventually, finally, first, second, . . ., last, later, meanwhile, next, now, since, soon, subsequently, then, when, while

Language

English is a rich language, one that gives the writer an opportunity to communicate thoughts with clarity and vigor. College professors evaluate language by looking at the effect created by the writer's words and sentences. Skillful word choice indicates the writer's ability to make precise mental distinctions. A thesaurus can be helpful in providing a list of suggested synonyms. Before substituting one word for another, you should check its specific meaning in a dictionary. Varied sentence structure demonstrates your ability to combine words that flow smoothly, clarifying interrelationships among ideas.

Writing Mechanics

As a college student, you are expected to have an understanding of Standard English. These writing conventions include grammar, punctuation, capitalization, usage, and spelling. In some classes, you may get peer reviews of your draft before you prepare a final copy. Sometimes your professor may note grammar errors on your paper, allowing you to make corrections. Most often, you are responsible for revising and proofreading. Many professors penalize points for grammatical errors.

Format Requirements

Length

If your professor indicates a paper of three to five pages, a two-page paper will not have enough depth and a seven-page paper will be too extensive to meet the demands of the assignment. In other words, less is not enough, but more is not necessarily better. When your assignment is given in terms of a required number of words, you can check the word count in your document. For example, in MS Word, click on file/properties/statistics to get a precise word count. Sometimes a professor will not provide page or word requirements, which means the scope of your topic will determine a suitable length. You are on your own with your common sense to guide you in terms of deciding the appropriate length of your paper.

Presentation

Don't underestimate the value of how your paper looks. You may be penalized for an otherwise excellent paper that is sloppy in appearance and ignores established formatting standards. Following instructions for the heading, format, and documentation style results in a paper that represents you well. Fancy fonts and graphics do not improve a grade.

> **EXAMPLE**
>
> **Women in U.S. History, 1620–1865, California State University, San Bernardino**
>
> Your papers must be 10–12 pages in length, double-spaced and type-written. It must have ONE-inch margins at the top, bottom, and on both sides. You should center page numbers at the bottom of each page. Please use a common 12-point font (i.e., Times New Roman, Arial, or Courier). You must properly document your paper using Chicago Manual of Style for footnotes or endnotes. You must also include a properly formatted bibliography. *Chicago Manual of Style* is the accepted standard of documentation for historical articles, books, and papers. Do not use any other style of documentation. I will automatically lower the grade on any paper using any other format by two full letter grades.[13]

WRITING PROCESS

"According to a Chinese parable, a rich patron once gave money to the painter Chu Ta, asking him to paint a picture of a fish. Three years later, when he still had not received the painting, the patron went to Chu Ta's house to ask why the picture was not done. Chu Ta did not answer but dipped a brush in ink and with a few strokes drew a splendid fish. 'If it is so easy,' asked the patron, 'why didn't you give me the picture three years ago?' Again, Chu Ta did not answer. Instead, he opened the door of a large cabinet. Thousands of pictures of fish tumbled out."[14]

Like the rich patron looking at the splendid fish, when you look at a piece of published writing, you see only the finished product. You do not see the numerous drafts that have come before it. As you know, most accomplishments, including effective writing, are achieved only with effort. Producing a piece of writing to be proud of involves working through a process. This process requires thoughtful writing and rewriting.

Sometimes you start with a main point and then write; other times you write until you discover your point. As you move through the process, be ready to loop back or rework an earlier step whenever the need arises.

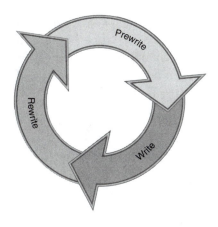

Every writing assignment involves three recursive steps: prewrite, write, and rewrite.

STEP 1: PREWRITE

Gather Information

Once you understand the writing task and narrow the topic sufficiently to develop it within the scope of the assignment, you gather information about the narrowed topic. If your information comes from personal experience, you can begin immediately to reflect about experiences that are pertinent to the assignment. If your writing assignment is based on facts from outside sources, you must schedule time to find information, read, and take notes. To generate ideas, try one or more of the following brainstorming techniques.

Listing

When you jot down a list of ideas, your goal is to create as long a list as possible. Include everything you can think about your topic, in any order, no matter how remotely it may be related. After compiling a list, read it over to see if the items on the list bring to mind other items that you can add. You may want to make an additional list based on an item in your first listing. Keep listing until you feel you have exhausted your supply of ideas.

Clustering

Clustering is a visual tool that gives you an expansive view of your ideas. You draw a representation of your ideas using lines to connect words with one another to show relationships. Start your clustering by inserting a word or phrase related to your topic in a box (or circle). Around the outside of your box write associated words, drawing lines to connect the new words to the box. Enclose these words in boxes and then draw individual lines from the boxes to more related ideas.

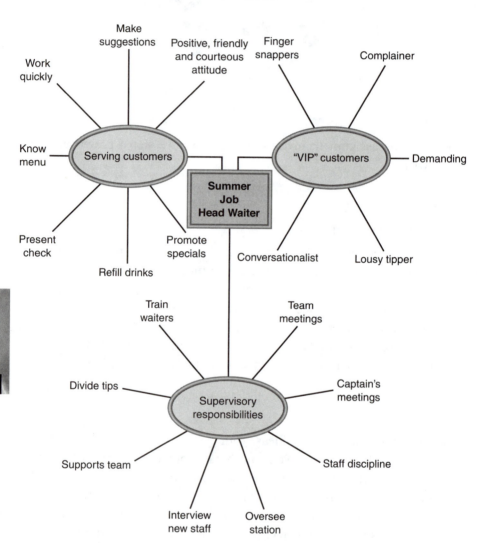

Asking Questions

Use the reporter's questions—Who? What? Where? When? How? Why?—to uncover information about a topic. Ask as many questions as you can.

One question can lead to another, and as long as you are uncovering new information, continue to ask questions.

Focused Free Writing

Focused free writing is both similar to and different from *free writing*. With free and focused free writing, you write for a period of time without being concerned about grammar, word choice, or spelling. With focused free writing, you focus your attention on your main idea. If you find yourself writing off the topic, shift your thoughts back to your subject. Do not confuse focused free writing with your first draft. Focused free writing is a brainstorming technique to help you generate ideas. Your first draft follows and develops a thoughtful topic or thesis sentence.

Decide Your Point

After you have gathered a sufficient amount of information, the next step is to sort through and organize this material. Which main idea do you want to develop? The focus of an essay is called a **thesis sentence**. A thesis sentence reflects your attitude toward or opinion about a topic and helps determine the organization and development of your writing. Start with a tentative thesis and be ready to revise it as you follow the steps of the writing process.

For some assignments, professors provide several thesis statements and ask you to agree or disagree with one of them. For other assignments, you may need to discover your own thesis. Sometimes you can decide on a thesis right away; other times, you need to explore your topic with prewriting techniques to formulate a working, or tentative, thesis. Because a thesis is the main point of your essay, it cannot be a fact or a question. Instead, facts and questions about your thesis are used to develop and support your essay.

The main idea of an essay is identified by many names.	Thesis sentence
	Dominant impression
	Statement of purpose
	Proposition statement
	Controlling idea

Organize Your Ideas

You may be asked to submit an outline, either formal or informal, with your completed paper that shows your organization plan. Even if an outline is not a specific part of your assignment, working with an outline is an effective technique for thinking through and planning support for your thesis.

You create an outline by first deciding what major points support your thesis. Then, you decide a logical order to arrange these major points and supporting details. A formal outline uses a standard format of Roman numerals, letters, and Arabic numbers to indicate different levels of detail. Each point is written as a sentence or a phrase. In the following examples, two outlines show how the same topic can be developed in two different ways.

EXAMPLE

Topic: TV Reality Shows
Thesis: TV reality shows exploit the participants.

1. Exposes private lives
   a. Unedited thoughts and emotions
   b. Embarrassing and compromising experiences
   c. Despair and disappointment
2. Promotes contrived situations
   a. Heavily edited
   b. Larger-than-life characters
   c. Unrealistic scenarios
3. Trivializes human experience
   a. Winner-takes-all mentality
   b. Sensationalizes fame
   c. Glorifies superficial values
   d. Degrading situations

EXAMPLE

Topic: TV Reality Shows
Thesis: TV reality shows provide enjoyable entertainment.

1. Colorful characters
   a. Characters are "real" people, not actors
   b. Highly motivated "type A" people
   c. Ordinary people in extraordinary situations

2. Unscripted drama
    a. Unpredictable outcome
    b. Interplay between contestants
    c. Arouses emotions
    d. No gratuitous sex or violence
3. Epitomizes American dream
    a. Find romance
    b. Become rich
    c. Compete hard
    d. Survive by your wits

Although you usually write an outline before you write the draft of a paper, sometimes you draft out your ideas first and then create an outline. An outline written before a draft serves as a working blueprint to follow. An outline written after the draft provides a means of testing the effectiveness of the draft's structure and development. Whether you outline before or after writing a first draft, an outline clearly displays whether you have a logical plan of development.

STEP 2: WRITE THE FIRST DRAFT

The first draft translates your thinking into writing. Be patient. This draft provides a preliminary record of your thinking on paper. As you draft for the first time, remain focused on ideas. Don't get sidetracked with perfecting your grammar, sentence structure, and spelling. Use your energy to think through what you want to say. The first draft is called a *rough* draft because it must be followed by other, more polished drafts.

At the draft-writing stage, the best advice is not to wait for inspiration but to start writing right away. Use your outline as a guide. As you write, think about what you are saying, changing order, and adding and subtracting ideas as you go. At any point in the process, you may see ways to refine your outline to make your finished paper stronger. The content and order of your outline needs to remain flexible throughout the drafting process.

Patterns of Development

Your thesis can be supported by using one or more patterns of development. These methods of development are helpful ways you can think about and relate information.

Writer's Purpose	Patterns of Development
To explain	Description
To inform	Example
To persuade	Classification
To narrate	Comparison
To entertain	Process
	Cause and effect
	Definition

Description Provides Details

In description, you describe what you observe using any of the five senses—sight, sound, taste, smell, or touch. Descriptive writing relies on concrete language to create a vivid picture.

Examples Show Evidence

The word *example*, derived from the Latin word *exemplum*, means *to take out*. When you select an example, you choose *to take out* one thing from a whole to represent or demonstrate this whole. You may choose several examples or one longer example to illustrate your points.

Classification Distinguishes among Types

Classification uses a basis for sorting ideas and information into categories. For instance, types or kinds of colleges, financial aid, or meal plans are categories that can be further developed using description or illustration.

Comparison Tells What Is Similar or Different

When two or more people, places, things, or ideas have something in common, you may compare them to examine their similarities and/or differences. Measuring one thing against another provides a way to analyze and evaluate ideas. Comparison can be arranged by comparing topic to topic or point to point.

Process Answers the Question How

Explaining how something works or how something happens requires dividing the process into its successive steps, stages, or methods. Begin by considering the entire process. Once you have established starting and ending points, list and explain the steps in the process.

Cause and Effect Determines Why

Using cause and effect as a method of development is a way to explain causal connections. An effect may be the result of multiple causes, just as a cause may have multiple effects. For example, you may have chosen your college (effect) based on several reasons (causes). Graduating from your college (cause) may result in many positive results (effects). Your goal in assessing causes or effects is to consider the possible reasons and results and focus on those that are most immediate and important.

Definition Examines Meaning

To define a word, start by understanding the word's literal (dictionary) definition. Expand this definition with various methods of development:

- Use personal or researched examples.
- Describe sensory detail to make the meaning of the word concrete.
- Discuss the steps, stages, or phases involved.
- Compare the word being defined with a word or concept the reader already knows.
- Explain the meaning of a word in terms of its cause and effect.

STEP 3: REWRITE

After you complete your first draft, put it away for awhile. You are more objective after a rest. Then rework the draft, making sure you give yourself plenty of time to write and rewrite. Figure out what times of day are more productive for you to write and whether you prefer writing in shorter blocks of time (15 to 20 minutes) or longer blocks of time (1 to 2 hours). If you set up a schedule, start well before the paper is due, so you are more likely to complete the project effectively. Rushing a writing assignment the night before it is due is a recipe for failure.

Revise

Often, only after you prepare a series of additional drafts will you be satisfied that what you have written is complete, unified, and understandable. Look carefully at your first draft. You may need to reconsider or reword your main idea and refine or reorganize some points.

Next, revisit your words, sentences, and paragraphs. Find answers to questions you may have regarding your use of Standard English. Make changes that enable readers to read fluently what you have written without having to stop to determine what you mean.

Proofread

Proofreading requires that you read your writing carefully to find errors and make corrections. Use the features on a computer, such as a spelling or grammar check, to assist your proofreading. If you use a grammar check, make sure you understand the suggested correction before accepting it. The computer's grammatical suggestion may be incorrect.

The best way to proofread is by reading a printed copy of your work. Try using a sheet of paper to block off your writing, leaving just a sentence visible. Viewing one line at a time can aid you in seeing errors in spelling and grammar. Reading your paper out loud can help you hear errors in your written work.

To complete the writing process, prepare a copy of your paper to submit to your instructor. At this stage, be conscientious about checking to see that all parts of the assignment are in order. Look at the copy of your paper. Is there an appropriate heading? Does the overall format conform to the assignment instructions? Have you included documentation for ideas you used from outside sources? Be sure that the pages of your paper, including a title page if requested, are numbered and in the correct order. If you hand in an outline, make a copy that reflects any changes you may have made during the drafting and editing stages of your writing. Check to see that the outline is consistent in format.

A final step in completing your paper is to look at the overall presentation to be sure the paper represents you well.

OCTOBER

Sunday	Monday	Tuesday	Wednesday	Thursday	Friday	Saturday
					1	2
Read five history articles, choose three.	Reread three articles, take notes, decide thesis.	Write draft.	Revise draft.	Proofread draft and print up.	History paper due.	

TYPES OF WRITING PRODUCTS

Write an essay, write a summary, and *write a report* are directions that refer to specific types of academic writing. The following tables provide guidelines and strategies for developing each type of essay assignment. Because terminology is open to interpretation, *always* check with your professor if you have any questions about the writing assignment. As you learned earlier in the chapter, depending on the assignment, the information you write may be based on *personal experience,* a *single outside source,* or *multiple outside sources.*

ACADEMIC ESSAY

Academic essay is a broad term that means a main point is developed in a logically ordered sequence of paragraphs. A **personal essay** is an informal development of a topic. A **formal essay** follows a traditional arrangement of paragraphs that develop a thesis.

Introduction	The introduction consists of one or more paragraphs that ■ capture the reader's attention; ■ establish the main point of the essay; ■ set a tone consistent with the essay; ■ contain the thesis sentence.
Middle section	The body paragraphs explain and expand a thesis by using one or more patterns of development, such as ■ examples; ■ description; ■ cause and effect; ■ classification; ■ comparison; ■ process; ■ definition.
Conclusion	The concluding paragraph may ■ remind reader of the thesis; ■ summarize important points; ■ restate the significance of the subject.

CRITICAL ESSAYS: RESPONSE, ANALYSIS, AND EVALUATION

A critical essay emphasizes critical thinking. *Critical thinking* does not mean that your purpose is to find fault or blame. Rather, when you think critically, you show insight and thoughtful reflection.

When your professor asks you to write a *critical essay*, he or she wants you to write a paper that demonstrates a higher level of thinking. A critical essay has many names: *analytical essay, response essay, reaction essay, interpretive essay, literary analysis*, and *evaluative essay.* Some professors may use these terms interchangeably; however, there are specific meanings for each type of critical writing. Once you understand these distinctions, you can make sure you know exactly what your professor expects for a critical essay writing assignment.

Critical Response, or Reaction, Essay

A response, or reaction, essay explains a writer's emotional and/or intellectual reaction to a specific reading or event. After reading a selection and taking notes, you identify the most important and interesting ideas. Then, you consider your reactions and observations about these ideas. Because this represents your personal response, there is no "right" or "wrong" reaction. The most important point to remember is to avoid vague generalizations by supporting your reactions with valid examples.

Introduction	The introduction ■ identifies the title, author, and publication; ■ briefly summarizes the work; ■ includes a thesis statement that presents a reaction.
Middle section	Each body paragraph includes ■ an argument that supports the thesis; ■ examples to support each argument.
Conclusion	The concluding paragraph may ■ reemphasize the thesis (response) to the work; ■ restate the overall response; ■ predict effects of the reaction.

EXAMPLE

English Course, Idaho State University

Write a response paper of no less than 500 words that discusses the ways "hero" and/or "healing" myths play central roles in our understanding of ourselves in relation to our culture. In what ways do we play out the roles such myths assign to us? How do we select which roles we will play? Are we stuck in such roles perpetually? Why or why not? Respond to Seger's article on at least two points.[15]

Critical Analysis Essay

In a critical analysis, or analytical, essay, you divide a subject matter into several parts and explain each part. Clue words indicating an analytical essay are as follows:

What are the parts or features of. . . ?
How is ____ related to___?
What is the theme of. . . ?
List and describe the main characteristics of. . . .
What is the function of. . . ?
What ideas support the conclusion that . . . ?
What inconsistencies or fallacies . . . ?

Introduction	The introduction consists of one or more paragraphs that
	■ capture the reader's attention;
	■ identify the topic and its parts to be analyzed;
	■ explain the approach in a thesis sentence.
Middle section	The body paragraphs may
	■ explain the function of the parts;
	■ determine connections and patterns;
	■ explain interactions among parts;
	■ recognize unstated meanings, fallacies, assumptions;
	■ use examples and details to show what, how, and why.
Conclusion	The concluding paragraph
	■ summarizes briefly;
	■ states the significance of the analysis.

Western Art History, Oberlin College (OH)

Write a concise (three-page) analysis of an advertisement, preferably a colored one, taken from a magazine or a newspaper. How does it communicate its message? Note everything contributing to its design. Consider such factors as the choice and placement of images, the use of scale and color, the style of the typeface, and the quality of the paper. What visual elements are important in its design?[16]

Critical Evaluation Essay

A critical evaluation, or evaluative, essay expresses the writer's judgment or opinion about a subject. Criteria used for the evaluation may be determined by the writer or may be specified in the assignment. The following clue words indicate an evaluative essay:

Describe the strengths and weaknesses of . . . .
Using the given criteria, evaluate . . . .
Which is the more important? Logical? Valid?

Introduction	The introduction consists of one or more paragraphs that
	■ capture the reader's attention;
	■ introduce the subject matter;
	■ establish the thesis.
Middle section	The body paragraphs may
	■ establish criteria by identifying –critical qualities for making an evaluative judgment, –standards of excellence;
	■ judge the subject matter using criteria –weaknesses, –strengths;
	■ provide evidence (proof) –specific details, –examples to prove.
Conclusion	The concluding paragraph
	■ reminds the reader of your overall evaluation;
	■ restates the thesis.

What is your opinion of . . .?
What would be better, . . .?
How would you evaluate . . .?
What judgment would you make about . . .?

EXAMPLE

Economics Course, George Mason University (VA)

This project will involve the selection and analysis of a song or poem from an economic perspective. It should include the following:

a. A brief summary of the work itself, and why you chose it.
b. The relevant economic concepts (and their definitions) that are mentioned or implied in the song.
c. Your reaction/reflection: Have the economic principles been applied correctly? Has the author/artist fallen in any pitfalls of economic thinking? Some research into the actual situation/time frame described may enhance your work in this section.[17]

INFORMATIVE REPORT

An informative report provides thorough information about a topic. Typically, you do *not* make conclusions or give recommendations in such a report.

Introduction	The introduction consists of one or more paragraphs that ■ introduce the subject matter; ■ define any relevant, special vocabulary; ■ include brief background information about the topic; ■ state the importance of understanding the subject matter (thesis sentence).
Middle section	The body paragraphs ■ present accurate, unbiased, clear information; ■ include all sides of a topic; ■ support points with evidence or facts.
Conclusion	The concluding paragraph ■ summarizes main points; ■ comments on the significance of the information.

Marketing Course, Yeshiva University (NY)

Imagine that you and a classmate are marketers for a major corporation (pick one you like). Decide whether your firm can/will expand internationally by entering the market in Mexico, India, Thailand, or China. If there already is a presence, examine the current situation and develop a plan to increase the company's market penetration. Describe the issues that your company must consider, based on the six areas that effect global trade: market demand, competition, economy, political-legal, social-cultural, and technology.

Your report should be keystroked and will most likely be between 25 and 30 double-spaced pages in length. Remember that you must cover each of the six areas mentioned above adequately. You may have additional pages of exhibits/illustrations, charts, etc. You must document and cite your sources of any data, conclusions, statistics, etc.[18]

SCIENTIFIC LAB REPORTS

You should write a scientific lab report in clear, factual scientific style. Instructors often provide a specific lab report format similar to the following template.

Front matter	Title Lab content
First section	Abstract ■ summarizes each part in order; ■ briefly describes the full report introduction; ■ presents the objectives of the report; ■ states an hypothesis and logical reasons for it.
Middle section	Procedures ■ identify materials used in lab procedure; ■ present description of lab procedure; ■ give sufficient details to enable lab duplication. Results ■ present overall findings; ■ include visuals (tables, graphs, drawings); ■ include citations and references, as appropriate. Discussion ■ compares hypothesis with results; ■ addresses issues pertinent to the lab.

Front matter	Title Lab content
Final section	Conclusion ■ summarizes what was learned in the lab; ■ includes supporting details.

SUMMARY, ABSTRACT, AND PRÉCIS

A summary and abstract are similar in that each presents original source material in a shortened version. A **summary** is usually the longer version, with 100 to 300 words. An **abstract**, also referred to as a **précis**, may have 50 to 100 words. You use your own words and typically do not cite information. Begin each type by identifying the title and author of the source material. Next, concisely present the main idea, major points, and conclusion of the subject matter. The objective is to give the most amount of information in the least number of words. You do not change the intent of the original or include your interpretation or perspective.

RESEARCH PAPER

The research paper is a staple of many college courses. Preparing a research paper represents the essence of education—using facts and ideas from various sources to create a fresh product, a new or different way of looking at a topic. A research paper often begins with a topic about which you have limited information or with a complex question for which you do not have a ready answer. When preparing to write a research paper, you discover a variety of source materials. After reading and assessing the source materials, you arrive at your own understanding of the topic or answer to the question, and you present your findings.

You can remove the mystique of producing a research paper when you let the steps of the research process guide your work. As you work through the process, you may find yourself circling back to an earlier step or thinking ahead to what comes next, but, in general, the process of writing a research paper can be divided into nine stages.

1. Lay the groundwork by choosing a topic, skimming general references and other sources for background information.
2. After you know something about your project, set up a working, or tentative, plan to research and write your paper.

3. Gather your material, selecting valid sources that can be helpful in your work.
4. Make a record of bibliographic data for each source, and note facts and opinions to support points you want to make in your writing.
5. Write the first draft.
6. Acknowledge the sources you have used with parenthetical documentation and a bibliography. Use the documentation style that is appropriate or that is required for your course. Although there are similarities in the way information is documented, each style of documentation provides specific format requirements:
   - American Chemical Society (ACS) style
   - American Psychological Association (APA) style
   - Chicago Manual of Style
   - Council of Science Editors (CSE) style
   - Modern Language Association (MLA) style
7. Prepare the final draft by revising and proofreading your work.
8. Create a final outline to submit with your paper.
9. Include a title page and bibliography.

Following this procedure helps you stay organized as you direct your attention to using sources as support for your thinking.

A research paper is sometimes called a **term paper** because writing it requires a period of time—often from the beginning to the end of a course. A secret to accomplishing the task creditably is scheduling plenty of time. You will need time to select, evaluate, read, and synthesize new information. You need to allow time in case your college library has to order materials through interlibrary loan. You will need time to document the sources in your research paper. Mostly importantly, you should complete your draft so that you have plenty of time for feedback from your professor, writing center tutor, or librarian.

If you begin to think about the topic as soon as it is assigned and assemble the materials you need shortly after that, you can work regularly on the project, completing it when it is due and eliminating the frustrating and nonproductive frenzy of "last minute-itis." Not only will you not feel rushed, you are more likely to earn a better grade on the project.

Front matter	May include (check with your professor) ■ separate title page; ■ formal outline; ■ abstract of the paper.
Introduction	The introduction consists of one or more paragraphs that ■ engage the reader's interest; ■ define any relevant, special vocabulary; ■ include brief background information about the topic; ■ state a point of view on a particular topic, traditionally in a thesis sentence.
Middle section	The body paragraphs ■ organize and synthesize multiple sources of information; ■ paraphrase, summarize, and quote source material; ■ present knowledge and understanding of the topic.
Conclusion	The concluding paragraph may ■ comment on the significance of the research; ■ suggest further related research.
End matter	May include (check with your professor) ■ appendix; ■ bibliography; ■ works cited (last page), listing all sources used to research the paper.

8
ACADEMIC WRITING

EXAMPLE

Literature Course, University of Michigan

This assignment asks you to choose some cultural-historical aspect of the Anglo-Saxon world and to write a paper that (1) provides an historical sketch of the topic; and (2) explains how that background informs and is informed by the literature. For example, if you are interested in political issues, you might investigate the institution of kingship in Anglo-Saxon England and then briefly discuss how the topic of kingship is treated in some Old English poem. All topics for this assignment must be approved by me; those that have not will not be accepted. You must choose your own topic; I will not choose one for you, though I will be more than happy to help you shape yours once you have chosen one.[19]

FOR DISCUSSION

Discuss which types of writing products in List A could be used to develop each of the writing topics in List B.

LIST A. WRITING PRODUCTS

Academic essay

Response essay

Analytical essay

Evaluative essay

Informative report

Scientific lab report

Summary, abstract, or précis

Research paper

LIST B. WRITING TOPICS

1. The reasons why you applied to the college you now attend
2. The function of freshman orientation at your college
3. How you felt the first week of college
4. Arguments for taking an open-book test in one of your courses
5. Your opinion of the student campus dining facility
6. The student parking system
7. The benefits and problems of commuting to college
8. The benefits and problems of living in a dormitory
9. How time management relates to college success
10. The positive and negative characteristics of the climate
11. Where your college is located
12. Briefly, the expectations of one of your courses
13. The desirable qualities in a roommate

WRITING SKILLS

To write well requires time, practice, and, most importantly, motivation. The more you work at your writing, the more skills you will develop. College freshmen begin their first semester with a considerable range of writing skills. Students who graduated from high schools that set high writing standards are well equipped to handle the rigors of college writing.

Students who weren't challenged to write well or who were "pushed ahead" in English may lack a number of basic language skills. You can improve your writing skills by taking writing courses and by using the services offered at your college writing center.

WRITING COURSES

Colleges offer credit and noncredit writing courses to help develop students' writing skills.

Noncredit writing courses are precollege courses. A developmental writing course covers basic writing skills, such as sentence, paragraph, and essay development, grammar, and usage.

Freshman English courses are designed to develop a writing standard consistent with academic writing. These courses may emphasize literature, persuasion, argumentation, and research.

EXAMPLE

English 111 Methods of Written Communication, University of Alaska–Anchorage.

Required for all baccalaureate degrees, English 111 is designed to introduce students to academic thinking and writing and to connect this new learning to the more personal thinking and writing of their community and culture. The reading and paper assignments have been chosen to help students find connections between their present language use and the language use of academia. The large issues of the curriculum concern language diversity, language conformity, and functioning in multiple speech/writing communities. The course work is also designed to give students a broad, interdisciplinary view of academic writing and to prepare them to write in other classes outside the discipline.[20]

WRITING CENTER

A wealth of college resources is available to help improve your writing skills. A writing center may provide one-on-one assistance either in person or through an e-mail writing service. One-on-one assistance gives you feedback on generating ideas, writing drafts, or developing papers. Writing center tutors do not proofread papers but instead work collaboratively with students.

You may find answers to your writing questions by attending writing workshops, reading hard-copy handouts, or accessing an online writing lab (OWL). OWLs offer comprehensive writing assistance, such as specialized writing guides for specific disciplines, a grammar guide to help with technical English questions, a style guide to help answer questions about citations, and useful online handouts on a wide range of writing topics, from How to Write an Essay Exam to Writing a Critical Essay.

ACTIVITIES AND EXERCISES

Log onto the On Campus Student Website at www.prenhall.com/fitton to determine how well you have studied and what you still need to learn.

1. **Defining Terms**
   Write the meanings of the following words.

   Exposition _____

   _____

   _____

   Persuasion _____

   _____

   _____

   Argumentation _____

   _____

   _____

   Explanatory _____

   _____

   _____

   Narration _____

   _____

   _____

Revision _____

_____

_____

Critical response or reaction essay_____

_____

_____

Critical analytical essay _____

_____

_____

Critical evaluation essay _____

_____

_____

Informative report _____

_____

_____

Scientific lab report _____

_____

_____

Summary, abstract, précis _____

_____

_____

Research paper _____

_____

_____

Documentation styles _____

_____

_____

2. Checking Your Understanding

a. How do you prepare differently for an open-ended topic versus a specific writing topic?

_____

_____

_____

b. Describe the steps involved in the writing process.

_____

_____

_____

_____

c. What are ways to brainstorm ideas?

_____

_____

_____

_____

d. What type of writing requires documentation of sources?

_____

_____

e. What language is used for academic writing?

_____

f. What criteria are typically assessed in a writing assignment?

_____

_____

_____

g. What are the different terms used to express the main idea of an essay?

_____

_____

_____

_____

_____

3. **Knowing Your Campus**

   a. What writing center and tutorial services are available for assistance in writing?

   _____

   _____

   b. What remedial/developmental writing courses are offered? Are the credits inputted or averaged in the GPA?

   _____

   _____

4. **Applying Chapter Concepts**

   a. Select one writing assignment due this semester. Answer the five questions outlined in this chapter for the paper.

     1. What is the topic? _____

     _____

     2. What is the source of information? _____

     3. Who is the intended audience? _____

     4. What is the purpose of the writing assignment? _____

     _____

     5. How is the writing assignment graded? _____

     _____

     6. Set up a schedule for accomplishing the assignment. _____

     _____

     _____

     _____

     _____

     _____

   b. Check _yes_ or _no_ for each item on the writing skills survey. What does your assessment tell you about your writing skills? If you are unsure, show the results to your professor or the campus writing center.

Yes	No	Don't Know	Are you satisfied with your ability to
			Use parts of speech (nouns, pronouns, verbs, adverbs, conjunctions, prepositions, adjectives, interjections)?
			Use subject-verb agreement?
			Use verb tense?
			Use pronoun agreement?
			Use commas?
			Use colons, hyphens, semi-colons, apostrophes, quotation marks, ellipses?
			Follow conventions of spelling?
			Capitalize sentences and proper nouns?
			Use prewriting strategies?
			Develop a focus or thesis?
			Organize ideas?
			Create outlines?
			Construct sentences that are not fragmented?
			Punctuate sentences to avoid run-ons?
			Use a variety of sentence structures?
			Use a varied and precise vocabulary?
			Use a variety of methods to develop and support a thesis?
			Present ideas coherently and logically?
			Employ basic editing skills to identify errors?
			Revise ideas and structure to improve meaning?

5. **Writing for Reflection**

Explore your feelings about writing in college. Write at least one paragraph in response to the following quotation or a meaningful sentence you select from the chapter.

Reading maketh a full man, conference a ready man and writing an exact man.

Sir Francis Bacon

6. Concerning College Athletes

What strategies can you use to write papers while you are traveling for athletic events?

_____

_____

7. Reading Further

The reading selections on the On Campus Student Website at www. prenhall.com/fitton explore different aspects of chapter topics. At the end of each reading selection are critical thinking questions. Your instructor will let you know whether you should print out your responses or use the online feature to email your answers.

Take This Fish and Look At It Samuel H. Scudder
Read this selection written by Samuel H. Scudder, a graduate of Harvard University in 1862, to understand what skills you need to become a good writer.

Notes

[1] D. Southgate, *Agricultural Environmental and Economic Development* Course Syllabus, Ohio State University, http://aede.osu.edu/clas/IS240/Southgate/writing-assignment.htm (accessed April 17, 2003; site now discontinued).

[2] Dean Ferguson, *History 1302: U.S. History Since 1877* Course Syllabus, Texas A&M University-Kingsville, http://users.tamuk.edu/kfdtf00/history_1302—web%20 syllabus.htm (accessed October 31, 2004).

[3] R. Dunkle, Classics 22 Writing Assignment, Brooklyn College, http://depthome. brooklyn.cuny.edu/classics/dunkle/courses/cl22wa.htm (accessed April 16, 2003).

[4] Hess Chung, E202: Introduction to Macroeconomics Course Syllabus, Section 1832, Indiana University, http://php.indiana.edu/~htchung/ (accessed April 17, 2003).

[5] University of Hawaii Manoa, Department of Anthropology, http://www.anthropology. hawaii.edu/faculty/graves/graves210/assignment1.htm (accessed April 16, 2003; site now discontinued).

[6] Princeton University, English Department (2000), http://www.princeton.edu/ ~eng366/paper1.html (accessed January 27, 2004).

[7] Lisa Norling, *U.S. History to 1880* Course Syllabus (2003), University of Minnesota, http://www.hist.umn.edu/hist1301/essay3.html (accessed January 27, 2004; site now discontinued).

[8] Alan Marshall, Cultural Anthropology Writing Assignments, Lewis-Clark State College, http://www.lcsc.edu/amarshal/classes/102/102_write.htm (accessed April 16, 2003; site now discontinued).

[9] T. Schmidt, *History 100 World History: An Introduction*, University of Kansas, http://www.kuce.org/isc/previews/hist/hist100_writing.html (accessed April 15, 2003; site now discontinued).

[10] D. Southgate, *Agricultural Environmental and Economic Development* Course Syllabus, Ohio State University, http://aede.osu.edu/clas/AEDE597.01/Southgate/writing-assignment.htm (accessed April 17, 2003; site now discontinued).

[11] Skidmore College, http://www.skidmore.edu/academics/classics/courses/1998fall/hi201w/pap3ques.html (accessed January 28, 2004).

[12] H. Hanson, *Women in U.S. History, 1620–1865* Course Syllabus, California State University San Bernardino, http://csbs.csusb.edu/history/history344/writing.htm (accessed January 13, 2003; site now discontinued).

[13] H. Hanson, *Women in U.S. History, 1620–1865* Course Syllabus, California State University San Bernardino, http://csbs.csusb.edu/history/history344/writing.htm (retrieved January 13, 2004; site now discontinued).

[14] S. Reid, *The Prentice Hall Guide for College Writers*, 5th ed. (Upper Saddle River, NJ: Prentice Hall, 2000).

[15] Draney, C., *ENGL 102 Critical Reading and Writing* Course Syllabus, Idaho State University, http://www.isu.edu/english/esweb/engl_102s/102_cdraney-su03/assignments/assign_2.htm (accessed January 29, 2004; site now discontinued).

[16] S. Kane, *ART 103 Approaches to Western Art History* Course Syllabus, Oberlin College, http://www.oberlin.edu/faculty/skane/Courses_9697/Art_103/Syllabus.html (accessed January 28, 2004).

[17] C. Smith, *Economics 103 Writing Assignment*, George Mason University, http://mason.gmu.edu/~csmith3/econ103writing.html (accessed January 29, 2004).

[18] F. Palumbo, *MAR 1001 Principles of Marketing Syllabus*, Yeshiva University, http://www.yu.edu/sssb/fall_03_syllabus20.htm (accessed January 28. 2004).

[19] *ENGL 401 Beowulf and Other Old English Poems Writing Assignments*, University of Michigan, http://www-personal.umd.umich.edu/~sdegreg/beowulf/bwf_assignments.htm (accessed January 28, 2004; site now discontinued).

[20] Department of English, University of Alaska Anchorage, http://english.uaa.alaska.edu/courses-comp.htm (accessed January 2, 2004; site now discontinued).

Notes

Notes

HIGHER EDUCATION

If you don't scale the mountain, you can't see the plain.

~ *Chinese proverb*

As a college student enrolled in an institution of higher education, you are part of one of the largest and most diverse institutions in the world. The term *higher education* refers to accredited programs of education offered for post–secondary school studies. In the United States, post–secondary school studies lead to degrees or certificates.

In 1965, when the Higher Education Act was signed into U.S. law "to strengthen the educational resources of our colleges and universities and to provide financial assistance for students in postsecondary and higher education" (Pub. L. No. 89-329), the opportunity to attend college became a reality for hundreds of thousands of people who would otherwise not have been able to afford college. Since 1965, the Higher Education Act has been reauthorized every four years, and each time the Act has been reauthorized, Congress adds and revises programs to benefit more people. If you are receiving any type of federal financial aid, then you, too, are benefiting from this historic act.

The Higher Education Act of 1965 includes a comprehensive legal definition of higher education that has, over the years, been expanded to include more institutions. According to U.S. Code, the term *institution of higher education* means an educational institution in any state that

(1) admits as regular students only persons having a certificate of graduation from a school providing secondary education, or the recognized equivalent of such a certificate;

(2) is legally authorized within such State to provide a program of education beyond secondary education;

(3) provides an educational program for which the institution awards a bachelor's degree or provides not less than a 2-year program that is acceptable for full credit toward such a degree;

(4) is a public or other nonprofit institution; and

(5) is accredited by a nationally recognized accrediting agency or association, or if not so accredited, is an institution that has been granted preaccreditation status by such an agency or association that has been recognized by the Secretary for the granting of preaccreditation status, and the Secretary has determined that there is satisfactory assurance that the institution will meet the accreditation standards of such an agency or association within a reasonable time.[1]

This formal definition can assure you that when you graduate from an accredited institution of higher education, your college degree or certificate has the value of widely established recognition.

INSTITUTIONS OF HIGHER EDUCATION

Since 1965, the number of institutions of higher education has increased by 90%. As the figures in the following table[2] show, the most significant increase is the number of two-year colleges.

Year	Total Institutions	Four-Year	Two-Year
1965	2,230	1,551	679
2004	4,236	2,530	1,706
Growth	90%	63%	151%

With more than 4,000 institutions, higher education in the United States is remarkably diverse. Throughout the country, thousands of colleges are located in urban, suburban, and rural communities. Some colleges enroll small numbers of students, and others enroll thousands of students. Some colleges have highly competitive admission requirements; others do not. Some colleges are private institutions, whereas others are public institutions. Some colleges are strictly liberal arts or technical, and others offer a wide range of programs. Higher education in the United States is unique because it is possible for students to start in one college, transfer credits to another, and graduate from a third. Because there is no central national university system in the United States that dictates curriculum and sets policies, colleges have independently developed their own.

TYPES OF INSTITUTIONS

A **university** comprises colleges and schools. It has the authority to grant bachelor's, master's, doctorate, and professional degrees. A **four-year college** is a postsecondary institution that offers a baccalaureate degree program that can be completed in four years of *full-time* study. A **community college** is a *two-year* postsecondary institution that grants associate degrees and offers certificate programs. Community colleges are sometimes called two-year colleges because their degrees can usually be completed in two years of *full-time* study. In addition to providing transfer programs to four-year colleges, a community college serves its surrounding community by providing credit and noncredit programs in high-demand occupations and lifelong learning opportunities. A few private **junior** colleges offer only the first two years of a baccalaureate education.

A **school** is a division in a university or college that includes several academic departments, such as the School of Engineering or the School of Fine Arts. A **department** is an academic division focused on a specific field of knowledge, such as the English Department, Mathematics Department, and Physical Education Department.

A **public college** is supported by taxes, state funds, and—to a lesser extent—tuition fees. **Public land grant colleges** are colleges built on 30,000 acres of public land granted to each state by the federal government. The land grant college system, established in 1862, consists of 73 land grant colleges in the United States.

A **private college** is not supported by state taxes. It depends on tuition and income derived from investments and donations for funding.

Ivy League colleges refer to eight private East Coast universities known for their high academic standards and social prestige. These colleges, which were among the first established in this country, are members of an athletic conference for intercollegiate football established in the 1870s.

Harvard University, founded 1636

Yale University, founded 1701

Princeton University, founded 1746

University of Pennsylvania, founded 1751
Columbia University, founded 1754
Brown University, founded 1764
Dartmouth College, founded 1769
Cornell University, founded 1865

The **Big Ten universities** consist of eleven world-class midwestern universities that share a common mission of intercollegiate athletics, research, graduate, professional, and undergraduate teaching, and public service.

Indiana University
Michigan State University
Northwestern University
The Ohio State University
Pennsylvania State University
Purdue University
University of Iowa
University of Illinois
University of Michigan
University of Minnesota
University of Wisconsin

ACADEMIC COMMUNITY

A college is a community comprising students, faculty, professional staff and administrators. Each part of the community contributes to the overall culture of the college. Look at the graphic overview of the academic community on the following page to see where you fit in.[3]

STUDENT BODY

Freshmen and sophomores in college are called **underclassmen,** and juniors and seniors, who take upper-level courses, are referred to as **upperclassmen.** At most colleges, students enrolled in a minimum of either 12 units per quarter or 12 units per semester are **full-time students.** Generally, students taking fewer than 12 credit hours in a semester are classified as **part-time students.**

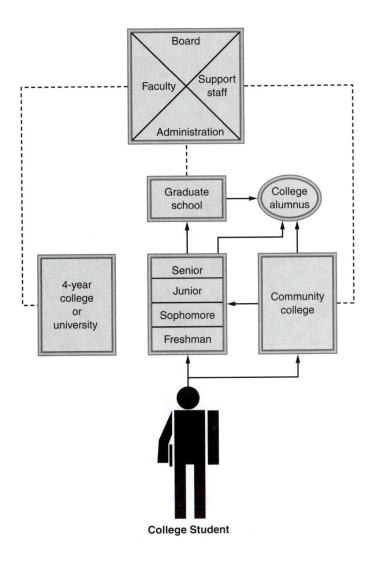

College Student

An **undergraduate** (**undergrad**) has matriculated in a degree-granting program but has not yet received a college degree. A student who graduates is an **alumnus** of his or her college. A student who matriculates in a master's or doctorate degree program is a **graduate student.** A **transfer student** is a student who changes colleges.

Class standing is determined by the number of credits a student earns toward a degree. Remedial or developmental-level courses usually do not count toward class standing. Each college sets its range for class standing.

FACULTY

College teachers are called **professors**. Most colleges have academic rank, titles that are given to faculty (full time or adjunct) who teach or do research. There are four professional ranks: instructor, assistant professor, associate professor, and full professor. To be promoted to a higher rank, a faculty member is evaluated by a faculty committee, which looks at the individual's achievements in teaching, research, and/or service. At most colleges, it takes faculty members many years to be promoted to a higher rank.

Adjunct faculty are part-time, temporary faculty members, who teach a large percentage of courses at U.S. colleges. In 2003, higher education institutions employed 1.2 million faculty members, of which 0.6 million were full time and 0.5 million were part-time.[4]

An adjunct may or may not have an office or be required to hold office hours. Because an adjunct may be piecing together several careers, you may find it difficult to meet with your instructor. For that reason, make sure to resolve any questions before or after the class.

Graduate teaching assistants (abbreviated **TA**) are graduate students appointed part-time by the university as part of a financial-assistance program. Graduate teaching assistants may lecture, lead discussion groups, serve as an assistant to laboratory classes, tutor students, proctor examinations, grade tests and papers, or provide general assistance in teaching.

PROFESSIONAL STAFF

Professional staff members provide comprehensive student services. You will learn more about these services in Chapter 12.

- An **academic advisor** is either a faculty member or a professional staff member who assists students one on one. This person answers academic questions, monitors student progress toward fulfilling degree requirements, and explains available support services. The academic advisor's focus is to keep students on track at college.

- **Career counselors** advise students about career options; **transfer counselors** advise about requirements for changing colleges.
- A **professional counselor** is a trained counselor skilled in helping students with individual problems on a strictly confidential basis.
- If you live in a college dormitory, you will get to know your **resident advisor (RA)** and **resident director (RD)**. Their goal is to help you make your dormitory experience a healthy and positive one.

COLLEGE ADMINISTRATION

College administrators direct the operations of their college. The administrative organization varies from one college to the next. Large university systems have multiple levels of administrators, with titles of chancellor, provost, or president.

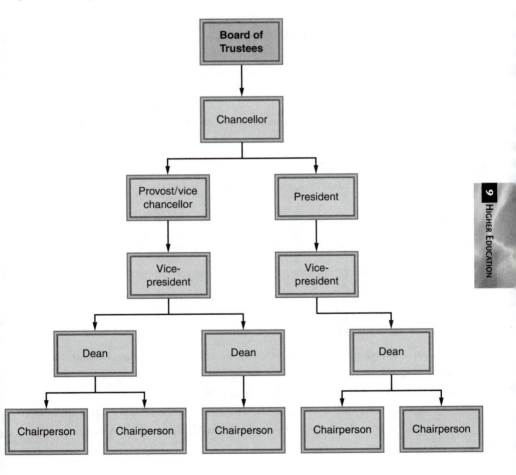

In many college systems, the **dean** supervises an academic college or a division and a **chairperson** is in charge of an academic department.

ACADEMIC DEGREES

A college degree is a title that is conferred to a student at graduation for satisfactorily completing an advanced concentration of study.

In the last half-century, hundreds of thousands of people have earned college degrees. The most dramatic growth has occurred with female students, who for centuries were traditionally denied or discouraged from attending college. Notice in the following tables[5] how female students are taking advantage of higher education opportunities.

Year	Associate's Degrees	Male	Female
1965	112,000	64,000	48,000
2004	665,300	260,000	405,000
Growth	494%	306%	744%

Year	Bachelor's Degrees	Male	Female
1965	520,000	299,000	221,000
2004	1,400,000	595,000	804,000
Growth	169%	99%	264%

ASSOCIATE'S DEGREE

An **associate's degree** is an academic degree conferred upon satisfactory completion of an undergraduate program of study designed to be completed in two or more years of full-time study.

A college may also specify the major area of study in the degree it grants, such as an Associate in Arts in Early Childhood or Associate in Science in Nursing.

College Degree	Abbreviation	Major Area of Study
Associate in arts	AA	Liberal arts, humanities, or fine arts "university-parallel" degree for someone planning to complete a bachelor's degree
Associate in science	AS	Science or mathematics university-parallel degree
Associate in applied science	AAS	An applied, often technical, field designed for someone seeking employment after finishing college

BACHELOR'S DEGREE

A **bachelor's (baccalaureate) degree** is an academic degree conferred by a college or university upon satisfactory completion of an undergraduate program of study designed to be completed in four or more years of full-time study. Depending on the major, approximately 120 to 136 total credits are needed for a bachelor's degree.

College Degree	Abbreviation	Major Area of Study
Bachelor of arts	BA	Liberal arts, humanities, or fine arts
Bachelor of science	BS	Science

Colleges also grant specific degrees, such as a bachelor of science in engineering (BSEE) or a bachelor of fine arts in music (BFA).

MASTER'S DEGREE

To be admitted to a master's program, you must have earned a bachelor's degree. A **master's degree** is an academic degree conferred by a college or university for those who complete in-depth study of a specific area of graduate-level work. A master's degree generally involves writing a thesis or research project and taking a comprehensive written or oral exam. Some graduate schools require both written and oral exams. Depending on the major, approximately 30 to 42 total credits are needed for a master's degree.

College Degree	Abbreviation	Major Area of Study
Master of arts	MA	Liberal arts, humanities, or fine arts
Master of science	MS	Science

Colleges also grant specific degrees, such as a master of business administration (MBA) or master of social work (MSW).

DOCTOR'S DEGREE

A **doctor's (doctorate) degree** is the highest degree awarded by a university. The number of years needed to earn this degree depends upon the specific doctorate degree. Usually, a PhD (doctor of philosophy) requires at least three years beyond a master's degree, with the candidate researching in a specific field, taking comprehensive exams, and/or presenting an original thesis, called a dissertation. The PhD is the most common doctoral degree; however, there are numerous equivalent doctoral degrees.

College Degree	Abbreviation
Doctor of philosophy	PhD
Doctor of medicine	MD
Doctor of divinity	DD
Doctor of laws	LLD, JD
Doctor of education	EdD or DEd
Doctor of computer science	DCS

GRADUATION

Camera lights are flashing. Sitting in the audience are the people who are the nearest and dearest to you, eager to see you as you proudly march across the platform toward the podium. It is commencement day, the date that your graduation degree is officially conferred. Your college degree is a title you earn after you satisfactorily complete a required program of study. Each degree represents a period of time and area of study, signifying an

☐ Graduate   ————————————————

☐ Graduate teaching
assistant   ————————————————

☐ Professional
counselor   ————————————————

☐ Professor   ————————————————

☐ Resident advisor   ————————————————

☐ Resident director   ————————————————

☐ Transfer student   ————————————————

☐ Underclassman   ————————————————

☐ Undergrad   ————————————————

☐ Upperclassman   ————————————————

c. College Degrees and Graduation

☐ Academic degrees   ————————————————

☐ Academic regalia   ————————————————

☐ Associate's degree   ————————————————

☐ Bachelor's degree   ————————————————

☐ Commencement   ————————————————

☐ Conferring of a degree ————————————————

☐ Doctorate degree   ————————————————

☐ Graduation   ————————————————

☐ Master's degree   ————————————————

2. **Checking Your Understanding**
The term *commencement* also means "beginning." What is the significance of this meaning as it relates to graduation?

————————————————————————————

————————————————————————————

————————————————————————————

accomplishment of critical thinking, problem solving, and communication indicative of higher education.

COMMENCEMENT

A **commencement** is a public celebration of graduation. Graduation ceremonies follow centuries of tradition, dating back to European universities during medieval times. Academic gowns, mortarboards, tassels, and hoods marked the colorful, formal pageantry of 12th- and 13th-century graduates.

The Processional

Candidates walk single file or two by two across a building or campus to their seats.

Conferring of Degrees

Candidates are recognized by name and academic honor as they walk across the stage. Often there is a speech by a designated graduating student, a keynote address by an invited significant guest, and a "charge" to all graduating students by the college president. Following the conferring of all degrees, the college president may instruct the candidates to shift their tassels from right to left. This ritual is done in unison, signifying the completion of commencement.

The Recessional

As a courtesy, college candidates and their guests do not leave the arena until the ceremony is completed. At the end of the ceremony, the academic procession leaves the arena in the reverse order of the processional.

Graduation ceremonies last one to two hours. Depending on the size of your graduating class, you may not actually receive your diploma at the commencement ceremony.

ACADEMIC REGALIA

At commencement, all individuals who participate in the ceremony wear specific academic attire, referred to as *academic regalia*. The academic gown, hood, and headwear formalize the ceremony and indicate the degree earned and, often, the conferring college. The National Committee on Academic Costumes and Ceremonies periodically reviews the code of attire and provides information and guidance to U.S. universities. Many colleges acknowledge the achievements of students who graduate with honors or who are student leaders with the addition of special stoles and tassels worn as part of their academic regalia.

Academic Gown

The academic gown recalls the gowns worn by medieval clergy, who comprised the majority of students attending universities in the 12th and 13th centuries. The color and style of the gown signify the degree.

Associate: gray or blue gown

Bachelor: black gown with traditional pointed sleeves

Master: fuller black gown with traditional oblong-shaped sleeves and wrist openings

Doctoral: black gown trimmed with velveteen panels; bell-shaped sleeves trimmed with chevrons

Academic Hood

Academic hoods, originally worn by clergy as head coverings, are today simply laid across the shoulders. The size, shape, and lining of the academic hood indicate the degree level being conferred. The doctor's is the longest at four feet, followed by the master's and the bachelor's. Generally, no hood is worn for an associate degree. The colors in the satin lining are those designated by the college or university. The color of the velvet border indicates the degree earned. Some colleges select their own color scheme for degrees.

Examples of Academic Colors

Communication	Crimson
Education	Light blue
Engineering	Orange
Fine arts, architecture	Brown
Humanities, liberal arts	White
Music	Pink

Academic Headwear

Mortarboard caps are worn for associate's, bachelor's, and master's degrees; soft, black velvet tams are worn for doctoral degrees. Candidates

wear their caps in the academic processions and during the ceremony of conferring degrees.

ACTIVITIES AND EXERCISES

Log onto the On Campus Student Website at www.prenhall.com/fitton to determine how well you have studied and what you still need to learn.

1. **Defining Terms**
   There are a number of college-related terms that you, as a college student, should know. Check off those terms you can define. Write the meaning of the terms you need to learn by writing its definition next to it.

   a. Institutions of Higher Learning

   ☐ Community college _____

   ☐ Department _____

   ☐ Four-year college _____

   ☐ Higher education _____

   ☐ Junior college _____

   ☐ Land grant college _____

   ☐ Private college _____

   ☐ School _____

   ☐ University _____

   b. College Community

   ☐ Academic advisor _____

   ☐ Adjunct _____

   ☐ Alumni _____

   ☐ Chairperson _____

   ☐ Chancellor _____

   ☐ Class standing _____

   ☐ Dean _____

   ☐ Faculty mentor _____

3. **Knowing Your Campus**
   a. Describe the type of college you attend.

   _____

   _____

   b. What are the different schools or departments that comprise your college?

   _____

   _____

   c. Who is the administrative head of your college? What is his or her title?

   _____

   d. What types of degrees are conferred at your college?

   _____

   _____

   e. What is the academic attire for your degree? Major? College?

   _____

   _____

   f. How often does your college have graduation ceremonies?

   _____

   _____

4. **Applying Chapter Concepts**
   What academic degree is needed for your chosen career? How many years of study will you need?

   _____

   _____

5. **Writing for Reflection**
   Explore your feelings about your college education. Write at least one paragraph in response to one of the following quotations or a meaningful sentence you select from the chapter.

   It is easier to begin well than to finish well.
   Plautus

Information cannot replace education.
Earl Kiole

6. **Concerning College Athletes**
   a. How many credits do you need to maintain your eligibility?

   _____

   b. What other academic criteria are necessary to maintain eligibility?

   _____

   c. Do you have specific time requirements for declaring and completing a major?

   _____

7. **Reading Further**
   The reading selections on the On Campus Student Website at www. prenhall.com/fitton explore different aspects of chapter topics. At the end of each reading selection are critical thinking questions. Your instructor will let you know whether you should print out your responses or use the online feature to e-mail your answers.
   a. *Higher Education Glossary* National Center Education Statistics
      Skim this selection to learn the meaning of words related to higher education.

   b. *Diploma Mills and Accreditation* U.S. Department of Education
      Read this selection to understand what individuals jeopardize when taking risky shortcuts to earn a college degree.

Notes

[1] "Title 20—Education Sec. 1001," GPO Access, http://www.gpoaccess.gov/index.html (accessed January 12, 2007).

[2] "Postsecondary Education Table 171," *Digest of Educational Statistic,* (Washington, DC: National Center for Education Statistics, 2005), http://nces.ed.gov/programs/digest/d05/ (accessed January 12, 2007).

[3] K. Yamamoto, *The College Student and His Culture: An Analysis,* Graphic adapted from *The College in American Society* graphic (Boston: Houghton Mifflin, 1968), 2.

[4] "Postsecondary Education Table 169 & 170," *Digest of Educational Statistics* (Washington, DC: National Center for Education Statistics, 2005), http://nces.ed.gov/programs/digest/d05/ (accessed January 12, 2007).

[5] "Postsecondary Education," *Digest of Educational Statistics* (Washington, DC: National Center for Education Statistics, 2005), http://nces.ed.gov/programs/digest/d05/ (accessed January 12, 2007).

Notes

Notes

ACADEMIC PROGRAMS

10

Be not afraid of going slowly; be afraid only of standing still.

~ Chinese Proverb

D o you remember when you applied to and were accepted by the college you are now attending? What were the requirements for admission? Did you have to write an application essay? Take a standardized test? Include letters of recommendation? When you compare your requirements with the admission requirements at Brown University (RI) in the 18th century, you will see how admission requirements have changed over the centuries.

Admission to the college in its earliest days was a personal encounter between the prospective student and the president. Solomon Drowne of the class of 1773, in an entry in his diary for June 30, 1770, described his examination by President Manning and tutor David Howell, which consisted of five verses in the Greek Testament, seven lines in Cicero's *Orations*, and five lines in Virgil's *Georgics*, after which he was pronounced fit to enter, which he did two days later.[1]

An academic program is a sequence of courses that comprise your course of study. The wide variation of academic programs is what distinguishes one college from another. Your choice of college determines the way your academic program unfolds until degree completion. For instance, if you want a strong liberal arts foundation, then you are best served by a college that offers a broadly based education. On the other hand, if you are looking for a specific career path, you might prefer a college that offers clearly defined professional concentrations.

MATRICULATION

When you enrolled at your college and matriculated into a program of study, you also agreed to follow the academic program in place. For that reason, it is your responsibility to make sure that your academic goals align with the college's academic programs. If you believe the college does not offer an academic program that meets your needs, you must speak to an academic counselor right away. It is possible that the college offers complementary programs of study that will serve you well. On the other hand, you may be advised to transfer to another college.

By definition, a matriculated student has applied for and has been formally accepted as a candidate for a degree in a specific program. **Matriculation** is an agreement between the college and you. The college describes the requirements for earning a college degree, and if you satisfactorily complete those requirements, the college awards you a degree. Matriculation requirements are explained in the college catalog.

THE COLLEGE CATALOG

Your college catalog is an encyclopedia of campus information. The catalog you start with as a freshman sets the requirements you need to complete in order to earn a degree. This is referred to as your **catalog year**. If specific requirements change any time after your freshman year, you still follow those set forth in your catalog year.

If you change your major or switch schools within the college, you may need to follow the catalog of the year of your latest change. The best advice is to check with your college for the specific requirements regarding catalog year, because the catalog year you follow may impact your ability to graduate on time. Some colleges put a ceiling on the catalog year. For example, the catalog year at the time you graduate may not be more than 10 years old.

Your catalog explains the curriculum, or **program of study**, approved for a specific degree or certificate. To earn a degree, you must complete all the requirements for that program. Colleges expect that students will be responsible for reading the catalog and asking questions, if necessary, about anything that needs to be clarified.

At the University of Arizona

The catalog is the University's primary official source of departmental, college, and university-wide information related to academic programs. Courses, programs, and policies that govern progress toward completion of an undergraduate degree are described in the catalog. . . . Each student is responsible for knowing and abiding by the policies described in the catalog chosen.[2]

At the University of Central Florida

Students must use a single catalog and not a combination of catalogs for graduation. In cases when required courses are no longer taught by the university, the appropriate department, college, or university office may designate a reasonable substitute. . . .[3]

Even though your college may duplicate its college catalog on the college Web page, keep a hard copy of your college catalog for later use.

STUDENT–ATHLETE HANDBOOK

In addition to publishing a college catalog, many colleges publish a student–athlete handbook. This handbook is designed to help student–athletes succeed in their dual role at college. If you are a student–athlete, make a point of reading through this resource book. You will learn about your additional student–athlete responsibilities and time commitments as well as national rules and regulations that you must follow. Many handbooks provide a list of academic resources available to assist you.

MAJORS AND MINORS

When you **major** in a subject, you study one field in depth. A major may be as specific as biomedical electrical engineering or as broad as elementary education. You may have already been admitted into a specific department, ready to begin your major in your freshman year, or you may still be undecided about your choice of major. As you think about a field of study, consider these points:

- Your choice of major should be based on *personal interest*. What subject(s) are you curious about? What fascinates you?
- Your choice of major should be *challenging*, not frustrating.
- Your choice of major is not a lifetime commitment. If you start taking courses in your major and realize that you do not enjoy the coursework, change your major.
- Your choice of major should be *your choice*, not your parents' or your high school counselor's. You, no one else, will be reading, thinking, and writing about your major. You are investing in yourself, not someone else.
- Your choice of major should fulfill a need that is *meaningful* to you. Don't base this need on the latest "hot" career or the "highest" paying salary. The former may disappear, and the latter, you may end up disliking.

Your college placement office provides valuable resources to help you learn about different majors and explore possible career paths. For instance, you learn which majors require a highly specific sequence of mathematics or science courses that begin with the fall semester. You find out what careers may be achieved through a broader range of study. Make a point of visiting your college placement office your first year. In addition, use the following resources to gather more information about a major:

- Interest inventories
- Seminars and workshops
- Career-exploration course
- Faculty members
- Organizations and clubs
- Internship or cooperative learning
- Volunteer experience

DECLARING A MAJOR

Each academic department determines if there are prerequisites that must be completed before you are accepted into that department. Find out the procedure for declaring a major from the department office. Colleges may require completing a form, earning a minimum grade point average, or interviewing with an advisor. Some majors fill up quickly and a quota is established, limiting the number of students who may major in that field. Many students attending colleges and universities change their majors at least once. If you are uncertain about your major or your career, you will have many experiences and opportunities in a year to explore what is right for you. If you choose a major that requires a strict sequence of courses (for example, engineering) and you do not start this sequence your freshman year, you can either take courses during the summer or complete your degree during extra semesters.

After you declare your major and are accepted into the department, you are typically assigned an academic advisor in that discipline. You learn about how many credit hours you need to take in your major and how these credit hours are distributed. In a two-year college, a major may consist of 18 credit hours; in a four-year college, a major usually totals 30 credit hours or more.

EXAMPLE

Yale University (CT)

Requirements of the major. To graduate as an art major, a student must have passed the sophomore review and have completed a total of four-teen term courses, including prerequisites. These fourteen term courses must include the following: (1) four prerequisite courses at the 100 level (at least one term must be Basic Drawing); (2) five 200- to 400-level courses; (3) three courses in History of Art; and (4) the senior project (ART 495a or b) for double credit. Suggested program guidelines for the various areas of concentration are available from the director of under-graduate studies.[4]

A major may be divided into specific concentrations.

EXAMPLE

University of Illinois at Urbana–Champaign

The Department of Business Administration offers eight separate under-graduate concentrations: marketing, organizational administration, produc-tion, management science, industrial distribution management, manage-ment information systems, entrepreneurship, and food and agribusiness management.[5]

With certain majors, depending on the sequence and number of courses you study, you can earn either a bachelor of arts or bachelor of science.

DECLARING A DOUBLE MAJOR

You may want to earn a double major for a single baccalaureate degree or a double baccalaureate degree by completing the requirements for two majors at the same time. Both majors may be within the same department, or they may be in different departments. At some colleges, it may be possible to complete two different majors simultaneously with no increase to the total credits beyond those required to satisfy both majors.

In addition to meeting the requirements established in the department for the second major, you must maintain a specific grade point average. If your GPA goes below the minimum, the college may cancel your double major/degree status and your program of study may revert to a single major. These guidelines are explained in the college catalog.

DECLARING A MINOR

A minor is a second subject area of concentration, usually consisting of 18 to 24 credits. The minor both complements and enhances a major.

EXAMPLE

Major Minor

English with Philosophy
History with Political Science
Physical Education with Health

GENERAL EDUCATION REQUIREMENTS

A universal goal for most colleges is to make sure that students—regardless of their major—receive a well-rounded, general education. Taking general education courses has many benefits. Not only will you graduate from college a more educated individual, you will learn lifelong skills in writing, speaking, and problem solving. Depending on the college and its mission, you may be required to take as few as 3 general education courses or as many as 30. **General education**, also referred to as *core curriculum*, includes courses in the liberal arts or humanities, fine arts, natural sciences, and social sciences. Make sure you understand the distinctions of each area of study.

Core curriculum refers to a distribution of courses in general education across the curriculum.

From Georgia College and State University

The purpose of the Core Curriculum . . . is to cultivate in our students those "Habits of Mind" that will prepare them to be responsible citizens and leaders in our republic and in the world. We seek to impart a deeper appreciation of the histories and cultural contributions of the diverse array of peoples that make up the civilizations of the world as well as to provide our students with a liberal arts education that enables them to understand and assess critically their own cultural inheritance. The Georgia College & State University student should emerge from the core with the ability to reason rigorously; with a heightened appreciation for the great literature of the world; with a deepened aesthetic sensibility; with the ability to write and speak with grace and clarity; with the skills to use and master modern technology; with a firm grasp of the methodology, theoretical postulates, and issues of the natural sciences, mathematics, and social sciences; and with the ability to see the interrelationships among the various areas of knowledge.[6]

Liberal arts does not refer to a "liberal" political philosophy but rather to the study of a traditional, broad-based education that includes anthropology, sociology, history, economics, arts, psychology, science, literature, foreign languages, and philosophy.

From Grinnell College (IA)

A liberal arts education has at its center four practices that distinguish it from other kinds of learning: critical thinking, examination of life, encounters with difference, and free exchange of ideas. By offering an education in the liberal arts, Grinnell College asserts the importance of lifelong learning characterized by sustained intellectual curiosity and an open mind for assessing the unfamiliar. At the same time, by using critical thinking to identify assumptions, to test logic, to evaluate evidence, to reason correctly, and to take responsibility for the conclusions and actions that result, a student of the liberal arts can grow personally as well as intellectually. A liberally educated person should be capable of principled judgment, seeking to understand the origins, context, and implications of any area of study, rather than looking exclusively at its application.[7]

The term **humanities** is sometimes used interchangeably with the term liberal arts.

From University of Calgary, Alberta, Canada

The Humanities are a cornerstone of education. Humanities disciplines emphasize expressive and logical communication . . . . Through the learning of languages and the study of images, artifacts, and texts and their historical contexts, students in the Humanities come to understand and appreciate their own and other cultures. Through exposure to multiple points of view and diverse methodologies and ideologies, they learn how to engage in critical enquiry, which by definition involves an honest attempt to examine divergent opinions. Humanities students gain a fuller appreciation of themselves and of the ways in which all of us shape and are shaped by our cultural circumstances. Work in the Humanities is intended to expand human awareness, an end that is both valuable in itself and useful in society.[8]

Fine arts are not limited to art, but include music, theatre, dance, and media.

From Marshall University (WV)

The fine arts are aesthetic responses to human nature and experience. They celebrate the best of human endeavor. They contribute to the individual and to society by reflecting and projecting values that shape every culture. They proceed from creation to experience and provide both the artist and the audience with deeper understanding of traditions of human existence and thought. Thus, the fine arts are essential to education.[9]

Natural science includes laboratory experience.

From University of Albany, (NY)

Natural Sciences: Approved courses show how understandings of natural phenomena are obtained using the scientific method, including data collection, hypothesis development, employment of mathematical analysis, and critical evaluation of evidence. Courses provide an overview of major principles and concepts underpinning a discipline's current base of knowledge and discuss major topics at the current frontiers of disciplinary knowledge. Courses show how answers to fundamental questions in science can change the world in which we live and often explore how social issues can influence scientific research. Opportunities for scientific inquiry within laboratory and/or field settings may be provided.[10]

Social science answers these questions: Who are we? How can we understand our behavior?

From Three Rivers Community College (CT)

Sociology has shown that all of us exist within a large collectivity called "society" and sociologists attempt to understand its origins and workings, as well as on the ways in which it shapes individuals. **Anthropology** focuses on origins of the social species, Homo sapiens, as well as on contemporary societies around the world. It uses the idea of "culture" to explain human similarities and differences. **Psychology** relates individual personality and behavior to the social and cultural context in which it is found. Psychology, as well as other social sciences, is also interested in the relationship of the human biological organism to its time and place and has concluded that the fundamental nature of humankind is social. All human societies must organize social systems that enable people to make a living and make collective decisions. Thus **Economics** and **Political Science** are more specialized divisions of social science. How these societies relate to their particular environmental and cultural conditions around the world is the province of **Geography**. Finally, all social scientists recognize that human individuals and societies exist in and change through the flow of time and thus acknowledge that no human behavior can be adequately understood without the perspective that **History** offers us.[11]

ELECTIVES

Electives are courses that you "elect," or choose to take, either within or outside your major area of study. Usually, you can take electives at any time during your undergraduate study. There are two types of electives.

A **free elective** is *any* course you choose to take, not one required by your program. Are you a biology major who likes to listen to jazz? Are you a music major interested in learning about the law? The goal of free electives is to encourage you to take a course in a subject you might not otherwise study.

A **restricted elective** allows you to choose a course as long as it falls within certain guidelines. Your college and department provide a list of acceptable electives from which to choose.

DELIVERY OF INSTRUCTION

The term *delivery of instruction* refers to the predominate method by which a course is taught. In addition to the traditional classroom and the lecture hall, college instruction can be delivered in a variety of ways.

Traditional

Lectures
Laboratory
Seminars

Off Campus

Cooperative education
Internship
Service learing

High Technology

Online
Hybrid courses
Telecourse
Distance interactive

Traditional Enhanced

Learning communities
Independent study
Writing intensive
Honors courses
International travel

Take advantage of the independence, enrichment, and flexibility these options provide by registering for courses that offer alternative instructional methods.

TRADITIONAL COURSES

Traditional instruction is based in the classroom, where many "smart" classrooms are equipped with integrative multimedia technology that enlivens lectures and discussions.

Lectures

In a traditional **lecture**, the instructor delivers content by telling you information. You listen and take notes while the instructor speaks. This didactic mode can be presented in a small classroom of 40 students or in a large lecture hall with hundreds of students. Lecturing is an efficient method of conveying a large amount of information. Lectures can be dynamic if presented by a captivating speaker or if enhanced with integrated media technology.

Laboratories

A **laboratory** section may be an additional required component for an art, foreign language, science, or engineering course. Labs provide practical, hands-on applications relating to the instructional part of the course. For science courses, you record experimental procedures and write lab reports on your experiments.

Seminars

A **seminar** is usually a small, informal, discussion-based class that emphasizes a thoughtful exchange of ideas. The instructor may sit with you and help facilitate discussions by posing questions. Because there are few, if any, tests in this type of instruction, participation is often a substantial part of your final grade.

ENHANCED COURSES

Enhanced courses typically meet in a traditional classroom setting, but there is an additional component to the instruction that enhances the course.

Learning Community

A **learning community** comprises a group of students and faculty who are learning and teaching collaboratively in several designated courses. Sometimes a common theme is explored across the disciplines. Although there are many different variations on how learning communities are structured, the commonality is a supportive network for learning.

Independent Study

If you discover a topic or a project not normally covered in a regular course and are self-disciplined and motivated to complete work independently, you might enjoy being challenged by independent study. After meeting with a faculty member to discuss credit hours and to agree on a plan of study for a specific amount of time, you work outside the classroom completing those academic requirements.

Writing-Intensive Courses

Depending on the college, **writing-intensive courses** are either optional or a program requirement. As the title implies, writing-intensive courses involve a great deal of writing. Typically, you prepare more formal and informal writing assignments than required in a traditional course. By enrolling in a writing-intensive course, you gain valuable writing experience while learning the subject matter.

Honors Courses

If you meet high academic standards, you are eligible to enroll in **honors courses**. These challenging courses provide more intensive study than is possible in most regular sections. Honors courses are intended to foster an advanced mastery of content and a higher level of critical thinking. If you are enrolled in an honors program, you are often eligible for academic scholarships and collegiate opportunities.

International Travel/Study

International study combines lecture and field experience in a foreign country. Studying in a foreign country enriches your understanding of other cultures in a way that cannot be duplicated by reading or watching a program. You may be able to take courses in a field of study not offered in the United States. It is important to understand your college's policy regarding the transferability of credit for courses taken abroad.

OFF-CAMPUS COURSES

Off-campus courses may have periodic, scheduled meeting times with the instructor on campus, but your learning experiences occur predominately in off-campus settings.

Cooperative Education (Co-Op)

Cooperative education is an academic program that integrates classroom studies with paid, real-life work experience. Working in a co-op gives you a practical view of a career you may be considering. You learn important job skills and gain a valuable understanding of the realities and responsibilities involved in their prospective career field. A successful cooperative experience can enhance your résumé as well as provide personal recommendations for future full-time employment. Many businesses support co-op programs to aid in their recruitment of talented students as future employees.

Internships

An internship is similar to a co-op program; however, generally, internships are nonpaid positions. As a student intern you work in consultation with a faculty member throughout the internship to connect the experience with the course objectives. Student teaching in a public school is an example of a nonpaid internship.

Service Learning Courses

In a **service learning course**, you receive credit for providing meaningful course-related community service outside the classroom. You are assessed on your experiential learning in a variety of ways, including class discussions and journals. Thoughtful reflection regarding the experience is an important learning component.

HIGH-TECHNOLOGY COURSES

High-tech courses take full advantage of technology to create more opportunities to experience learning outside the classroom.

Online Courses

An **online course** is asynchronous. That means you, your classmates, and your instructor attend class at different times during the day or night.

Asynchrony offers convenience and flexibility. You can check on and submit assignments in just minutes. You can pop in for an online classroom discussion any time of the day. You still have deadlines; for instance, your instructor may state, Assignment 3 is due at 12:00 a.m. To succeed in an online course, you must be a capable reader. Instructors replace lectures with lecture-type information posted on the course Web site. You also need to be comfortable writing frequently because written assignments and ongoing e-mail discussion "threads" document classroom "attendance." Last, lacking the regimen of regularly scheduled classes, you need the self-discipline and motivation to keep up with the online coursework on a timely basis. Some colleges require students to attend an orientation session and to take exams on campus.

Hybrid Courses

In a sense, **hybrid courses** offer the better of two worlds: face-to-face instruction combined with online learning. The time you spend online has the advantage of being asynchronous because you decide when to log onto the Web. The online component reduces the amount of time you spend in the traditional classroom. At the same time, the face-to-face component enables you to ask real-time questions and to participate in real-time discussions.

Telecourses

With the convenience of learning from home, **telecourses** offer self-paced instruction broadcast on public television. Guided by a faculty member, students view pretaped video lectures, follow a study guide, and complete assigned textbook readings and additional coursework. Students may be required to attend some on-campus class sessions for orientation, reviews, and exams.

Distance Interactive Courses

An interactive video classroom allows a class to be offered on more than one campus at the same time. Instruction is synchronous, meaning you can talk to, see, and work together with classmates and instructors who may be hundreds of miles away. These classrooms are equipped with state-of-the-art automated technology and allow real-time interactive instruction to be delivered to different remote sites. Video monitors are used in conjunction with telephones, computers, fax machines, or television to communicate with one another. Distance interactive courses offer the advantage of allowing you to take courses with instructors who might not otherwise be available at your college.

PROGRAM OF STUDY

Many colleges offer a computerized degree audit system that generates individualized detailed progress reports. Using the audit system, you can

1. understand the degree requirements in your major;
2. track the progress you are making toward degree requirements for your college or program;
3. view approved courses for your major and program;
4. enter "what-if" situations for program changes. For instance, if you decide to switch majors, the system generates a new report that lists the requirements you have already fulfilled and the courses you need to take to in order to complete your new major.

This system has various names, including

Academic Progress Audit System (APAS)

On Course System

Interactive Degree Audit (IDA)

When you already understand your college and program requirements, the time spent meeting with your academic advisor to discuss your program will be more productive. Remember, even if your college provides a student degree audit system, you are still required to meet with your advisor and to file an application for graduation at the beginning of your final semester.

Develop your own plan of study if your college does not provide an automated system. The following example shows the process for completing a BA in American Studies at the College of Staten Island (State University of New York), where students must satisfactorily fulfill state, college, and program requirements.

Step 1

Look up college requirements for a degree. These may be listed as general education, core requirements, or general education distribution.

General Education Requirements

PART I = 12 total credits
    ENG 111 Communications Workshop (3)
    ENG 151 College Writing (4)
    COR 100 United States Issues, Ideas, Institutions (4)
    PED 190 Fitness for Life (1)
PART II = 28–47 total credits
    Scientific Analysis; Social Scientific Analysis; The Contemporary World;
    Textual, Aesthetic, and Linguistic Analysis; Pluralism and Diversity
    requirements

Step 2

Look up any premajor requirements. These may be listed as premajor or prerequisite courses.

EXAMPLE

Premajor Requirements = 3 total credits
    AMS 101 America: An Introduction (3)

Step 3

Look up the program requirements for the major. These may be listed as curricular requirements, major requirements, course requirements, track courses, and related courses.

EXAMPLE

Major Requirements = 32 total credits
    American literature = 8 credits
        ENH 203 Literary History of the US to 1855 (4)
        ENH 204 Literary History of the US since 1855 (4)
    American history = 8 credits
        HST 244 US History: 1607–1865 (4)
        HST 245 US History: 1865–present (4)
    American Studies = 16 credits
        16 credits beyond AMS 101, including at least two courses at
        the 300 level or above.

Step 4

Look up elective requirements.

Electives = 26–48 total credits

Step 5

Use the major categories of requirements to make a plan of study. Under each category list both required and restricted elective courses.

Area of Concentration: American Studies

Requirement	Required Credits	Credits by Semester							
		1	2	3	4	5	6	7	8
Gen Ed I	12								
ENG 111		3							
ENG 151			4						
COR 100			4						
PED 190		1							
• • •									
Gen Ed II	28–47								
ECO 252				4					
BIO 106/107			4						
• • •									
Pre-Major	3								
AMS 101		3							
Major	32								
ENH 203						4			
ENH 205							4		
• • •									
Totals	138	15	18	18	18	18	18	18	15

SEQUENCE OF COURSES

The sooner you understand the sequence of courses for a program of study, the more equipped you will be to balance your course load in subsequent semesters and to graduate in a timely manner. For instance, if your major has courses that require a lot of reading, you would be wise to spread these out throughout the semesters. Or, if your major has a rigorous sequence of mathematics courses, you will need to judge the number of credits you can handle well each semester. Finally, if you are taking any noncredit preparatory courses, you may need to see how taking summer classes can help you "catch up" to the program sequence.

If you are attending a two-year college and intend to transfer to a four-year college for a bachelor's degree, you should look ahead and understand the requirements at the transfer college. Many colleges have established articulation agreements between two-year and four-year colleges. Should you want to transfer to a college that does not have an articulation agreement with your college, be sure to find out what courses you should be taking during your first two years.

Planning a sequence of courses when you are a freshman may take time. Your efforts will pay off later because you will have a clear picture of all the courses you need to take to graduate. For example, you will know which required courses are offered only once a year and avoid extending your graduation date because you have to wait to take these classes. In addition, you will be able to determine the impact of attending summer sessions on your graduation date. And, finally, you will avoid taking courses that do not fulfill your program requirements.

ACTIVITIES AND EXERCISES

Log onto the On Campus Student Website at www.prenhall.com/fitton to determine how well you have studied and what you still need to learn.

1. **Defining Terms**

   There are a number of college-related terms that you should know. Check off those terms you can define. Study each term you need to learn by writing its definition next to the term.

a. *Academic Programs*

- Class standing _____
- Core curriculum _____
- Fine arts _____
- Free elective _____
- General education _____
- Humanities _____
- Institutional mission _____
- Liberal arts _____
- Major _____
- Matriculation _____
- Minor _____
- Natural science _____
- Restricted elective _____
- Social science _____

b. *College Courses*

- Cooperative education _____
- Honors course _____
- Hybrid course _____
- Independent study _____
- International study _____
- Internship _____
- Lab _____
- Learning community _____
- Lecture _____
- Online course _____
- Seminar _____
- Service learning _____
- Telecourses _____
- Writing-intensive course _____

2. **Checking Your Understanding**

   Next to each course, write whether it is classified as *liberal arts, fine arts, social science,* or *natural science.* If you are unsure, check your college catalog.

   a. Art appreciation   _____

   b. Principles of public speaking   _____

   c. Fundamentals of general chemistry _____

   d. Introduction to the theatre   _____

   e. Principles of microeconomics   _____

   f. Intermediate Italian   _____

   g. Social anthropology   _____

   h. Field geology   _____

   i. Modern world history   _____

   j. Calculus for business   _____

   k. Philosophy and logic   _____

   l. Introduction to music history   _____

3. **Knowing Your Campus**

   a. In what department or school are you matriculated?

   _____

   b. Does your college have a policy regarding catalog year? If so, what is it?

   _____

   _____

   c. What is the procedure for declaring a major?

   _____

   _____

   d. How does your college distinguish among college majors when granting a degree?

   _____

   _____

4. **Applying Chapter Concepts**

   a. Choose at least two types of classes that interest you and that are offered at your college. Next, find one course for each type of class. How do you register for the courses?

   _____

   _____

   _____

   _____

   b. Create a plan of study for your program of study. If you are undecided about your major, select a program of study, such as liberal arts, that offers wide latitude regarding your choice of courses. Print a copy of your computerized student course report, or create and complete a table similar to the one in the text.

   c. Follow these steps to determine a semester-by-semester sequence of courses that satisfy college requirements and meet your individual needs.

   > ***Step 1.*** Make a list of your college and program requirements.
   >
   > ***Step 2.*** Identify the requirement headings at your college. The headings may be similar or different to the ones used in the figure in the text.
   >
   > ***Step 3.*** Look up advanced courses to determine which ones have prerequisites.
   >
   > ***Step 4.*** Sequence your courses over the number of semesters you will attend college. Find out which of these courses are offered alternate semesters and years.

Area of Concentration:

Term 1		
Course	**Credits**	**Requirement Being Met**
Total Credits:		

Term 2		
Course	**Credits**	**Requirement Being Met**
Total Credits:		

Term 3		
Course	**Credits**	**Requirement Being Met**
Total Credits:		

Term 4		
Course	**Credits**	**Requirement Being Met**
Total Credits:		

Term 5		
Course	**Credits**	**Requirement Being Met**
Total Credits:		

Term 6		
Course	**Credits**	**Requirement Being Met**
Total Credits:		

Term 7		
Course	**Credits**	**Requirement Being Met**
Total Credits:		

Term 8		
Course	**Credits**	**Requirement Being Met**
Total Credits:		

5. Writing for Reflection

Explore your feelings about your choice for a college major. Write at least one paragraph in response to one of the following quotations or a meaningful sentence you select from the chapter.

> *The road to happiness lies in two simple principles;*
> *find what interests you and that you can do well,*
> *and put your whole soul into it—every bit of energy*
> *and ambition and natural ability you have.*
> John D. Rockefeller

6. Concerning College Athletes

Explain what this quotation means to you:

> *A decade after graduation, almost everyone will have forgotten*
> *where and what (athletes) played. But every time they speak,*
> *everyone will know whether or not they are educated.*
> Theodore M. Hesburgh, C.S.C., Johnson State College,
> Johnson, Vermont

_____

_____

_____

7. Reading Further

The reading selections on the On Campus Student Website at www.prenhall.com/fitton explore different aspects of chapter topics. At the end of each reading selection are critical thinking questions. Your instructor will let you know whether you should print out your responses or use the online feature to email your answers.

The Meaning of the Baccalaureate Degree Margaret A Miller
Read this selection to find out what good questions you can ask.

Notes

[1] Martha Mitchell, Encyclopedia Brunoniana, Brown University News Service Web site: http://www.webstar.brown.edu/Administration/News_Bureau/Encyclopedia/Lasso.acgi (accessed March 17, 2004; site now discontinued).

[2] Academic Policies, Choice of Catalog, University of Arizona Web site, http://catalog.arizona.edu/2002–03/policies/catchoice.htm (accessed April 12, 2003).

[3] Undergraduate Degree Requirements, University of Central Florida Web site, http://www.ucf.edu/catalog/9697/undergrad_requirements.html (accessed April 12, 2003).

[4] Art Program, Yale University Web site, http://www.yale.edu/ycpo/ycps/A–D/artFM.html (accessed December 22, 2003).

[5] *Curriculum in Business Administration*, University of Illinois at Urbana–Champaign Web site, http://www2.uiuc.edu/admin_manual/pos/current/ugrad/commerce/ba.html (accessed December 22, 2003; site now discontinued).

[6] Core Curriculum, Georgia College and State University Web site, http://www.gcsu.edu/acad_affairs/coll_artsci/core.html (accessed April 12, 2003; site now discontinued).

[7] Education in the Liberal Arts, Grinnell College Web site, http://www.grinnell.edu/academic/catalog/education/(accessed February 18, 2004).

[8] University of Calgary, http://www.ucalgary.caUofC/faculties/HUM/Faculty/mission.html (accessed April 12, 2003; site now discontinued).

[9] *College of Fine Arts Mission*, Marshall University Web site, http://www.marshall.edu/cofa/(accessed April 12, 2003).

[10] General Education Requirements, SUNY Albany Web site, http://www.albany.edu/undergraduate_bulletin/general_education.html (accessed April 12, 2003; site now discontinued).

[11] Social Sciences Mission, Three Rivers Community College Web site, http://www.trcc.commnet.edu/acad_depts/soc_sciences/mission.htm (accessed April 12, 2003).

10 ACADEMIC PROGRAMS

Notes

COLLEGE POLICY

Ignorance of the law is no excuse.
~ Latin legal phrase

Every organization, including college, has rules and regulations designed to maintain standards and civility within its structure. If you believe your college's regulations are strict, take a look at the rules imposed at Yale in the late 19th century. Notice the last sentence regarding student athletes. What does that exception suggest?

College discipline. Every morning you must be at chapel at ten minutes past eight, at half-past eight everybody has a recitation. All the work of the Freshman and Sophomore years is prescribed; you sit with the same men and all your class has the same tasks and the same teachers. There is a regular tariff of black marks for offences of negligence, so many for tardiness at chapel, so many for absence, so many if you cut more than six lectures in a course, so many if you cut successive lectures, and most of all—eight marks—if you are absent from church on Sunday. When twenty marks are received a letter is written to your father; forty-eight marks in one term involve suspension, unless the ruling powers can be mollified, as they perhaps might be by a good athletic record.[1]

At college, you will discover there is a policy for just about everything—attendance, bicycles, grades, posters, parking, and withdrawal. At your pre-college orientation, counselors or peer guides explained many of these policies. You are expected to learn the rest on your own.

If you need assistance in understanding any policy at your college, you can find answers at your college's counseling center, advising center, registrar, academic affairs, or department office.

COLLEGEWIDE POLICIES A TO Z

College policies of U.S. colleges share similarities regardless of the college. Make sure you know the specific details of policies at *your* college.

APPEAL PROCESS

You initiate an appeal process for a variety of reasons. For example, if you believe you received an incorrect grade in a course, your first step is to meet with the instructor and discuss your reasons for requesting a grade change. Many colleges impose a deadline, typically two weeks, during which time you may appeal a grade. After that time, the grade is recorded permanently on your transcript.

Find Out

1. For what situations does your college have an appeal process?
2. What is the process of appeal?
3. What are the time requirements?

ATTENDANCE

Colleges set a generic attendance policy that can be made more restrictive by individual faculty members. Often, state funding regulates attendance policies.

Find Out

1. What is the college attendance policy at your college?
2. Which of your courses have an attendance policy different from that of the college?

CLASS RANK

Your class rank is based on your GPA, as compared with that of the other members of your class. For example, in a graduating class of 1000, the student with the highest GPA has rank 1; the person with the lowest GPA, 1,000. Class rank becomes part of the permanent record.

Find Out

1. If your college has class rank, how is it determined?
2. What is the policy if two or more students have an identical GPA?

DROP/ADD

Drop/add refers to a short period of time during which you can add or drop a course. Depending on the college, drop/add may or may not be noted on your transcript. Usually, during this short window of time, you can drop or add a course without financial penalty.

Find Out

1. What is the drop/add time period at your college?
2. Are there any consequences for dropping a course?
3. How does dropping a course differ from withdrawing from a course at your college?
4. What might be some concerns about adding a course late, after the start date of that class?

FINAL EXAMINATIONS

Study days and final examinations are scheduled on your academic calendar. If you miss a final, you need to know the process for contacting your professor.

Find Out

1. When are final examinations scheduled for this semester?
2. What is the college policy regarding missed finals?

HOLIDAYS

Universities and colleges schedule the observance of secular as well as some religious holidays on the college calendar. Policies are designed to address the diversity of beliefs and traditions present at a college.

Find Out

1. What holidays does your college recognize and observe?
2. What is the policy regarding scheduling tests on religious holidays?
3. What rights do you have if you miss class to observe a religious holiday?

INCOMPLETE GRADES

An incomplete grade represents a postponement of the deadline for completion of a course. Your college has guidelines that determine under which conditions an incomplete can be granted and under which conditions you can complete the course. These guidelines are usually published in the college catalog and often require a signed agreement between the faculty member and you. Typical reasons for giving an incomplete are unavoidable interruption of academic work:

- Prolonged illness or other incapacity
- A personal or family emergency
- An illness or similar incapacity in the final days of a course
- Military leave

If you are granted an incomplete, you must complete the coursework by a specific date. After you complete the work for the course and the instructor submits the grade, the incomplete grade is changed to the appropriate grade. If you do not complete the work, depending on college policy, your professor may convert the incomplete to the default grade (the grade you earned up to the point of the incomplete) or an F.

Find Out

1. How does your college policy for granting an incomplete compare with the reasons cited in this section?
2. What is the process for requesting an incomplete?
3. How is the final grade determined?
4. What is the deadline for completing course requirements?
5. What specific accommodations are made for students on military leave?

LIBRARY SERVICES

Libraries have policies regarding what materials you may borrow and the length of time you may borrow them, as well as policies covering student conduct within the library.

Find Out

1. What is the library policy regarding borrowing course-related materials?
2. What are the consequences of not returning library materials on time or not paying library fines?

PARKING REGULATIONS

Parking regulations outline speed limits and parking zones on campus. An unpaid parking ticket can, for example, prevent the release of an official transcript you may need in the future, such as for a job or graduate school application.

Find Out

1. What are important parking regulations on your campus that you should know?
2. What is the towing policy?
3. How do you appeal a parking ticket?

PASS OR FAIL

To encourage students to try courses they might not otherwise take, many colleges allow students to enroll in courses on a pass or fail basis. You may earn credit for the course, but the P/F letter is not calculated in your GPA.

Find Out

1. Can you take a pass/fail course in your major?
2. What is the maximum number of credits that may be taken on a pass/fail basis?
3. What is the minimum grade you must earn to receive a pass for a class?

4. Can you change a course you are taking for a grade to pass/fail? If so, what is the deadline?
5. Can you change a pass/fail course you are taking to one with a letter grade calculated in your GPA?
6. Do your instructors know if you are taking pass/fail? Or, do you need to tell them?
7. Should you take preprofessional requirements (example, premed or prebusiness courses) as pass/fail?

PROBATION OR SUSPENSION

A college may put you on probation or suspension for academic or disciplinary reasons. The sanctions imposed depend on the severity of the violation or academic problem.

Find Out

1. What is the difference between probation and suspension at your college?
2. What restrictions exist while a student is on probation or suspension?

REGISTRATION

Colleges have priority registration if you are an upperclassmen to make sure you can register for courses you need in order to graduate on time. Some colleges have online registration; others prefer in-person registration with an academic counselor.

Find Out

1. When can you register for courses next semester?
2. What is the registration process?

REPEATING A COURSE

There are many ways colleges handle repeating a course.

- Each time a course is repeated, the previous grade is removed from GPA calculation. That means if the repeated grade is lower than the previous grade, the lower grade stands.
- All grades received for the same course are recorded on the transcript and calculated in the GPA.

If you decide to repeat a course, make sure you change the conditions that caused the low grade. Consider retaking the course with another instructor. Spend more time studying the material for the course. If necessary, get a tutor. Unless you make changes, you risk repeating a course without changing your last grade.

Find Out

1. What is the college policy regarding repeating a course?
2. What happens if the grade for a repeated course is lower than the first grade?
3. What are the benefits of repeating a course besides improving the grade?

TRANSCRIPTS

Your transcript lists, by semester, the specific courses for which you were registered and the final grade you received in each course. A student copy is an unofficial transcript. An official transcript has a raised stamp and is typically enclosed in a sealed college envelope. Many colleges charge a fee for an official transcript.

Find Out

1. How does your college differentiate between a student copy and official copy of your transcript?
2. How do you obtain an official copy of your transcript at your college?

WITHDRAWAL

Suppose you realize halfway through the semester that (a) your work load is too heavy, (b) you are going to fail a course, or (c) you need to work more hours. You stop going to one of your courses, concentrating your efforts fully on your remaining credits. What you may not realize is that even though you no longer attend the class and did not take any more tests, you can still earn an F for the course. One of the most common mistakes you might make is to believe that if you stop attending class, your professor will give you a W for a grade or that the college will automatically drop you from the course. Make sure you understand the conditions and procedures for withdrawing from a course at your college.

Find Out

1. What is the process for withdrawing from a course?
2. What is the deadline for withdrawal this semester?
3. For what types of situations should you consider withdrawing from a course?
4. How does withdrawal impact your GPA and financial aid?

ACADEMIC CODE

Honesty is a choice. People are honest because of their sense of morality and personal ethics. In college, you are going to be tested not only in the content of your courses but also in your resolve to behave honestly. You are familiar with the term *cheating*. It means sneaking answers to tests, copying answers, falsifying class attendance, lying to a faculty member, and falsifying data or evidence in a paper, presentation, or lab report. You may be less familiar with the term *plagiarism*, using another person's words or ideas as if they were your own. Helping other students cheat also violates the academic honesty policy, subject to the same consequences as if you were the one who cheated. This includes letting students copy your homework or giving them answers on a test.

EXAMPLE

Example from American University (DC)

Academic integrity lies at the heart of intellectual life. As members of a diverse community committed to the advancement of knowledge, we affirm the importance of respecting the integrity of one another's work. The Academic Integrity Code for American University describes standards for academic conduct, rights, and responsibilities as members of an academic community and procedures for handling allegations of academic dishonesty. As an institution of higher learning, American University views academic integrity as an educational as well as a judicial issue.[3]

Example from the University of Virginia

The Honor System directly expresses the principle of student self-governance. Founded in 1842, the Honor System has succeeded for more than 150 years as an entirely student-run system. Stewardship of the system rests not only with the elected members of the Honor Com-

COLLEGE POLICY
11

mittee, but it also lies with each student's decision to act honorably and to hold fellow students to the same standard. The Honor System works best when each student actively reaps its benefits and consciously strengthens its principles.[4]

You may be asked to write out and sign your college's honor code, signifying an agreement to abide by the code, as students do at Kansas State University:

> On my honor, as a student, I have neither given nor received unauthorized aid on this academic work.[5]

FOR DISCUSSION

At the University of Georgia, researchers administered an *Academic Honesty Questionnaire*[6] to learn about faculty and student perceptions regarding academic honesty. Take the survey yourself to see what your perceptions are regarding academic honesty.

Part 1

Read each statement in the following *Academic Honesty Questionnaire* and circle each number that you believe is cheating. Write a question mark in the column if you believe it depends on the circumstances.

Part 2

After you complete the survey, discuss your answers with your group. Were there specific situations that influenced some of your answers?

Academic Honesty Questionnaire

1. When typing a paper for a friend, changing words or phrases in order to improve how the paper reads
2. Discussing a paper with a friend while in the process of writing it
3. Discussing a paper with a friend who is in the same class and is writing on the same subject
4. Changing laboratory results to reflect what the results should have been
5. Turning in the same paper for two different courses during the same quarter
6. Turning in the same paper for two different courses during different quarters

7. Turning in two different papers based upon the same library research for two different courses
8. Studying from old exams from the same course and professor
9. Maintaining a test file of old exams for students in an organization to use to prepare for exams
10. Asking someone who has already taken the same exam (e.g., during an earlier class period) about what is on the test
11. Making arrangements with other students to take turns going to the lecture and taking notes
12. Purchasing lecture notes from a note-taking business to supplement one's own notes
13. Purchasing lecture notes from a note-taking business instead of going to class
14. Copying lecture notes from a friend after missing a class
15. Asking another student how to do a homework assignment
16. Collaborating with other students to complete homework assignments
17. Preparing for exams with a study group in which each person develops review materials for a portion of the course
18. Including an article in a reference list when only reading the abstract
19. Asking someone to proofread a draft of a paper for a writing course and circle errors
20. Asking someone to correct a draft of a paper for a writing course
21. Asking someone to proofread a draft of a term paper and circle errors
22. Asking someone to correct a draft of a term paper
23. Using published summaries and/or study guides to assist in understanding reading assignments
24. Using published summaries and/or study guides instead of reading assigned works of literature
25. Watching videotaped films of famous works of fiction rather than reading an assigned book

STUDENT CODE OF CONDUCT

Student life refers to all activities—both academic and social—that occur on a college campus. To maintain civility and mutual responsibility on a college campus, formal policies describe acceptable and unacceptable conduct and explain the consequences for violating these policies. If you are admitted to and matriculated on a college campus, you are obligated to follow the established student conduct code.

As the Student Conduct Code from the University of Washington illustrates, students are obliged to abide by the code set forth by their college.

WAC 478-120-010 Student Conduct Code—Authority

Pursuant to Chapter 34.05 RCW and the authority granted by RCW 28B.20.130, the Board of Regents of the University of Washington has established the following regulations on student conduct and student discipline on the University campus.

WAC 478-120-020 Standards of Conduct

(1) The University is a public institution having special responsibility for providing instruction in higher education, for advancing knowledge through scholarship and research, and for providing related services to the community. As a center of learning, the University also has the obligation to maintain conditions conducive to freedom of inquiry and expression to the maximum degree compatible with the orderly conduct of its functions. For these purposes, the University is governed by the rules, regulations, procedures, policies, and standards of conduct that safeguard its functions and protect the rights and freedoms of all members of the academic community.

(2) Admission to the University carries with it the presumption that students will conduct themselves as responsible members of the academic community. As a condition of enrollment, all students assume responsibility to observe standards of conduct that will contribute to the pursuit of academic goals and to the welfare of the academic community.[7]

ALCOHOL

For students who are at the legal age to drink, colleges encourage responsible decisions about the consumption of alcoholic beverages while promoting safe and healthy social interactions.

Find Out

1. What is your college's position regarding alcohol consumption?
2. What sanctions are imposed for violations?

DRUGS

Colleges expect drug-free campuses in accordance with state and federal laws.

Find Out

What sanctions are imposed for individuals violating the antidrug policy?

HAZING

Hazing is any conduct or method of initiation into any student organization that deliberately or recklessly endangers the health or well-being of any other person. As a consequence of hazing, students have, tragically, died on U.S. college campuses.

Find Out

Does your college have a strong antihazing policy? Explain.

RESIDENCE HALLS

When you applied for and were accepted into a college dormitory, you also agreed to abide by established rules and regulations for living on campus. Resident advisors are careful to make sure you understand specific residence hall policies.

Find Out

What policies did you *not* expect when you first moved into your dormitory?

HARASSMENT

Sexual harassment—unwanted sexual attention—is not tolerated by any member, student, faculty, or staff, of a college campus. Given the differences in people's perceptions, it is important that you understand how it is defined on your campus.

Find Out

How does your campus define sexual harassment?

ACQUAINTANCE RAPE AND SEXUAL VIOLENCE

Colleges have zero tolerance for acquaintance rape and sexual violence and impose severe sanctions for those who violate the policy.

Find Out

1. How does your college define acquaintance rape and sexual violence?
2. What sanctions are imposed for violations?

BIAS OR HATE CRIMES

Northwestern University (IL) provides definitions that explain the similarities and differences between bias and hate.

> Bias incidents and/or hate crimes involve behavior that is motivated by race, religion, sexual orientation, ethnicity, national origin, ancestry, gender, age, or disability. Bias incidents include those actions that are motivated by bias but may not meet the necessary elements required to prove a crime. Hate crimes are also motivated by bias and they include property damage, personal injury, or other illegal conduct.
>
> A hate crime is a bias incident that has risen to the level of a violation of criminal statue. All hate crimes are bias incidents, but not all bias incidents are hate crimes.[8]

Find Out

1. What is the college policy regarding bias and hate incidents?
2. Do you believe your college provides adequate coverage of this topic either on the college Web site or in workshops? Explain.

COMPUTER CODE OF CONDUCT

With the inclusion of computers on the college campus, colleges have developed specific codes of conduct if you use college computers or college e-mail. For example, at Monroe Community College, a comprehensive code of conduct for users of the college computer systems begins as follows:

> Individuals who use MCC computer facilities and systems must assume the responsibility for using these resources in an appropriate manner for college related work only. Misuse of computer facilities is considered a violation of College policy and may also be a violation of state and federal law. Please note that MCC computers are public access computers where you should have no expectations of privacy.[9]

You must have a thorough understanding of those computer activities that your college characterizes as unethical, unacceptable, and just cause for disciplinary action.

FOR DISCUSSION

For each of the following situations, discuss these four topics:

1. What *problem* does the student face? What makes it difficult?
2. What *college policy* covers the issues in the situation?
3. What *actions* might resolve or improve the situation?
4. How could the student have been *proactive* rather than reactive? What steps could the student have taken before this situation arose that might have prevented or lessened the conflict the student faces?

Situation 1

Tanya receives a notice from the college health office indicating that because Tanya did not submit verification of her MMR immunization to health services, she is being withdrawn immediately from all her courses. Tanya cannot understand why this is a final notice. She does not remember receiving previous ones. She is also positive that she had submitted all the required immunization records during the summer by making the necessary phone calls to her doctor's office. When Tanya attends classes the next day, her mathematics and sociology professors do not permit Tanya to stay in either class, explaining that she was withdrawn by the college. Tanya misses taking her math test, and now does not have important lecture notes she will need for her sociology midterm.

Situation 2

Tiffany is a single mother who is working 30 hours a week. She has to add one more class in order to have the 12 credit hours required for financial aid. She signs up for an elective art course because she enjoys art, and the class fits well in her tight schedule. At the end of the first week, one of her "wait-listed" classes has an opening. Because the course is required for her major, she decides to take that one instead. With her busy schedule, Tiffany forgets to drop the art class. When she finally remembers a week later, she figures because she never attended a class, the professor would automatically drop her. At the end of the semester, Tiffany discovers she is still registered for the art class and has received an F. She contacts the professor and explains her situation, but the professor refuses to change the F to a W, insisting it was Tiffany's responsibility to withdraw from the course. Now Tiffany finds out that the F may jeopardize her financial aid.

Situation 3

The first day of math class, Michelle sits next to a male student who appears friendly and helpful. After the third class, the male student asks for her phone number, suggesting that they study together. Because Michelle feels uneasy, she does not share her phone number and changes her seat in class. The male student also changes his seat and proceeds to make suggestive sexual comments. After class, Michelle mentions the situation to her professor. When the professor speaks to the male student, he angrily comments that Michelle is actually the one leading him on.

Situation 4

Mike is an honor student who received a merit scholarship. During the first eight weeks in chemistry class, while Mike's professor is out on medical leave, a young graduate assistant teaches the class. Because the graduate assistant encourages collaborative learning for classwork and assignments, Mike forms a study group with two other students. The three students work on their assignments together. When the professor returns, Mike hands in an assignment in collaboration with his group, as he has been doing all along for the substitute instructor. The professor accuses the three of cheating and submits their names to the academic dean for disciplinary action. All three students are sanctioned for cheating and are withdrawn from the course.

Situation 5

Sean is a senior in his last semester at college. He is a high-honors student majoring in chemistry and has already been accepted to graduate school. Two years earlier when he had transferred from the College of Engineering to the College of Liberal Arts, Sean stopped off at one of the offices to make sure he had met all his liberal arts requirements. The person working in the office assured Sean that he had fulfilled his liberal arts requirements. Now, at the beginning of his last semester, Sean completes an intent-to-graduate form. With graduation less than three months away, Sean is shocked to learn that because he is short one fine arts course, he has failed to satisfy all the general education requirements. He cannot graduate in June.

Situation 6

During the fourth week of the semester, Adam receives a phone call from his sergeant requesting that he join his National Guard unit for two weeks of military training. Adam speaks to each of his five professors before leaving college for military exercises. All but two professors are understanding and supportive. The psychology instructor tells Adam to bring his textbook to military training so he "doesn't fall behind." Because this was not practical, when Adam returns to college, he struggles trying to catch up on the missed chapters as well as to keep up with current reading assignments. His biology instructor gives him one additional week to make up two weeks of online assignments. The professor expects the current week's work to be handed in on time. Finding it impossible to keep up with all the assignments, Adam barely passes his English exam and fails his biology test. Adam explains his predicament to each of the professors, but he is not granted extensions. If he cannot improve his GPA, Adam is in jeopardy of losing his financial aid for next semester.

Situation 7

Amanda has 3.5 GPA and wants to keep her GPA high because she is applying for scholarships. In her communications course, the professor has assigned a group project that is worth 25% of their grade. The group has to do research and give a presentation on a specific topic. There will be one grade given to the entire group based on their presentation. Amanda is not pleased that Joe is assigned to her group. Joe always fools around and doesn't seem to take the class seriously. Amanda asks her professor if Joe can be moved to a different group, but the professor refuses, stating that because students have to learn to work with all kinds of people in life, this would be a good experience. Amanda's group decides to divide the project and assigns each group member a different part. Amanda works hard on her section. The day of the presentation, Joe brings only a few sentences written for his part. Another group member is absent. The presentation is weak. Some major pieces of information are missing, and the presentation does not flow. The group receives a C−. Amanda is upset because she worked hard on her section and thinks she deserves a better grade. She talks to the professor, but he reminds her that the rubric states only a single grade is given to the entire group.

Situation 8

Keith has had an extremely busy week. He has been working overtime hours each day. On Thursday, he manages to finish a five-page paper for English due on Friday. He also has a math assignment, a take-home test due the next day, but he knows he cannot complete the test later at work. Keith talks to his friend Josh, who is in the same math class, and asks if he can copy his homework. Josh agrees. Josh figures Keith would return the favor if need be. Later that week, when the teacher returns the papers, Josh sees the professor has given him a zero. He talks to the professor, who points out that Keith's and Josh's papers are identical, including the same incorrect answers and identical work shown. She concluded that the two students had cheated on the assignment and gave them both zeros. Josh protests and explains that he had done the original work. He believes he should earn a B on the take-home test. The professor refuses to change the grade. A zero on this test will bring Josh's class average from a C+ to a D−. Josh needs a C average in this class in order to take the next math course.

Situation 9

Carlotta struggles in math, and she is taking an introductory math course. Several students in her class understand the material easily and are always joking around and whispering amongst themselves. Carlotta finds this behavior very distracting, and she sometimes has trouble hearing or understanding the instructor. She sits in the front row, but no matter where she sits, she still finds herself distracted by the constant talking from students while the instructor is teaching. The professor just ignores the talking. If Carlotta asks a question when she doesn't understand something, she hears chuckles and snide comments from some of the other students. Carlotta talks to her professor after class about the distractions. The professor says she will try to keep the talkers quiet, but the next class is no different. Carlotta finds herself falling behind because of the distractions.

Situation 10

Al is taking a political science class. He has very strong political beliefs. His professor is also very firm in her political beliefs, which are vastly different from Al's. Al can't prove it, but it seems to him that the professor tries to control the class discussions by calling on students who agree with her opinions and cutting off students who hold other opinions. When Al tried to express his personal political opinions, the professor stated that Al is narrow-minded and has not done all of the reading. From that point on, Al stopped participating in class discussions. The midterm is all essay questions, and Al only receives a 58. Al talks to other students in the class and finds that all of the students who share his political beliefs received low grades on the midterms, whereas those of the professor's persuasion all passed. Al also finds that his class participation points are low because he hasn't been contributing in class lately.

ACTIVITIES AND EXERCISES

Log onto the On Campus Student Website at www.prenhall.com/fitton to determine how well you have studied and what you still need to learn.

1. **Knowing Your Campus**

    Answer the *Find Out* questions throughout the chapter to learn more about your college.

2. **Applying Chapter Concepts**

    a. Locate the academic code at your college. Explain the policy. Is there a more specific academic honesty code in any of your courses? Explain.

    _____

    _____

    _____

    _____

    _____

    _____

    b. Locate the student code of conduct at your college. Explain the policy.

    _____

    _____

    _____

c. Locate the code of conduct for computer users at your college. Explain the policy.

_____

_____

_____

_____

_____

d. What policies do you believe students should know *before* the first day of classes? Explain why.

_____

_____

_____

_____

_____

e. Based on your observations and understanding of college code, to what extent does your college enforce its academic code and code of conduct on campus? Include examples.

_____

_____

_____

_____

_____

3. **Concerning College Athletes**
   a. What are four pieces of critical information emphasized in your student athlete handbook?

_____

_____

_____

b. Does your college have specific policies for student athletes initiating a withdrawal?

_____

_____

c. What is the college policy regarding attendance for athletes?

_____

_____

Notes

[1] "A Glimpse of Yale by George Santayana," *The Harvard Monthly* (December, 1892), Collected by J. Ballowe, Barnard Electronic and Archive Teaching Laboratory, http://beatl.barnard.columbia.edu/learn/99AHLstuff.htm/Santayana.htm (accessed March 22, 2004; site now discontinued).

[2] *Undergraduate Regulations,* Santa Clara University, http://www.scu.edu/bulletin/undergraduate/regulations.cfm?menu=reg (accessed April 12, 2003; site now discontinued).

[3] *Academic Integrity Code*, American University, http://www.american.edu/academics/integrity/code01.htm (accessed April 12, 2003).

[4] *The Honor Committee*, University of Virginia, http://www.student.virginia.edu/~honor/intro/welcome.html (accessed April 12, 2003).

[5] *Honesty & Integrity Peer Educators*, Kansas State University, http://www.ksu.edu/hipe/(accessed April 12, 2003; site now incorporated into http://www.ksu.edu(hono).

[6] J. L. Higbee and P. V. Thomas, "Student and Faculty Perceptions of Behaviors that Constitute Cheating," *NASPA Journal* 40(1), Article 3 (2002), http://publications.naspa.org/naspajournal/vol40/iss1/art3 (accessed March 22, 2004).

[7] *Student Conduct Code*, University of Washington, http://www.washington.edu/students/handbook/conduct.html (accessed January 13, 2007).

[8] *Hate Crimes and Bias Incidents*, Northwestern University College, http://www.northwestern.edu/noplaceforhate/hatecrimes/definition.html (accessed January 14, 2007).

[9] *Code of Conduct for Users of MCC Computer Systems*, Monroe Community College, http://www.monroecc.edu/depts/elc/Code.htm (accessed January 14, 2007).

11 COLLEGE POLICY

Notes

Notes

CAMPUS RESOURCES AND ACTIVITIES 12

Seek advice but use your own common sense.
~ Yiddish proverb

Ith an abundance of resources and activities available on your campus, your college years should be filled experiencing these diverse opportunities. Higher education is much more than the information you learn in class:

College is two things.
It is a Place and it is an Idea.
It is situated in the Heart of Knowledge.
It offers everything in the way of Reflection.
This is the time in your Life
for the Remarkable,
the Inspirational,
and the Extraordinary.
Make it happen Now.

Diane Fitton

As illustrated by the following mission statements, colleges and universities want you to become a citizen of your campus community.

EXAMPLE

Bowdoin College (ME), a Small Liberal Arts College

One real benefit of Bowdoin is the immediate access to a wide range of quality services and caring staff that make a difference in the daily lives of students. Whether you are looking for some coaching in writing, struggling with issues at home, or discovering a new interest in a craft or career field, there are people and programs here to help you grow your skills and achieve new goals.[1]

Monroe Community College (NY), a Large Community College

The Division for Student Services strives to offer services that combine learning and student life. We believe that the college experience assists in the transformation and development of a student's quest for learning, career expectations, life goals, cultural understanding, personal growth and future vision. Student Services is committed to the business of helping students develop and build character that encourages them not only to believe in themselves, but to strive to be distinguished members of our community.[2]

CAMPUS RESOURCES

The figure shows a variety of campus resources, which we discuss in more detail in following sections.

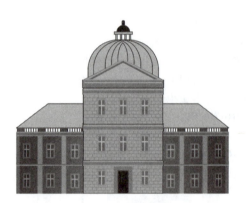

Campus Resources

College website
Financial aid
Student health services
Career services
Residence life
Academic advising
Library services
Counseling services
International student services
Student services

COLLEGE WEB SITE

Your college Web site functions as a valuable means of communication between your college and its academic community. Revised at regular intervals, a college Web site is a dynamic portal. By accessing your college Web site, you can link to a huge depository of information, including calendars, daily news, events, academic resources, financial resources, support services, libraries, organizations, college facts, policies and regulations. In addition, on most college Web sites you can access your e-mail, check your grades, monitor completion of your program requirements, and register for next semester's classes.

FINANCIAL AID

Simply stated, financial aid is money to help pay for a college education. The basic philosophy underlying student financial-aid programs is that the primary responsibility for funding your education rests with your parents and yourself. Financial aid is designed to help complement, not substitute for, your family's ability to pay the cost of your college education.

The college financial-aid office will work with you to assess your financial needs and to assist you in applying for all forms of aid for which you may be eligible. In addition, the student financial-aid staff can help you with your personal financial planning while you are in college. The four sources of financial aid are federal, state, college, and private.

The starting point for all federal aid and many state aid programs is to complete the online **Free Application for Federal Student Aid (FAFSA)** at http://www.fafsa.ed.gov/. Depending on the state, data from FAFSA may be released by the federal processor to the state where you are a resident. Some states, such as New York and Vermont, have separate applications for their financial aid programs that must be filed in addition to FAFSA.

Grant

A **grant** is financial aid that you do *not* have to repay. The amount you receive is based on a formula that calculates need, cost of attendance, and enrollment status. You may qualify for both state and federal grants. Academic competitive grants are awarded on the basis of scholastic achievement.

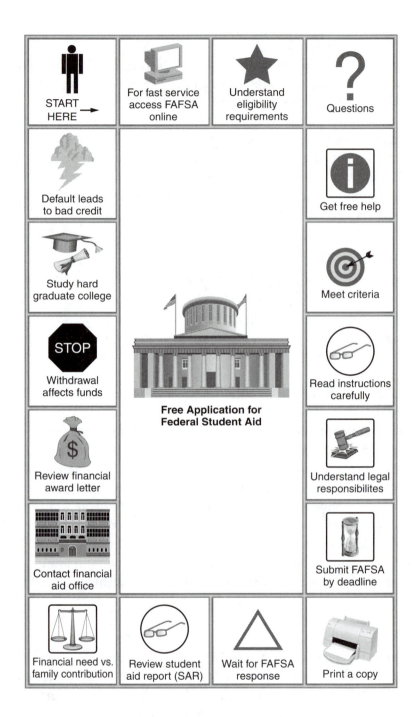

START HERE →

For fast service access FAFSA online

Understand eligibility requirements

Questions

Default leads to bad credit

Get free help

Study hard graduate college

Meet criteria

STOP
Withdrawal affects funds

Read instructions carefully

Free Application for Federal Student Aid

Review financial award letter

Understand legal responsibilites

Contact financial aid office

Submit FAFSA by deadline

Financial need vs. family contribution

Review student aid report (SAR)

Wait for FAFSA response

Print a copy

Federal College Work-Study Program

Work-study is a federally funded program that provides part-time jobs for students. During the summer, if you participate in a work-study program, you do not need to be registered for classes. The number of hours you work per week and the amount of money you earn are established in your federal work-study award. Work-study may be on campus at your school or off campus with either a private nonprofit organization or a public agency in the public interest.

Scholarship

A **scholarship** is financial aid that you do *not* have to repay. There are many sources for scholarships: colleges, companies, labor unions, religious organizations, fraternities or sororities, sports/athletics, and local, state, and federal organizations. Your financial aid office can provide sources of private scholarship. Be wary of Web sites that offer to search for scholarship money for a fee. You should not have to pay for this service.

Benefit

A **benefit** is an educational assistance fund that is awarded in conjunction with some type of work or assignment. AmeriCorps Program awards funds to pay current educational expenses or repay federal students loans in return for community service. The government awards educational assistance for active military duty or serving in the selected reserve. Your place of employment may provide benefits for tuition and fees. Each provider sets the requirements as well as the amount and length of the benefit.

Loan

A **loan** is financial aid that you borrow and repay with interest. You may apply for an educational loan from a bank or financial institution, or you may qualify for a *federal, state* or *local* **government educational loan**. A **subsidized government loan** means the Department of Education pays the interest while you are in school and during grace and deferment periods. With an **unsubsidized loan**, you are responsible to pay for the interest on your loan starting from the time you borrow money. Although you must repay the money you borrow, remember that this loan is an investment in your future. For that reason, borrow money that you must have only for your *educational* expenses.

When you receive financial aid, it is your obligation to maintain satisfactory academic progress toward the completion of your degree to maintain your financial aid eligibility. Failing, dropping, withdrawing, and repeating courses, as well as receiving incomplete grades, can result in the loss of financial aid.

Find Out

1. What services does your financial aid office offer?
2. For what types of federal loans are you eligible?
3. For what types of state loans are you eligible?

STUDENT HEALTH SERVICES

Student health services typically provide health promotion, education, and medical care to you if you are a registered student. These health services may be offered through a campus health service, community agency, or hospital:

- Evaluation and treatment of illness and injury
- Medications and medication refills ordered by the health services
- Referrals to specialists as needed
- Allergy injections
- Contraception/sexual counseling
- Treatment of sexually transmitted infections
- Pregnancy testing
- Anonymous HIV testing
- Diagnostic tests, available at a college or local lab
- X-rays performed at local facilities
- Immunizations
- Nutrition and eating-disorder information
- Alcohol- and drug-use information and counseling

Find Out

1. Does your college provide health insurance? What type is it?
2. Review the preceding list and check off those services that are offered at your college.

CAREER SERVICES

Career services departments provide resources to support your career development at all stages of your education. In addition to providing personal career counseling, the career development office will help you to do the following:

- Identify your interests, skills, and values.
- Research career fields and academic majors.
- Build résumés and write cover letters.
- Practice interviewing skills.
- Apply to internships and jobs.

Find Out

1. What types of career services does your career office offer?
2. How often can you make an appointment for personal career counseling?

RESIDENCE LIFE

Residence life programs help students cope with the transition of living in a community away from home. Residence halls are staffed with professional members, who live in the halls. Each head resident typically works with resident advisors (RA) to enhance the on-campus living experience and provide educational and recreational programming.

RAs help organize activities that promote mutual support and peer learning for residential life. During the semester, planned events may include social activities as well as workshops on life and study skills.

Find Out

1. What types of programs does your dorm or residential life office offer?
2. What are the qualifications needed to become a resident advisor?

ACADEMIC ADVISING

The purpose of **academic advising** is to promote student development and success by helping students to identify, clarify, and achieve their academic goals. Academic advising may be offered at a separate central office, or it may be provided by faculty in academic departments. Some colleges assign a professional advisor with whom you will meet until you graduate.

An academic advisor will help you to do the following:

- Identify your degree requirements and options.
- Evaluate your transcripts.

- Monitor your progress.
- Assist in considering career options.
- Make appropriate referrals to other campus offices.

Your responsibilities are to do the following:

- Meet with an advisor at least once a semester.
- Schedule an advisement appointment.
- Prepare for advisement by keeping a personal academic file of records.
- Ask questions.
- Keep the appointment.

Find Out

1. How do you obtain academic advisement at your college?
2. What should you keep in your academic file of records for advisement?

LIBRARY SERVICES

Twenty-first century college libraries are designed to advance learning, scholarship, and research. To assist the college community, libraries include comprehensive, high tech services:

Resources
- Online catalog
- E-resources
- Databases
- Periodicals (magazines, journals, newsletters, or newspapers published on a regular basis)
- Libraries across America (WorldCAT)

Research Help
- Research guides
- Tutorials
- Research papers

Services
- Individual research consultations
- Reserves
- Interlibrary loan

- Reference instruction
- Library instruction
- Media

Collections
- Archives
- Special (AIDS, women, Holocaust, career)

Find Out

1. Review the preceding list and check off those services that are offered at your college.
2. What special collections does your college library own?

COUNSELING SERVICES

College counseling centers are staffed by counselors and interns trained to help you understand and work through personal issues ranging from mild difficulties to serious problems.

Counseling services can help you with issues that involve academic stress, depression, anxiety, romantic relationships, family members or friends, eating disorders, sexuality (or sexual orientation), and alcohol and/or other drug use.

A college counseling center does not give out information about participation in or the content of counseling to faculty members or parents unless a student gives written consent.

Find Out

1. What is the process for receiving counseling services at your college?
2. What are the qualifications of the counselors at your college?

INTERNATIONAL STUDENT SERVICES

International student services help international students with travel, registration, financial aid, and housing. Orientation programs and programs of special interest help international students make a successful adjustment to the campus and community. At many colleges, the International Student Service Center (ISSC) offers information about programs of study abroad.

Find Out

1. Does your college provide specific services for international students?
2. What information do you need to know for study abroad opportunities?

STUDENT SERVICES

Learning Center and Tutoring Resources

The National College Learning Center Association defines a learning center as "a place where students can be taught to become more efficient and effective learners. Learning Center services may include tutoring, mentoring, supplemental instruction, computer aided instruction, success seminars/ programs, advising and more."[3]

Many colleges provide

- individual and group review sessions for specific courses;
- free and/or fee-based tutoring;
- peer tutoring;
- a reading lab;
- a writing center;
- specific course learning centers (psychology, chemistry, etc.);
- academic success workshops.

Federal TRIO Program

Federal TRIO programs are educational-opportunity outreach programs designed to serve and assist low-income, first-generation college students and students with disabilities.

Student Support Services (SSS) programs provide opportunities for academic development, assist students with basic college requirements, and serve to motivate students toward the successful completion of their postsecondary education.

Services for Students with Disabilities

Most colleges provide specific services to assist students with disabilities and students with Individual Education Programs. For example, students with disabilities may be entitled to

- use special test accommodations (such as extra time, Braille copy);
- take a reduced course load without losing financial aid;
- make adjustments in seating arrangements;
- receive copies of lecture notes;
- have a helper take notes for a student with a hearing impairment.

To qualify for services offered at college, students must be able to document their specific disabilities. Students should speak with the Services for Students with Disabilities Office to understand what services are provided at the college. In addition, students should contact their instructors before or during the first week of classes regarding any special needs.

Find Out

1. Review the preceding list. What services are offered at your college?
2. Through what office(s) are these services organized at your college?

 FOR DISCUSSION

1. What information about types of services, benefits, or rules surprised you after you found out about resources available on your campus?
2. What is your responsibility for taking advantage of campus resources?
3. Which campus resources can help position you to be proactive at college?
4. How do campus resources double the value of your education?

CAMPUS ACTIVITIES

College offers you a unique opportunity to try many free and inexpensive activities in one place. You can enjoy the fun of joining others in clubs and organizations. You can compete in intercollegiate or cocurricular athletics and intramurals. You can derive satisfaction from community service or share your opinions in student publications. The friendships you form, the activities you pursue, and the interests you embrace all contribute in positive ways to the person you are now and will be when you graduate. The more you become involved in out-of-class activities, the more you get out of your education.

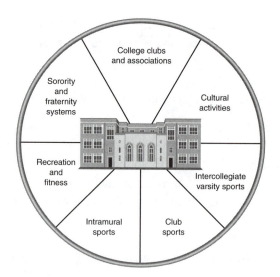

COLLEGE CLUBS AND ASSOCIATIONS

Membership in a college club or association provides opportunities for friendship, leadership experience, scholarship, community service, and networking (making contacts that may be useful for future employment). These organizations are chartered by student government. Many clubs are free; some have a nominal fee. Typically, to join a club, you attend a meeting and/or complete an interest form. If you don't find something to fit your interests, there is usually a process for starting a new club. Schedule an activity into your week just as you do other events.

Following is a small sampling of college clubs and associations.

Academic Groups. Math Club, American Chemical Society, Physics Club

Arts and Performing Groups. Ceramics Club, Glee Club, Jazz Ensemble

Cultural Heritage Groups. Asian Students Association, Black Students' Alliance, Nosotras (Latina students)

Professional Groups. Business Club, Black Educators of Tomorrow

Recreational Groups. Sailing, Croquet, Ice Hockey, Chess Club

Religious Groups. Christian Fellowship, Hillel, Newman Association

Social and Political Action Groups. Amnesty International, Habitat for Humanity, Spectrum (lesbian, bisexual, and transgender alliance), Student Leadership

Special-Interest Groups. American Sign Language and Deaf Culture Club, Investment Club

Find Out

1. How can you find out information about clubs and associations at your college?
2. How do you join a club?
3. Given enough time in your schedule, what activity would you join? Why?

FRATERNITY AND SORORITY SYSTEM

Depending on the college, Greek-letter societies may dominate the overall campus social life, take on a low profile, or not exist at all. Many students who join a sorority or fraternity are attracted to the social aspects as well as the organization's particular values and focus.

Fraternities and sororities, similar to college clubs and organizations, provide friendship, leadership experience, scholarship, community service, and networking. Unlike college clubs, Greek-letter organizations are selective. Both you and the Greek-letter organization must have a mutual interest in your membership. After you receive and accept a bid (invitation), then you pledge the Greek organization. Membership fees are often required. Elaborate initiation rituals may be an important part in gaining entry.

Find Out

1. How large a presence is Greek life on your campus?
2. What is the process for joining a fraternity or sorority?

COLLEGE ATHLETICS

Recreation and Fitness

The primary goal of **college fitness programs** is to promote a lifelong pursuit of health, wellness, and fitness. College programs may include weight training, group exercise, aerobics, triathlons, swimming, spinning, yoga classes, and fitness assessments.

College fitness facilities often include a physical activity center, regulation playing floors, pool, gymnasium, weight room, walking track, and racquetball courts.

Intramural Sports

College **intramural sport programs** offer structured leagues and tournaments for all college students. The level of competition ranges from competitive to recreational, where more emphasis is placed on participation than on winning. Intramural sports provide the opportunity for physical activity and fellowship while promoting wellness and the positive use of leisure time. Intramurals may be either men's, women's, or corecreation leagues with individual, dual, and team competitions.

Intramural sports include, among others, basketball, bowling, ultimate Frisbee, soccer, badminton, bowling, dodge ball, flag football, tennis, ice hockey, billiards, and volleyball.

Club Sports

Club sports are nonvarsity teams and organizations. Depending on the college, club sports range from serious intercollegiate competition to informal, instructional competition. Club teams may compete in leagues against other local and regional teams or at national competitions.

At many colleges, students organize club sports. The college helps to promote, develop, and support the clubs, but students provide the primary administration and management of the sport.

Club sports include, among others, ultimate Frisbee, rugby, racquetball, figure skating, sailing, golf, crew, volleyball, badminton, archery, cycling, rowing, water polo, table tennis, tae kwon do, kickboxing, volleyball, ice hockey, and soccer.

Intercollegiate Varsity Sports

Highly structured and intensely competitive, intercollegiate varsity sports mean big business for colleges in terms of expenditures and revenues. Every institution that participates in intercollegiate sports is a member of one of the collegiate sport-sanctioning organizations: the National Collegiate Athletic Association (NCAA), the National Association of Intercollegiate Athletics (NAIA), or the National Junior College Athletic Association (NJCAA). The NCAA is further divided into divisions that categorize schools into groups based on criteria such as size, number of participants, and type of sport. The largest subdivision is Division IA; the smallest is Division III.

Intercollegiate varsity sports include cross country, field hockey, football, soccer, volleyball, basketball, bowling, fencing, gymnastics, ice hockey, rifle, skiing, swimming and diving, indoor track and field, wrestling, baseball, golf, lacrosse, rowing, softball, tennis, outdoor track and field, volleyball, and water polo.

Find Out

1. What services are offered for recreation and fitness at your college?
2. If your college offers intramurals and club sports, what is the mission of each?
3. If your college has intercollegiate sports, what sports are played?

CULTURAL ACTIVITIES

Colleges offer a wide variety of cultural events to the academic and surrounding community. Your involvement in cultural activities contributes significantly to your quality of life and well being. When you participate in cultural activities, you share in the ingenuity and enjoy the creativity of the human mind and spirit. Cultural activities include

Drama	Dance
Film	Musical programs
Lectures	Art
Exhibits	Museums

Find Out

1. How prominent are cultural activities on your campus?
2. From the preceding list, what activities does your college offer?
3. What are other reasons, not explained in this section, to participate in cultural activities?

GOVERNING AND REPRESENTATIVE ORGANIZATIONS

STUDENT GOVERNMENT ASSOCIATION

The Student Government Association (SGA) provides continuous interaction among students, faculty, and administration. By representing the student body, SGA communicates an organized expression of student opinion on concerns and issues relating to student welfare. In addition, SGA may influence the college's decision-making process by serving as a liaison between the students and administrative governing bodies.

Student government attracts motivated individuals who want to share ideas, meet people, communicate information and enrich the campus

Student government association
Off-campus student services
Community service clubs
Service learning
Veterans affairs office

community. To become involved in the Student Government Association, you may run for election to the SGA or may be appointed to any open seat on one of the standing committees. Time commitments will vary based on the position.

Find Out

1. How is student government structured at your college?
2. What are the benefits of becoming involved in student government?
3. How can you become involved?

OFF-CAMPUS STUDENT SERVICES

Colleges recognize that commuter students are a diverse population of students whose family and working status, living, and commuting arrangements may present challenging situations. Commuter students balance multiple roles, commuting to campus, attending classes, and finding time to study. The mission of off-campus student services is to enhance the educational experience of commuter students by providing practical, social, and advocacy assistance.

Many colleges have a separate organization, such as the Commuter Student Union (CSU) or Commuter Student Affairs (CSA), that provides a variety of services and programs. These organizations strive to make the commuter's experience on campus more enjoyable and convenient as well as to help the commuter become an active and involved participant in college.

Find Out

What types of off-campus student services are available at your campus?

VOLUNTEER SERVICE AND CIVIC ENGAGEMENT

Your college experience can be greatly enriched by engaging in civic activities. Whether you participate in service learning or volunteerism, these learning experiences result in meaningful personal, professional, leadership, and citizenship skills. Many colleges provide opportunities for students to get involved both on and off campus.

Community Service Clubs

Volunteer service is nonpaid, part-time work in your community. Examples of volunteer activities include helping out with literacy programs, delivering food to the Salvation Army kitchen, dedicating several hours per week to work with children in a neighboring town, donating blood for the Red Cross blood drive, and helping to build a home for Habitat for Humanity.

Service Learning

Many college courses are enriched with a service learning component. You participate in real-world application of your learning by providing meaningful community service that you can relate to your studies. For example, at the University of Connecticut, as part of a service learning project, students enrolled in engineering and environmental geology service learning courses investigated the preservation of historical landmarks to benefit the local community. At Miami Dade Community College, in a service learning project for a music appreciation course, students interacted one on one with the children of migrant workers. Both the college students and children developed a mutual appreciation of music.

Find Out

1. What types of volunteer opportunities does your college provide?
2. What types of service learning courses are offered at your college?

VETERANS AFFAIRS OFFICE

The Veterans Affairs Office serves as a liaison between veteran students and the Department of Veteran Affairs. The office assists veteran students in applying for educational benefits for veterans and veterans' dependents, certifying school attendance to the regional VA office, maintaining individual student's files, assisting with any questions concerning veteran educational benefits or educational experiences, and reporting to regional and state VA offices.

Find Out

Does your college provide specific services for veterans? If so, where is the Veterans Affairs office located?

LOOKING *OUT*, LOOKING *IN*

Throughout this textbook, the focus has been *looking in* on you. Why are *you* in college? How do *you* stay motivated? How do *you* plan a workable schedule? How do *you* take useful notes? How do *you* read, write, and study effectively? How do *you* earn a college degree? How do *you* finance a college education? How can *you* get involved at college?

Looking out is responding intelligently and compassionately to the world around you.

Looking out is making wise decisions that follow your dreams and aspirations.

Looking out is choosing to do things that make you a healthier and happier person and bring you more opportunities.

Looking out is acknowledging that many decisions result in immutable consequences dictated by the laws of nature and society.

Looking out is taking care of yourself. No one but you can do this for you.

 FOR DISCUSSION

What are the extrinsic and intrinsic values of getting involved in campus activities?

How would you address each of the following reasons that students give for not getting involved in campus activities?

1. I already have friends.
2. I am shy.
3. I keep to myself.
4. I don't have extra time to spare.
5. I don't have extra money to spend.

Activities and Exercises

Log onto the On Campus Student Website at www.prenhall.com/fitton to determine how well you have studied and what you still need to learn.

1. **Knowing Your Campus**

   Answer the *Find Out* questions throughout the chapter to learn more about your college.

2. **Applying Chapter Concepts**

   Learn about one college resource, activity, or event at your college.

   a. ***Get the Facts.*** Visit the location to obtain materials, observe, and speak to someone. Check the college Web site for additional information.

   b. ***Present Information.*** Use PowerPoint or poster board to present information to your class.

   - Would you recommend this place or event as worthwhile? Why or why not?
   - What should students know before visiting this resource or participating in this event?
   - What is *one* valuable or useful piece of information you can share with the class?

3. **Writing for Reflection**

   Write at least one paragraph in response to the following short poem.

   As I walked by myself,
   And talked to myself,
   Myself said unto me:
   Look to thyself,
   Take care of thyself,
   For nobody cares for thee.

I answered myself,
And said to myself,
In the selfsame way to me:
Look to thyself,
Or not look to thyself,
The selfsame thing will be.[4]

4. **Reading Further**

The reading selections on the On Campus Student Website at www.prenhall.com/fitton explore different aspects of chapter topics. At the end of each reading selection are critical thinking questions. Your instructor will let you know whether you should print out your responses or use the online feature to e-mail your answers.

a. *Getting a Credit Card* Arthur J. Keown

b. *Credit Card Habits Quiz* Arthur J. Keown

c. *Examining the Culture of College Drinking* National Institute of Alcohol Abuse and Alcoholism

d. *The Health Consequences of Smoking on the Human Body* National Center for Chronic Disease Prevention and Health Promotion

Notes

[1] *Student Life*, Bowdoin College, http://www.bowdoin.edu/studentlife/studentResources. shtml (accessed December 27, 2002; site now discontinued).

[2] Student Service Division, Monroe Community College, http://www.monroecc.edu (accessed January 3, 2004).

[3] National College Learning Center Association, http://www.nclca.org (accessed January 14, 2006).

[4] From an old folksong, "As I Walked By Myself," *Folksongs of Various Countries*, http://ingeb.org/folksong.html (accessed April 9, 2004).

Notes

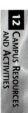

12 CAMPUS RESOURCES
AND ACTIVITIES

Notes

Index

INDEX

INDEX